DATE DUE

DEMCO 38-296

THE MOVEMENT TOWARDS SUBVERSION

The English History Play from Skelton to Shakespeare

Eric Sterling

University Press of America, Inc.
Lanham • New York • London

Copyright © 1996 by
University Press of America,® Inc.

                                         Way
                                         nd 20706

                                         Street
                                         ,U England

                                         erved
                                         ates of America
British Cataloging in Publication Information Available

Library of Congress Cataloging-in-Publication Data

Sterling, Eric.
The movement towards subversion : the English history play from
    Skelton to Shakespeare / Eric Sterling.
                       p.   cm.
       Includes bibliographical references and index.
1. Historical drama, English--History and criticism. 2. Literature and
  history--England--History--16th century. 3. English drama--Early
  modern and Elizabethan, 1500-1600--History and criticism. 4.
  Skelton, John, 1460?-1529--Dramatic works. 5. Shakespeare,
          William, 1564-1616--Histories. I. Title.
    PR658.H5S74   1996   82'.051409 --dc20   96-24716   CIP

          ISBN 0-7618-0448-X (cloth: alk. ppr.)
          ISBN 0-7618-0449-8 (pbk: alk. ppr.)

For my parents (Robert and Marianne), Jill, Sheldon and Michelle, and Carla

CONTENTS

ACKNOWLEDGMENTS

While writing this book, I have had the pleasure and the privilege of receiving help from several outstanding scholars.

I wish to thank Charles Forker for his assiduous help from the beginning of this book project through its completion. I appreciate his advice and his encouragement.

I thank Albert Wertheim for his advice and suggestions in regard to my book and my career. He has been an exemplary role model for me.

H. James Jensen read the first several drafts of my book very carefully and gave me a great deal of help. I am also grateful for his advice regarding my teaching.

I thank Richard Nash for his challenging comments and astute observations regarding my book. I also appreciate his good humor and advice regarding my career.

I appreciate the manifold kindnesses of Terrance Kearns and the faculty and secretaries (Barb Whisnant and Charlene Bland) of the English Department at the University of Central Arkansas. I am thankful for the encouragement and advice I received from colleagues such as Phillip Anderson, Jay Curlin, Raymond Frontain, Kate Kamakahi, John Lammers, Mike Schaefer, and Wayne Stengel. I completed most of my revisions while a member of this department. I am grateful to Robert Lowrey, editor of *Publications of the Arkansas Philological Association*, for permission to include my chapter on *Richard the Second*, part of which appeared in the Spring 1993 issue of that journal.

I thank my outstanding department head, Alan Gribben, for his support and encouragement. I also thank my wonderful colleagues at Auburn University at Montgomery for their help and support. Mary Jane Curry provided me with several good ideas regarding my introduction, and Jeff Melton and David Walker have been quite helpful. I have also benefitted from discussions with learned AUM colleagues such as Joseph Crowley, Gerald Morton, and Susan Willis. Angie Thurmond has provided me with good advice regarding the preparation of this book for publication.

Most of all, I wish to acknowledge Robert Evans, who took time from his busy schedule to read the manuscript and offer many helpful suggestions. He has been an outstanding colleague and a wonderful friend, and I am grateful for all he has done for me.

I wish to thank my wonderful wife Jill for all the love and support she has given me.

Lastly, I wish to thank my parents (Robert and Marianne), as well as my brother (Sheldon), my sister-in-law (Michelle), and my grandmother (Carla), for their encouragement and love.

INTRODUCTION

Such is in man the greedy mind to reign,
So great is his desire to climb aloft,
In worldly stage the stateliest parts to bear,
That faith and justice and all kindly love
Do yield unto desire of sovereignty,
Where egal state doth raise an egal hope
To win the thing that either would attain.
---*Gorboduc, or Ferrex and Porrex*[1]

This book explores the theme of power in the Renaissance English history play, a fascinating genre whose earliest works include John Skelton's *Magnificence* (c. 1516-18) and John Bale's *King Johan* (1538). My study analyzes the growing subversion of the sociopolitical hierarchy in Renaissance drama from *Magnificence* to William Shakespeare's *King Lear* (c. 1605). When Shakespeare begins writing history plays in approximately 1589-90, he inherits a tradition that has evolved for more than half a century. As the genre of the history play progresses, it becomes more politically subversive, for the dramas begin to question the sociopolitical hierarchy (of which the monarch is the apex) instead of reinforcing the social order. Richard Helgerson suggests "a special relation between popular revolt and the theater. Clearly a significant portion of the Elizabethan theater audience liked seeing such plays, and . . . the theater was a willing bearer of a radically subversive peasant, or more generally commoner, ideology."[2]

Scholarship tends to focus heavily on the most famous and well-known plays of the Renaissance, especially those of William Shakespeare. I discuss a combination of some familiar, "canonical" works and lesser-known, often neglected plays. Virtually no articles have been published in more than a decade on dramas such as Skelton's *Magnificence*, Bale's *King Johan*, and the anonymous *Troublesome Raigne of King John* and *King*

ix

Leir. My study explores the lesser-known Renaissance historical plays for what they can tell us about political and religious attitudes in sixteenth-century England; I also attempt to throw light on the evolution of Renaissance historical drama. Unlike many previous scholars, I analyze the plays on their own terms instead of merely discussing them in regard to their relationships with, and influences upon, Shakespearean drama. My thesis is that Renaissance history plays become increasingly seditious politically and that Shakespeare's historical drama exemplifies this trend; as the playwright's career develops, his dramas of this genre increasingly challenge established ideologies, such as the belief in divine right, in the king's two bodies, and in history as providential. His plays are more subversive than earlier Tudor works containing similar themes, and as his historical dramas begin to undermine traditional hierarchies with greater force, the genre itself shifts, blending history with tragedy. Consequently, *King Lear*, the last play involving English history that Shakespeare wrote during the prime of his career, possesses many tragic elements and frequently has been labeled as a tragedy only; actually the play is a tragical history, a merging of the two genres. In fact, throughout my discussion I deliberately blur reductive demarcations between genres, for as playwrights increasingly demystify received notions of teleological design and challenge religious and political ideologies of kingship, they create dramatic conclusions that imply a correspondingly more tragic view of English history.

   Parts of my book emphasize the distinction between literary texts and other aspects of culture, such as politics, history, and religion. I sometimes employ traditional methodology to explore the subversive nature of Tudor history plays; yet sometimes the conclusions I reach in regard to how playwrights question ideologies that justify authority are similar to the findings of contemporary literary theorists, such as the New Historicists and the Cultural Materialists. For instance, in the chapter on *Richard II*, I discuss Shakespeare's demystification of divine right and the king's two bodies through the playwright's purposeful telescoping of history, through his altering of chronicle history, and through his characterization of Richard. The dramatists disclose an increasing disapproval of rulers, and more and more they portray kings not as divinely ordained monarchs who govern in accordance with metaphysical fiat but as incompetent human beings who have acquired power by cultural means. By questioning the metaphysics of kingship and by characterizing kings as ineffective leaders who lead their country to the brink of ruin, these playwrights implicitly justify usurpation as necessary. The civil wars, foreign invasions, and murders that often arise from such usurpations almost always, therefore, imply tragic scenes or a tragic ethos.

Wolfgang Clemen says, "Shakespeare not only handled episodes from the historical past, but he translated into drama elements inherent in history itself. For history demonstrates how the past grows into the present and leads on to the future."[3] Clemen's point about the history plays written by Shakespeare holds true for those by his contemporaries as well. The plays I discuss are quite political:[4] we may regard any drama that deals with the issue of kingship as such. Jonathan Dollimore claims that a Renaissance play

> is related to the contexts of its production--to the economic and political system of Elizabethan and Jacobean England and to the particular institutions of cultural production (the court, patronage, theatre, education, the church) .... What the plays signify, how they signify, depends on the cultural field in which they are situated.[5]

Some of the dramas (such as *Gorboduc*) contain allusions to contemporary governmental situations and employ history to manifest their viewpoints concerning affairs in sixteenth-century England.

Others deal with historical events that are seemingly unrelated to contemporary England but that are actually quite relevant because they dramatize politically important events such as successions, usurpations, and civil wars. These historical incidents (for instance, the forced abdication of Richard II and his subsequent murder) have nothing to do with the reign of Queen Elizabeth--at least on the surface. Political subversion exists in *Richard II*, however, because usurpers may conceptualize the idea of seizing their monarch's power after observing the dramatization of a rebellion and because conceivably subjects may identify a ruler in a history play with a contemporary monarch, as Queen Elizabeth did. David Bevington claims that Elizabeth's "sensitivity, combined with her fascination for allegorical subtlety, inevitably altered the method of political allusion."[6] The Queen, for instance, expressed anger about the staging of *Richard II*, perhaps because the demonstration of a historical deposition could set a precedent and introduce subversive ideas into the minds of the audience; she complained, "I am Richard II. know ye not that? . . . [And that] this tragedy was played 40tie times in open streets."[7] Barbara Hodgdon correctly points out that Elizabeth's "comment reveals some anxiety about staged performances occurring in city spaces where--unlike either the licensed theaters or her own pageants of state--neither she nor her censors had control over the royal image or the circumstances of its representation."[8] The content of *Richard II* is politically charged, yet the productions of the plays in open streets are also crucial. These unlicensed productions manifest a desire by those involved with the performances and by the playgoers to conduct and witness politically sensitive entertainment (such as a play that contains a deposition of a king) without monarchical control or influence; in the above statement, Elizabeth acknowledges her vulnerability to unlicensed performances that could freely subvert her ideological strategies.

The Queen's remark about the staging of the play in the streets is also noteworthy because such public performances may blur the distinction between reality and drama, between fact and fiction. When playgoers attended the performance of *Richard II* at the Globe Theatre, they realized that they were witnessing a drama. The theatre is an environment for "the willing suspension of disbelief." But people see actual events in the streets. The performances in the "open streets" irked Elizabeth justifiably, for, as Stephen Greenblatt notes, "the play had broken out of the boundaries of the playhouse, where such stories are clearly marked as powerful illusions, and moved into the more volatile zone--the zone she calls 'open'--of the streets. In the streets the story begins to lose the conventional containment of the playhouse where audiences are kept at a safe distance. . . from the world beyond the walls."[9] Removed from its fantastic environment and thrust into the setting of actuality, *Richard II* conflates the real with the unreal, the actual with the dramatic, and the contemporary with the past.

Drama could shape history through its effect upon its playgoers, as Essex's follower who commissioned the performance of the drama hoped. In the Renaissance, people believed that an audience member's observation of a character's noble and courageous deed onstage could readily influence that viewer to perform a similar action in real life. Thomas Heywood claims:

> To turne to our domesticke hystories, what English blood seeing the person of any bold English man presented and doth not hugge his fame, and hunnye at his valor, pursuing him in his enterprise with his best wishes, and as beeing wrapt in contemplation, offers to him in his hart all prosperous performance, as if the Personater were the man Personated, so bewitching a thing is liuely and well spirited action, that it hath power to new mold the harts of the spectators and fashion them to the shape of any noble and notable attempt.[10]

If the noble action performed onstage is a nobleman's (such as Bolingbroke's) heroic rebellion against an incompetent and cruel monarch (such as Richard II), Heywood implies that the action could stir or "bewitch" the audience to emulate such a deed. Such a drama would be politically subversive, for if the noble action is a deposition, the play could incite an actual usurpation. Perhaps that is one reason why Elizabeth labeled the drama, which appears in the first folio of 1623 as a history, a tragedy.[11]

Historical and political events influence drama regarding plot and genre. *King Johan* is a prime example, for Bale defends Henry VIII's break with Rome and the monarch's claim to be the head of the Church of England. Carole Levin reminds us that "King John, regarded for centuries as a monster, could be transformed into a hero to suit the new religious and political climate."[12] A growing distrust of the teleological order and of the quality of monarchical government in early seventeenth-century England permeates Shakespeare's *King Lear*--a drama about pre-Christian English history. The dark play's challenging of Providence and of the ability of rulers to govern effectively renders the outcome of the drama tragic; the play, however, concerns English history and issues such as kingship, succession, political marriages, civil war, and foreign invasion, which Holinshed discusses in his *Chronicles*. Most of Shakespeare's audience would have considered the historical account fundamentally truthful. The classification of *King Lear* as a tragedy is an oversimplification, for the work, a blending of the two genres, is as much a history play as a tragedy. The play follows Holinshed's account loosely, but the dramatist, perhaps influenced by the growing distrust of monarchy and of political and religious ideology, alters the plot, rendering the outcome tragic.

I explore the movement towards the subversion of political power in the English history play in the following manner: in the first part, I discuss John Bale's *King Johan*, the anonymous *Troublesome Raigne of King John*, and Shakespeare's *King John*. My second part consists of chapters on John Skelton's *Magnificence*, the anonymous *Woodstock*, Christopher Marlowe's *Edward II*, and Shakespeare's *Richard II*. In part three, I investigate Thomas Sackville's and Thomas Norton's *Gorboduc, or Ferrex and Porrex,* the anonymous *King Leir*, and Shakespeare's *King Lear*. A summary of the three parts follows:

I begin with a discussion of plays that deal with King John because I am interested in the correlation that Reformation polemicists made between the medieval king and contemporary Tudor monarchs and because of the marked transformation of John's reputation after Henry's break from the

Church of Rome. Bale's *King Johan* functions as a transition between the medieval morality play and English historical drama. I focus on Reformation influences and the playwright's religious and political viewpoints, so far as these can be inferred. As Levin correctly points out, "The recreation of John as a hero was one part of the changing of historical images and the propaganda campaign of the English Reformation;"[13] the play, commissioned by Thomas Cromwell, is quite polemical, and Bale, ahistorically, glorifies King John in his attempt to demonstrate why the state should possess power over the church.

The anonymous author of *The Troublesome Raigne of King John* (c. 1588-89) also concentrates heavily upon John's defiance of the Roman Catholic Church; the playwright's disdain for Catholics is not as fanatical as that of Bale, but his religious views are less moderate than those of Shakespeare. This play utilizes historical events more than does *King Johan* and concerns itself more with historical fact than its predecessor. The unknown dramatist supports the Tudor dynasty and exposes the papal hypocrisy and political ambition of King Philip of Spain that he considers threats to the established Protestantism of Elizabethan government.

Shakespeare's perspective on religion is more moderate than Bale's and that of the anonymous author of *The Troublesome Raigne*. *King John* expresses virtually no anti-papal sentiment. Shakespeare focuses more on the dangers of commodity and on the necessity of unwavering loyalty of subjects to their sovereign. Although Protestant writers such as William Tyndale and John Foxe regarded John as a hero, Shakespeare presents the king as a usurper, thus undercutting the parallel between John and Henry that the Tudor monarchs perpetuated. In *King John*, Shakespeare's portrayal of the king resembles that of Catholic chroniclers such as Polydore Vergil more than that of the Protestant polemicists mentioned above. The presentation of John as a tyrannical usurper may be considered radical, for many people in Tudor England identified him with Henry and with Elizabeth.

Part two of my study deals with plays in which kings cause their own loss of power by subjugating themselves to parasites. I begin with Skelton's *Magnificence*, the earliest of the four plays and the least politically subversive. *Magnificence*, a political morality play and a political allegory, demonstrates the importance of "measure" and the dangers of a king's reliance on flatterers rather than on worthy advisors. Magnificence is an Everyman figure but also a king, the leader of a nation. There are allusions to King Henry VIII and Cardinal Wolsey; but I do not agree with Irving Ribner's and David Bevington's identifications of the characters in the play with these historical figures.[14] This political drama is an influential precursor to the English history play although it is not specifically of that genre.

I believe that the propagandistic *Woodstock*, like *Magnificence*, is a political allegory containing allusions to contemporary historical figures. I investigate why the anonymous playwright might have glorified Woodstock, whom Holinshed describes as "a sore and a right seuere man, who might not by any meanes be remooued from his opinion and purpose, if he once resolued vpon any matter,"[15] and why the author takes such liberties in his unnecessary conflation of time. My thesis is that the dramatist, who is not a staunch royalist, defames Richard II in an effort to demonstrate the necessity of deposing an ineffective ruler. I draw parallels between the plot of *Woodstock* and the contemporary political situation involving Queen Elizabeth and the Earl of Essex; furthermore, I suggest evidence to support the idea that Essex may have commissioned the anonymous dramatist to write the play in order to illuminate the similarities between Richard and Elizabeth and between Woodstock and the earl.

Next, I discuss Christopher Marlowe's *Edward II*, a drama which, like *Magnificence*, *Woodstock*, and to some extent *Richard II*, examines the precarious situation of a king when he subjugates himself to the influence of flatterers. All four of these dramas demonstrate the fall of a monarch who relies on sycophants. In Marlowe's play, Edward II's obsession with Gaveston and the Spensers leads to the king's ill treatment of Isabella and the nobles, and subsequently to his forced abdication and murder. I also explore Marlowe's deviations from his historical sources and the reasons for these changes, such as why he chooses to make Younger Mortimer the main usurper in the play when, historically, the chief overreacher was the Earl of Lancaster; my theory leads to discussions on sexual politics and the blending of history with tragedy.

Part two concludes with discussions of the merging of history with tragedy and of the theme of kingship in Shakespeare's *Richard II*. As with Marlowe's play, the genre shifts along with the transferal of sympathies. Part of the complexity of the title character lies in the questions raised by the theory of divine right and by the effects of usurping power. Is Bolingbroke's behavior a sin against God and England because he forces King Richard to abdicate, indirectly orders his murder, and commits a crime that ultimately leads to the War of the Roses? Or are Bolingbroke's actions justified because Richard is an incompetent ruler who is leading his country to destruction? I believe that Shakespeare's viewpoint correlates more with the latter perspective, and I support this thesis by examining how the playwright uses and omits historical information in this drama. Shakespeare defames Richard by omitting crucial historical information concerning the Lords Appellant, thus portraying the king as an incompetent and cruel ruler. Shakespeare shows Richard's deeds, such as his banishment of Hereford and his seizure of Gaunt's (actually Henry's) property, but the playwright purposefully suppresses the fact that Hereford, as a member of the Lords Appellant, committed treason by usurping the throne. The playwright also demystifies ideologies that legitimize kingship, such as the theory of the king's two bodies, as we witness the king coming to terms with his earthly body.

Part three focuses on plays involving English legendary history. These works concern Pre-Christian kings who foolishly relinquish power to children whom they have misjudged, offspring who abuse their authority. I begin with a section on *Gorboduc, or Ferrex and Porrex* (1561). The character Gorboduc is not only an abstraction to embody the unity of a kingdom but also a historical king. Hermon and Tyndar represent in combination the morality figure Vice, but they also play a role in Norton's and Sackville's political allegory. In this drama, we see the dangers of the division of a kingdom, but although Gorboduc is indirectly responsible for his own demise because of his foolish self-deposition, an important theme is that "no cause serves whereby the subject may / Call to account the doings of his prince" (V.i.42-43). In addition, I draw parallels between the plot of *Gorboduc* and the issue of succession in Elizabethan England and show how the dramatists employ the historical plot in their presentation of nationalistic and Protestant propaganda regarding the contemporary political situation.

The anonymous *King Leir* is a play read and valued as the main source of Shakespeare's *King Lear*, but it is an intriguing and effective play in its own right. Like *Gorboduc*, *King Leir* concerns a historic English king who has devastated his country by unwisely abdicating the throne. The anonymous playwright follows his source, the 1587 edition of Holinshed's *Chronicles*, in that King Leir ultimately regains power after he learns from his social and political errors of judgment. The play is largely a conservative romantic history, quite unlike Shakespeare's later tragical history, for it clearly supports the theory of providential history. Actually, the anonymous *King Leir* resembles Shakespeare's *Cymbeline* more than *King Lear* since the play, whose origins lie in pre-Christian English history, concerns itself more with familial relationships than with the politics of kingship and possesses elements of a romance.

My final chapter concerns Shakespeare's *King Lear*. Obviously, this drama also deals with the mistake of dividing a kingdom, but Shakespeare deviates from the works of Holinshed and the anonymous author of *King Leir*, for in this play King Lear dies. Several possibilities exist for this change, including Shakespeare's implication of the ineffectiveness of monarchical government and the playwright's denial of historical accuracy (which monarchs used as a means of legitimizing their authority). Furthermore, Shakespeare's tragical history clearly challenges the concept of Divine Providence.

The book concludes with an analysis of the development of historical drama.   The plays manifest a growing subversiveness--a movement towards the questioning of political and religious ideology.   It will be apparent from the interpretations of these ten dramas that history plays become increasingly more anti-establishment, more politically subversive, and consequently more tragic. My study ends with a short discussion on how the politically subversive plays reflect the growing distrust of political institutions in Renaissance English history.

INTRODUCTION: NOTES

1. Thomas Sackville and Thomas Norton, *Gorboduc, or Ferrex and Porrex*, ed. Irby B. Cauthen, Jr. (Lincoln: University of Nebraska), I.ii.262-68.

2. Richard Helgerson, *Forms of Nationhood: The Elizabethan Writing of England* (Chicago: University of Chicago Press, 1992), p. 210.

3. Wolfgang Clemen, "Past and Future in Shakespeare's Drama," *Proceedings of the British Academy*, 52 (1966), 233.

4. The anonymous *King Leir* is an exception, yet the drama plays an integral role in my study nonetheless.

5. Jonathan Dollimore and Alan Sinfield, eds., *Political Shakespeare: New Essays in Cultural Materialism* (Ithaca: Cornell University Press, 1985), p. viii.

6. David Bevington, *Tudor Drama and Politics: A Critical Approach to Topical Meaning* (Cambridge, Mass.: Harvard University Press, 1968), p. 8.

7. Peter Ure, Introduction, *King Richard II* by William Shakespeare (London: Methuen, 1969), p. lix.

8. Barbara Hodgdon, *The End Crowns All: Closure and Contradiction in Shakespeare's History* (Princeton: Princeton University Press, 1991), p. 127.

9. Stephen Greenblatt, Introduction, *The Power of Forms in the English Renaissance*, ed. Stephen Greenblatt (Norman, Ok: Pilgrim, 1982), pp. 3-4.

10. Thomas Heywood, *An Apology for Actors*, in *An Apology for Actors; A Refutation of the "Apology for Actors"* (New York: Garland, 1973), sig. B4.

11. Although Shakespeare does label the play a tragedy in the quarto, we cannot assume that Elizabeth would have read the play.

12. Carole Levin, *Propaganda in the English Reformation: Heroic and Villainous Images of King John, Studies in British History*. Vol. 11 (Lewiston, New York: Edward Mellen Press, 1988), p. 2.

13. Levin, p. 2

14. See Irving Ribner, *The English History Play in the Age of Shakespeare*, rev. ed. (New York: Barnes & Noble, 1965), pp. 32-33. See also Bevington, pp. 56-63.

15. Raphael Holinshed, *Holinshed's Chronicles of England, Scotland, and Ireland* 6 vols. (London: J. Johnson, et al., *1807-1808*), II, 794.

PART ONE

THE RE-EVALUATION OF KING JOHN

IN REFORMATION ENGLAND

CHAPTER ONE

THE SHIFT OF ALLEGIANCE FROM POPE TO KING:

Bale's *King Johan* as Political Propaganda

I

John Bale's *King Johan*, the anonymous *Troublesome Raigne of King John*, and William Shakespeare's *King John* are sixteenth-century dramas that treat the issues of kingship, the conflict between the powers of church and state, political ideology, and the allegiance subjects owe to their monarch. Bale's play, written shortly after the beginning of the Reformation, uses the figure of King John as a character because of the analogy Reformation polemicists made between John and the current ruler, Henry VIII: both defied the Pope and subsequently experienced the wrath of Rome. Bale manifests his allegiance to Henry by glorifying John and by defending the medieval king in his struggle with Pope Innocent III. In doing so, Bale disregards the medieval chronicles that portray John as an evil usurper and creates a new, Reformation version of the history of King John's reign. Approximately fifty years later, *The Troublesome Raigne* appears onstage. The anonymous play, written in approximately the same year that England defeated the Spanish Armada (1588), possesses some anti-Catholic sentiment but clearly not as much as Bale's drama. Perhaps the unknown playwright includes two anti-Catholic scenes because of the frequent attempts by King Philip of Spain and the Pope to overthrow Elizabeth's government; but with the Reformation movement established in England for half a century, the dramatist would not have needed to propagandize against Roman Catholicism as his predecessor had.

Shakespeare, writing *King John* several years after England had defeated the Armada convincingly, omits the two anti-Catholic scenes and criticizes commodity (political self-interest), not Catholicism. Shakespeare's play parallels the growing religious toleration that ensued in England several years after the nation's glorious triumph over Spain at sea.

Since *King Johan* is a pro-Reformation play and Bale clearly identifies John with Henry, the playwright portrays the medieval ruler as a heroic leader whom God has selected as England's king. Bale employs historical figures to propagandize on a contemporary political situation and to support political ideologies that Henry perpetuated. Contrariwise, the anonymous *Troublesome Raigne* and Shakespeare's *King John* deal with history mostly for its own sake and, despite possessing contemporary political agendas, focus predominantly on the reign of the medieval king. Neither of the two plays glorifies John, and both works permit the audience to ponder whether John has usurped power from his nephew Arthur--a character whom Bale purposefully omits. The authors of *The Troublesome Raigne* and *King John* portray John as a cruel tyrant and demystify the belief in the divine right of kings, an ideology Bale supports vehemently.

Bale advocates the belief in divine right in his attempt to persuade his audience of the importance of allegiance to one's king--as opposed to one's loyalty to the Catholic Church. In his defense of Tudor ideology regarding monarchical government, Bale characterizes John as a virtuous and almost Christ-like leader who loses power because of his subjects' disloyalty. The dramatist implies that England may only prosper when subjects support their king. The anonymous playwright and especially Shakespeare demystify the belief in divine right by implying that John may be a usurper and by showing his cruelty and his inability to govern well. Although they challenge Tudor ideology by portraying John in a negative light, the two dramatists indicate that subjects must be loyal to their king--even if he is evil and illegitimate. These two dramatists, therefore, simultaneously subvert and support Tudor polemics. John is more evil and possesses less of a right to the throne in Shakespeare's play than in *The Troublesome Raigne*; a trend develops, with the dramas portraying John increasingly as a cruel and illegitimate monarch. Thus, the Reformation plays regarding King John become more subversive and less supportive of Tudor ideology. In the following three chapters, we shall see a steady progression towards a questioning and a complication of the issues regarding the reign of King John and the concept of kingship.

II

Bale's *King Johan* of approximately 1538 unwaveringly presents John as king and as God's appointed minister on earth. The playwright glorifies John and purposefully suppresses the medieval king's evil actions and contestation with Prince Arthur for the throne, implying that John is clearly Richard's rightful heir. Bale writes this polemical drama to support Henry's break with the Church of Rome by glorifying King John's earlier defiance of Pope Innocent III and by defaming the Catholic clergy. Commissioned to write the play by Henry's ministers Cromwell and Cranmer, Bale attempts to influence his audience members about the validity of Henry's policies towards the Roman Church, the necessity of the supremacy of the State's power over that of the Church in its own affairs, and the importance of loyalty to one's king. Bale's religious views are quite radical, but his political stance is actually conservative because he fervently propagandizes in support of the established Tudor government.

During the reign of Henry VIII, England broke free of its allegiance to Rome, and Pope Clement VII excommunicated Henry. These developments hastened the Reformation in England. Outraged by, and jealous of, the wealth attained by Catholic clergy as a result of their abuses, many English citizens harbored anti-clerical attitudes. Some wished to plunder the churches and monasteries in order to acquire wealth for themselves; others were genuinely upset by the manifold deceptions performed by those who claimed to perform God's will. This Tudor movement, which was as much anti-clerical as Protestant, resulted in a decline in the authority of the Roman clergy and the concomitant dominance of the State over the Church. It is noteworthy that such anti-clerical sentiment was later allied with Protestantism. The anti-clerics were upset by the Catholic clergy's abuse of power, such as the misuse of pardons, absolution, papal bulls, and other such manifestations of ecclesiastical authority. Furthermore, for several reasons Pope Clement VII refused to grant King Henry VIII a divorce; these included the papal dispensation that permitted the king to marry his brother's widow as well as Clement's subservience to Charles V, Katharine of Aragon's nephew. The Pope's denial of Henry's request, moreover, showed the English sovereign the undesirability of permitting a foreign leader to exert political power over him. In order for England to prosper, it seemed essential to reject a papal authority that was heavily influenced, if not controlled, by England's foreign enemies. Because of the nation's growing nationalistic spirit, the English were reluctant to acknowledge foreign laws when they considered England fully capable of governing itself. Henry VIII's subsequent breach with the Church of Rome led to his claim in 1534 to be the Supreme Head of the Church of England. The change made obvious England's new policy of subordinating Church to State.

Not everyone, of course, agreed with Henry's actions--his breach with Rome, his desire for a divorce, his ransacking and looting of monasteries, and his anti-clerical policies. Many Catholics, including Henry's nobles in northern and southwestern England, disapproved of his actions. In such a time of religious conflict and zealotry, the creation and dissemination of propaganda was inevitable. Graham Holderness notes:

> When Henry VIII substituted his authority for that of the Pope as Head of the Church, the king automatically assumed complete control of the drama: and the history of drama under the Tudor state is partly a history of increasing state interference and tightening bureaucratic control, centralising the cultural power of the state enormously.[1]

David Bevington says that "the party of victory in the 1530s, composed of zealous episcopal reformers such as Cranmer and ambitious politicians such as Cromwell, rapidly discovered the need for strong propagandistic countermeasures against their opponents to right and left."[2] These two Protestant leaders "had patronized companies of players who performed heavily-loaded plays and interludes (like those of John Bale) on village commons and at market squares."[3] Peter Happe and John King add that "As the king's chief minister and vicegerent in religious affairs, Cromwell patronized a group of Protestant publicists who wrote in favor of the royal supremacy, the disestablishment of the monasteries, and the campaign against pilgrimages and religious images."[4] Seymour Baker House adds that under Cromwell's patronage, Bale's plays

> became potential weapons in a program of religious reform which was promulgated under the guise of a return to the purity of the early Church, free from its medieval accretions--accretions which included not only various sacramental and traditional matters, but also the dramatic aspects of medieval Christianity such as pageants, cycle plays, and processions.[5]
>
> Although King Henry never commissioned such literature, his chief officials, who believed strongly in the Reformation, provided financial assistance to English propagandists who supported the Reformation.

Bale's *King Johan*, probably written in 1538,[6] is noteworthy because it is both a morality play and perhaps the first English historical drama. Since it possesses elements of the medieval morality play and contains historical facts as well as ideological politics, it marks a transition between the two dramatic genres. Bale wished to write a polemical work about contemporary religious and political controversies. He could have written a pamphlet or a poem to promote his views, yet he chose drama as a means of accomplishing his objective. Bale probably chose theatre as his vehicle because drama is the genre that would affect the greatest number of people. Given the high rate of illiteracy in early Renaissance England, a play would capture the attention of more people than prose writings or poetry. Unlettered men, women, and children could not, of course, comprehend Bale's writings, but they could witness and be swayed by the presentation of his works onstage. Bale's pro-Reformation propaganda becomes more powerful when we consider that drama had been previously a vehicle that promoted Catholic ideologies. The images and visual satire, such as with respect to the costumes and religious paraphernalia, permit Bale to use the stage, a Catholic polemical vehicle, to attack Roman Catholicism.

We assume that *King Johan* was composed by Bale specifically for performance because the stage directions explicitly call for the doubling of characters; obviously actors were needed. For example, a stage direction reads, "Go owt Ynglond and drese for Clargy" (l. 154).[7] The play was probably performed throughout London so that its pro-Reformation and anti-clerical sentiments would reach as many citizens as possible. Many English citizens would have witnessed *King Johan* if J. H. P. Pafford is correct in his assumption that "on his expulsion from the living of Thorndon in 1537 or 1538 [Bale] may have collected a travelling troop to perform his plays as Protestant propaganda."[8] Pafford's statement is credible, especially when we consider Richard and Helen Leacroft's point that the first permanent English theatre, that of James Burbage, was not built until 1576,[9] which was thirty-eight years after Bale's play was first performed. Adams notes, furthermore, that *King Johan* was performed before Archbishop Cranmer January 2, 1539, and paid for by the playwright's patron, Cromwell. He also reports that Queen Elizabeth witnessed it at Ipswich in 1561.[10]

To present his anti-Catholic point of view in *King Johan*, Bale uses elements of the morality play, for that was the genre with which he was familiar, the English history play having not yet evolved. The morality play, however, had been a flourishing genre in medieval England; and

Bale's appropriation of the morality play to satisfy his purposes is an example of propagandistic ingenuity, for he employed a genre used by Catholics to instruct audiences about morality and the Catholic way of life as a means of attacking the Catholic Church and its abuses. In addition, the morality play genre is in some respects analogous to historical drama. Morality plays present allegorized universal characters, such as Everyman and Mankind, who struggle between representations of good and evil--characters who are actually abstractions and who externalize basic conflicts within the psyche. But this battle for dominance within man symbolizes a macrocosmic struggle, for, as Janet Hertzbach points out, "the resolution which the Renaissance figure, frequently a sovereign, strives to attain is important for himself but more generally for the welfare of the political realm."[11]

Bale's contribution to English historical drama in *King Johan* is his inclusion of historical "facts" from Robert Fabyan's *New Chronicles of England and France*, William Tyndale's *The Obedience of a Christen Man*, John Major's *A History of Greater Britain as well England as Scotland*, and Polydore Vergil's *Anglica Historia*. The playwright uses information from these sources to revise history in a light favorable to the contemporary Protestant Tudor government. Carole Levin claims that the alteration of King John's reputation was part of the English Reformation's propaganda and that "an analysis of this changing image opens a window to the culture of the English Renaissance and Reformation. . . . King John, regarded for centuries as a monster, could be transformed into a hero to suit the new religious and political climate."[12] Bale, in his satire on Roman Catholic hypocrisy and abuses, adulates King John for his initial refusal to capitulate to what the playwright considers the unjust and ambitious demands of Pope Innocent III. Thus the villains of the play are abstractions (typical of the morality play) of vices Bale attributes to Catholicism, but they are also historical Catholic individuals (who reflect the more realistic approach of historical drama) whom the playwright wishes to attack. Furthermore, Bale's modification of the morality play is important religiously and politically because *King Johan*, a powerful example of pro-Reformation polemics, alters the figure to whom the audience must show its political and spiritual submission: A.P. Rossiter notes that in Tudor propagandistic drama, "The old allegory of man's duty towards God, within His Catholic and universal Church, was narrowed towards the allegory of men's duties as subjects under a God-representing King."[13]

Several elements of the morality play genre appear in Bale's drama. Many of the playwright's stylistic devices are primitive in comparison with those of other Renaissance dramatists. The characters, for instance, frequently ask each other to state their names. When Verity castigates Civil Order for his disobedience to King Johan, Civil Order inexplicably interrupts him to inquire, "Sir, my bretherne and I woulde gladly knowe your name" (l. 2281). Another of Bale's methods of introducing characters is for someone to ask where a character is and for him to appear onstage immediately afterwards, as if by coincidence. After Sedition says, "I maruele greatly where dissymulacyon is," the character who has just been named retorts from offstage, "I wyll come anon if thu tarry tyll I pysse," and Dissimulation then enters (ll. 2006-07). Although Sedition has told King Johan his name at line 90, the sovereign asks again at line 185 in order to remind the audience. These dramatic devices may be viewed as mechanical, but we must also acknowledge their necessity. Since characters such as Dissimulation and Sedition are abstract and not historical figures, they would be unrecognizable to their viewing audiences and must be introduced in this manner.

The abstract nature of the characters--another aspect of the medieval morality play--is apparent in *King Johan*. Sedition, Dissimulation, Private Wealth, and Usurped Power are clearly evil characters who behave in a manner true to their names. Although they change their names and their costumes, their comportment and sinister values remain the same. King Johan and England are unmistakably virtuous figures, and, like the villains, are flat characters. Nobility, Clergy, Civil Order, and Commonalty are the "Everyman" figures torn between the opposite forces representing vice (the Roman Catholic Church) and virtue (the King of England). When virtuous King Johan asks for Nobility's support, the latter cannot comply:

> for I am sworne thervnto [i.e., to the Church]:
> I toke a great othe whan I was dubbyd a knyght
> Euer to defend the holy churches ryght.
> (ll. 361-63)

And when the spiritually blind Commonalty is with his mother (England) and King Johan, the Cardinal orders him to leave. King Johan asks the simple-minded Commonalty, "Why wylt þou forsake þi prince or þi prince leve the?", to which the latter responds, "I mvst nedes obbay whan holy chirch commandyth me" (ll. 1608-09). Commonalty's submission to Pandulph indicates his reluctance to disobey the Cardinal, but,

nevertheless, his words demonstrate his recognition of his duty to his king:
he "must nedes obbay." After King Johan's murder, however, Nobility,
Clergy, and Civil Order, like the universal protagonists of the medieval
morality play, discover their sinful error caused by Vice's enticement (in
this case, Sedition, Dissimulation, Usurped Power, and Private Wealth)
and experience a spiritual awakening. Verity reviles them for their sins
against God and his ordained minister on earth, King Johan, which causes
them to repent. This moral reformation, an integral element in the
morality play genre, represents the Reformation in England in the 1530s.

Bale, a former prior of the Carmelite order and a holder of a bachelor's
degree from Cambridge, became a vehement, even bilious, spokesperson
for the Reformation after his defection from Roman Catholicism.
According to Adams, his anti-papal propaganda is so extreme that it
shocked audience members.[14] Bale portrays his Roman Catholic
characters as hypocritical, deceitful, avaricious, lustful, ambitious, and
unholy anti-Christs. We realize that they are duplicitous, for they are the
only characters who have two names--their allegorical name (of the vice
they embody) and their historical one, which they use to influence people.
Sedition, in fact, uses a third name--Good Perfection. These hypocritical
characters, while in the guise of their historical personages, employ their
religious functions to dupe and corrupt others by convincing them of their
holiness. The evil characters' clothes, like their religious beliefs and holy
behavior, are external appearances that the villains use to deceive others.
Adams notes that "One of Bale's principal concerns in *King Johan* is to
disparage the Roman clergy, and the association of evil figures with
religious habits provides a suitable kind of continuous visual satire."[15]
Usurped Power dresses in his Pope's apparel when he desires to exert his
authority over others, but he admits that he sometimes wears other
clothing:

> [I] must haue sum dalyaunce and playe,
> For I am a man lyke as an other ys.
> Sumtyme I must hunt, sumtyme I mvst Alysen kys.
> (ll. 840-42)

Sedition uses appearances to trick Nobility into committing the treasonous
act of disobeying his king; and he seduces Nobility to take the side of the
Roman Catholic Church against King Johan by convincing him, with the
help of his ecclesiastical clothing, that he is Good Perfection. Nobility
says to Sedition, "Yowr habyte showyth ye to be a man of relygeon" (l.
1135). In fact, the Roman Catholic characters are so duplicitous that Bale

himself occasionally finds it difficult to keep the allegorical and historical identities of the characters straight: in Pafford's, Creeth's, and Happe's editions of *King Johan,* Bale mistakenly lists the allegorical persona Sedition as the speaker of a passage actually spoken by the historical figure Stephen Langton.[16]

The deceitful Roman Catholic Vice characters also employ materialistic paraphernalia and what Bale considers superstitious rituals of the Catholic Church in order to persuade King Johan's subjects to help depose their lawful sovereign. The Pope curses King Johan "wyth crosse, boke, bell and candle" (l. 1035). The monarch, Bale's spokesperson in this instance, is unabashed by the curse and the Roman Catholic "superstition"; he later tells Private Wealth:

> Take to ye yowr traysh, yowr ryngyng, syngyng and pypyng,
> So þat we may haue the scryptures openyng.
> But þat we can not haue; yt stondyth not with yowr avantage.
>
> (ll. 1392-94)

Bale satirizes the Roman Catholic ceremonies of absolution and auricular confession. After King Johan capitulates to the pressure of Usurped Power, Stephen Langton gives him absolution:

> *Dominus papa noster te absolua, et ego absoluo te auctoritate eius, et apostolorum Petri et Paui in hac parte mihi comissa, ab omnibus impietatibus tuis, et restituo te corone et regno, in nomine domini pape, amen.*
>
> (ll. 1797-1800)

In this satirical absolution Langton substitutes the Pope for God and implies that the ecclesiastical leader overreaches his authority as if he were God. The satirical absolution is Bale's attack not only upon Roman Catholic doctrine, but, more importantly, upon the pride and ambition of the Catholic clergy.

Although Bale's disdain for Catholicism, which precipitated his conversion to Protestantism, may account for his aforementioned attacks upon the Roman faith, it only does so in part. The playwright satirizes Roman Catholicism mercilessly because he views it as a threat--not merely from a religious perspective, but from a political standpoint as well. He sees the Pope's ambition as a threat to the supremacy of the monarchical system of government. Bale is concerned with the Catholic clergy's desire to influence and control English politics and government. *King Johan* is a play about kingship and the duty owed to a sovereign. Sedition, Dissimulation, Private Wealth, and Usurped Power are not only villains because of their religious hypocrisy but also because of their usurpation of the sovereign's power. They employ their religious rituals to achieve their political ambition. In his effort to force King Johan to yield to the demands of the Roman clergy, Sedition declares:

> To all that wyll fyght I proclame a Iubyle
> Of cleane remyssyon, thys tyraunt here to slee.
> Destroye hys people, burne vp both cytie and towne,
> That the pope of Rome maye haue hys scepture and crowne.
> In the churches cause to dye thys daye be bolde;
> Your sowles shall to heauen ere your fleshe and bones be colde.
>
> (ll. 1644-49)

Bale's audience would have readily noticed the religious hypocrisy of Sedition's statement that the Church of Rome will grant a jubilee (a remission from punishment for sins) and eternal salvation to anyone committing regicide, mass murder, and arson so that the Pope might acquire hegemonic power. This passage is extremely telling when we consider the fact that Bale's audience, an English crowd, was hearing a disguised Roman Catholic archbishop trying to persuade people to massacre their own citizens and destroy their own country in the name of the Pope. The audience also was listening to these Catholic villains plot to overthrow the English monarchy by manipulating vulnerable characters, through papal hypocrisy, to shift their allegiance from their rightful king to the Pope (Usurped Power).

In *King Johan*, Bale implies that the Roman Catholic clergy's desire for political power is unholy and heretical. In order for the Catholic characters to claim the allegiance of King Johan and his subjects, they must deny the Scriptures and the ideology of the divine right of kings, which they do on several occasions. King Johan points out to the audience that God's Scriptures frequently mention

> that all pepell shuld shew there trew alegyauns
> To ther lawfull kyng Christ Iesu dothe consent,
> Whych to þe hygh powres was evere obedyent.
>
> (ll. 5-7)

Consequently, in their efforts to subdue King Johan and to make him "an obedyent chylde" (l. 1805) to the Church of Rome, the Catholic clergymen ignore the Holy Scriptures and prevent their followers from reading them.

Furthermore, Verity lectures his audiences, the "Everyman" characters onstage (Nobility, Clergy, and Civil Order), and the playgoers and readers of the play on the theory of divine right:

> For Gods sake obeye lyke as doth yow befall,
> For in hys owne realme a kynge is iudge ouer all
> By Gods appoyntment, and none maye hym iudge agayne
> But the lorde hymself. In thys the scripture is playne.
> He that condempneth a kynge condempneth God without dought;
> He that harmeth a kynge to harme God goeth abought;
> He that a prynce resisteth doth dampne Gods ordynaunce
> And resisteth God in withdrawynge hys affyaunce.
> All subiectes offendynge are vndre the kynges iudgement;
> A kynge is reserued to the lorde omnypotent.
> He is a mynyster immedyate vndre God.
> Of hys ryghteousnesse to execute the rod.
>
> (ll. 2346-57)

This passage is worth quoting in its entirety because it is integral to Bale's primary theme in *King Johan*. Bale strongly believes in the explicit meaning of the passage and also wishes his audiences to accept the sentiment expressed as true. That is why the playwright names the speaker "Verity": no one can dispute the words of Truth. If Bale's audience shared his views of divine right, they believed that the Roman Catholic characters--Pope Innocent III, Cardinal Pandulphus, Archbishop Stephen Langton, and the monk Simon of Swynsett--are not merely guilty of crimes against King Johan and England but also of crimes against God; sovereigns are the Lord's viceroys and are accountable only to Him. In this instance, as with the satirical absolution, the Catholic clergy are also guilty of the sin of pride because they attempt to usurp God's role.

The ideology of divine right is prominent in *King Johan* because of the sixteenth-century Reform movement in Henry VIII's England. Bale's play focuses on King Johan's dispute with the Roman Catholic ecclesiastics of thirteenth-century England because of Henry VIII's sixteenth-century struggle with Pope Clement VII; like Henry, John opposed the Church of Rome and her desire to subjugate the secular monarch to her own ecclesiastical power. Honor McCusker's assertion that Bale's inspiration for *King Johan* came from William Tyndale's *The Obedience of a Christen Man* is significant because the early reformer's treatise strongly supports the ideology of divine right.[17] In fact, Verity's passage asserting the cause of divine right, quoted previously, paraphrases a part of Tyndale's pro-Protestant treatise, a prose tract unique in its defense of King John for his defiance of the Pope. It is quite conceivable, according to McCusker, that Bale discovered an appropriate allegorical figure for Henry "in Tyndale's passing eulogy of King John, and welcomed a plot which gave him opportunity to display both his reformed doctrine and his loyalty to the crown."[18]

As a political propagandist for the Reformation, Bale despised Pope Clement VII's attempt to control and to exert power over King Henry; and the playwright views King John's earlier confrontation with Pope Innocent III as an appropriate historical analogy. This analogy was implicitly acknowledged by the Tudor government. Friar Geoffrey Turner, for instance, was arrested in 1538 for claiming that the poisoning of King John by a monk was justifiable because of the sovereign's evil conduct.[19] Tudor authorities must have clearly identified Henry with the medieval king since the friar's arrest involved a statement concerning a ruler who died 322 years previously. When we view the Pope's ambition to dethrone King Johan in Bale's morality-history, we should recognize the frequent allusions to the political conflict of the author's own time. Bale's drama thus reveals an understanding of history as cyclical, a conception that arises naturally from the eternal allegory of the morality play. We see Bale's connection between the two kings in Sedition's prophecy about the Roman clergy: "by owr craftes kyng Iohn wyll so subdwe / That for iij .C. yers all Englond shall yt rewe" (ll. 775-76). Bale asserts that the Catholic ecclesiastics will subjugate and control English monarchical government, thus making it possible for their superstitious and hypocritical doctrine to rule England for three hundred years--until the magnificent character, Imperial Majesty (Henry VIII), permits the Reformation to curb Catholic dominance in English political affairs. Since Sedition claims that England will rue the dominance of Roman Catholicism for those three hundred years, Henry's defiance of Pope Clement VII is glorious; he acts as a savior who rescues his nation from its unfortunate subjugation to the rule of the hypocritical and anti-Christian papists.

The desire for freedom from subjugation to the Church of Rome began with the disapproval of ecclesiastical wealth and abuses on the part of the anticlerical party but was precipitated by Henry's failure to obtain an annulment of his marriage to Katharine of Aragon. As stated earlier, Pope Clement VII chose not to grant the divorce because of political pressure from the powerful Charles V and because of reluctance to nullify the original papal dispensation that had allowed the marriage to occur in the first place. Although Henry wanted a divorce because he had tired of Katharine and had fallen in love with Anne Boleyn, he also had a political motive for his actions.[20] As Peter Saccio notes, "after many years of wedlock and many pregnancies, [Katharine] had produced only one child surviving infancy, the princess Mary. As few thought that a woman could rule England, Katharine had failed in her one essential duty."[21] Since Henry did not have what many considered a suitable heir, he obviously ran the risk "of a dynastic failure, of another bout of civil war, perhaps, or . . . of England's union with a continental power" after his death.[22] Thus, Pope Clement's refusal to grant the divorce and so open the way for a new marriage was potentially injurious to the future of England.

After Cardinal Wolsey and Henry's other agents failed to secure a remedy for this dangerous political situation through papal negotiation, Thomas Cromwell succeeded in recommending a unilateral solution to the problem. Saccio says that "Henry's difficulties [in securing a divorce] really arose from Rome's jurisdiction over much of England. English ecclesiastics owed allegiance to Rome as well as to Henry. . . [so] Cromwell's solution was essentially simple: he used parliament to abolish Rome's jurisdiction in England." Parliament passed bills limiting ecclesiastical jurisdiction, and subsequently, in 1533, according to Saccio, "Cromwell got the decisive bill through parliament: the act of appeals, which prohibited litigants in cases concerning wills and marriages from appealing to Rome."[23] Thereafter, Thomas Cranmer, the Archbishop of Canterbury, voided Henry's marriage to Katharine. The bills passed in parliament are important, for, by limiting the power of the Church of Rome, they proportionately increased the supremacy of the monarchy. It is no coincidence that in the following year, 1534, Henry announced that he was the Supreme Head of the English Church; the vague qualification, "so far as the law of Christ allows," was no longer necessary because Henry realized that his subjugation to Roman Catholic ecclesiastical authority had come to an end.

In *King Johan*, Bale is preoccupied with the ideology of divine right and with the sovereign's superiority over Roman Catholic ecclesiastics not only for religious reasons but also because of the political situation in Tudor England. Bale effectively employs the analogy of King John as a means of influencing his audience regarding the political dangers of Roman Catholicism in Reformation England.   Bale envisions that his propagandistic plot would persuade audience members to despise the Church of Rome, to correlate that religion and its priests with treason, and to feel a strong sense of allegiance towards their Protestant monarch.

CHAPTER ONE: NOTES

1. Graham Holderness, *Shakespeare's History* (Dublin: Gill and Macmillan; New York: St. Martin's, 1985), p. 154.

2. David Bevington, *Tudor Drama and Politics: A Critical Approach to Topical Meaning* (Cambridge, Mass.: Harvard University Press, 1968), p. 96.

3. J.J. Scarisbrick, *Henry VIII* (Berkeley: University of California Press, 1968), p. 367.

4. Peter Happe and John N. King, ed., Introduction, *The Vocacyon of Johan Bale* (Binghamton: Medieval & Renaissance Texts & Studies, 1990), p. 3.

5. Seymour Baker House, "Cromwell's Message to the Regulars: The Biblical Trilogy of John Bale, 1537," *Renaissance and Reformation* 26 (1991): 124.

6. Barry B. Adams, ed., Introduction, *King Johan* by John Bale (San Marino, Cal.: The Huntington Library, 1969), p. 23.

7. Bale, *King Johan*, ed. Adams. All quotations from *King Johan* are from this edition unless otherwise noted and are cited by line number parenthetically in the text.

8. John Henry Pyle Pafford, ed., Introduction, *King Johan* by John Bale (Oxford: Oxford University Press, 1931), p. xvii.

9. Richard Leacroft and Helen Leacroft, *Theatre and Playhouse: An Illustrated Survey of Theatre Building from Ancient Greece to the Present Day* (London: Methuen, 1988), p. 53.

10. Adams, pp. 20, 24.

11. Janet Stavropoulos Hertzbach, *From Congregation to Polity: The English Moral Drama to Shakespeare*, Diss. Indiana University, 1978, p. 2.

12. Carole Levin, *Propaganda in the English Reformation: Heroic and Villainous Images of King John*, Vol. 11. *Studies in British History* (Lewiston, New York: Edwin Mellen Press, 1988), p. 2.

13. A.P. Rossiter, *English Drama from Early Times to the Elizabethans: Its Background, Origins and Developments* (New York: Barnes & Noble, 1959), p. 115.

14. Adams, p. 20.

15. Adams, p. 42.

16. See Edmund Creeth, ed., *Kyng Johan*, in *Tudor Plays: An Anthology of Early English Drama* (New York: W.W. Norton, 1972), pp. 97-213; Part II, l. 687; see Peter Happe, ed., *King Johan*, in *The Complete Plays of John Bale* 2 vols. (Cambridge: D.S. Brewer, 1985-86), I, 76, l. 1804; and see Pafford, p. 90, l. 1756. We know that Bale made the mistake because it is written in "Hand B," which Pafford proves to be the handwriting of the playwright (p. xi).

17. Honor McCusker, *John Bale: Dramatist and Antiquary*, Diss. (Bryn Mawr University, 1942), p. 90.

18. McCusker, p. 93.

19. James Gairdner, ed., *Letters and Papers, Foreign and Domestic, of the Reign of Henry VIII. Preserved in the Public Record Office, the British Museum, and Elsewhere in England* (London: Eyre and Spottiswoode, 1892), XIII, 252.

20. Henry claimed he wanted a divorce since the marriage was incestuous because of Katharine's marriage to his brother, Arthur. Henry cited Leviticus 18:16 and 20:21, which state respectively, "Thou shalt not uncover the nakedness of thy brother's wife; it is thy brother's nakedness" and "If a man shall take his brother's wife, it is an impurity: he hath uncovered his brother's nakedness; they shall be childless." According to Scarisbrick, Henry's supporters claimed that "The miscarriages, the still-births, the denial of a son were clearly divine punishment for, and proof of, transgression of divine law" (p. 152). Deuteronomy 25:5, however, states that "When brethren dwell together, and one of them dieth without children, the wife of the deceased shall not marry to another; but his brother shall take her, and raise up seed for his brother."
Most probably Henry was not genuinely concerned about the issue of incest. The fact that his alleged fear of the ramifications of his theologically questionable marriage coincided with his interest in Anne Boleyn and his realization that Katharine was becoming too old to bear him children is significant. If Henry were truly concerned about the illegality of his marriage, he would not have sought a papal dispensation and would not have waited many years to mention his fears. Furthermore, Henry proved he had no qualms about incest by having an affair with Anne Boleyn's sister, Mary. Scarisbrick insists, "That Mary was at one time Henry's mistress, and this presumably after her marriage, is beyond doubt"; there

is also evidence that she gave birth to his bastard (p. 148). Charles R. Forker discusses the implications of the incest problem in *Fancy's Images: Contexts, Settings, and Perspectives in Shakespeare and His Contemporaries* (Carbondale: Southern Illinois University Press, 1990), pp. 154-57.

21. Peter Saccio, *Shakespeare's English Kings: History, Chronicle, and Drama* (New York: Oxford University Press, 1977), p. 217.

22. Scarisbrick, p. 150.

23. Saccio, p. 224.

THE (IL)LEGITIMACY OF JOHN:

AMBIVALENCE TOWARDS KING JOHN IN
THE TROUBLESOME RAIGNE

The anonymous *Troublesome Raigne* (c. 1588-89)[1] represents in many respects a transition between the plays of Bale and Shakespeare. The play is not as extreme in its religious perspectives as *King Johan* but is an anti-Catholic play nonetheless, as the scenes involving the Bastard's encounters in the monastery and the poisoning of John indicate. The anonymous play is more political and less polemical than Bale's, for the unknown dramatist, unlike Bale, distinguishes political from religious issues of loyalty and disobedience. The character of John is more complex and round than Bale's two-dimensional portrayal of the saintly King John. In *The Troublesome Raigne*, John, who is possibly the rightful king, acts sometimes in a villainous and tyrannical fashion. The king, however, occasionally comports himself in a heroic manner, especially when he defies the papal legate Pandulph; the dramatist intends the audience to admire him for this behavior because the playwright presents the Catholic characters as immoral and evil. The play, first performed during the Armada years, is a patriotic drama. It implies that John, despite his flaws, would never have surrendered his crown to Pandulph had he the support of his barons. *The Troublesome Raigne* demonstrates to its Elizabethan audience the dangers of the ambitious Roman clergy and the necessity of subjects' allegiance to their ruler.

Like Bale's *King Johan*, the anonymous *Troublesome Raigne of King John* is a drama concerned with pro-Reformation propaganda, but unlike its predecessor of 1538, the later work is very much a history play. The development of the chronicle history play during the fifty-three year interval between the two dramas is readily apparent when we contrast Bale's work with that of the anonymous playwright; several of the historical characters in *The Troublesome Raigne* are three-dimensional, not abstract; that is, they are figures who develop as the play progresses. One such example is King John. He is not the flat, idealistic, ahistorical saintly martyr of *King Johan*; in the anonymous play, he is a curious conflation of an unheroic rebel to the Church of Rome and an evil tyrant.

An additional evidence of the development of the history play involves the anti-papal propaganda in the two works, for the anonymous writer presents his polemics in a much more subtle manner than Bale. The speeches denouncing Roman Catholicism are not as extreme as those in *King Johan*, and they blend better with the plot and dialogue. In *The Troublesome Raigne*, we have a sense that the characters are talking to each other (with the audience eavesdropping on the exchange) rather than conversing directly with the audience. Furthermore, the anonymous play is concerned with actual historical events for their own sake. Although *The Troublesome Raigne* conflates historical time (for by its very nature the dramatic genre involves the compression and alteration of history), it nevertheless takes a greater interest in thirteenth-century England than does *King Johan*, which uses the situation of the medieval sovereign solely to analogize Tudor political conflicts. This is not to say that Bale's drama is inferior to *The Troublesome Raigne* but rather that it has different objectives. This chapter analyzes the playwright's ambivalent attitude towards his protagonist and demonstrates how the evil and heroic aspects of John's character, along with political and religious issues, reflect the dramatist's conception of the allegiance subjects owe to their monarch.

Bale omits the question of the legitimacy of John's title to the throne. If we are intended to identify Bale's King Johan with Henry VIII, it is obvious why he chooses to ignore the debate over whether the title of the medieval king is rightful. Yet the subject is a major one in *The Troublesome Raigne*. In this history play, John's nephew, Arthur of Brittany, claims the throne because his father was Geoffrey, an older brother of John. John claims the crown because his eldest brother, Richard I, allegedly bequeathed it to him: Queen Elinor declares that she "can inferre a Will, / That barres the way he [Arthur] urgeth by discent" (Part I, ll. 519-20).[2] She refers to the belief that just before Richard's death, the king altered his will, making John, not Arthur, his heir. Holinshed reports: "Vnto his brother Iohn he assigned the crowne of England, and all other his lands and dominions, causing the Nobles there present to sweare fealtie vnto him."[3] Constance, Arthur's mother, disputes the will because according to the concept of primogeniture, her son should be king. As Arthur states, "The law intends such testaments [i.e., Richard's will] as voyd, / Where right discent can no way be impeacht" (Part I, ll. 527-28). The problem of John's legitimacy, therefore, rests upon the question of whether the sovereign's last wish or primogeniture takes precedence.

There were no established laws to determine the line of succession in thirteenth-century England. Peter Saccio points out:

> The real or supposed wishes of the dying king, the preferences of the leading magnates, the strength and celerity of the various heirs, and sheer luck were all potentially powerful elements in the highly fluid situation created by a demise of the crown. The situation was all the more fluid because the crown governed a conglomerate empire whose various provinces maintained different feudal customs.[4]

John Neville Figgis presents a different perspective, claiming that in the Middle Ages the sovereign asserted himself as the indirect or direct landowner of England; consequently, "The elective character of kingship began to fall into the background, and the influences, leading to a rigid rule of primogeniture in the case of land, tended to the same result in regard to the succession."[5] It is important to ascertain when this process occurred, but as Foucault notes concerning discontinuities, "any limit we set may perhaps be no more than an arbitrary division made in a constantly mobile whole."[6] In Elizabethan England, when *The Troublesome Raigne* was written, primogeniture was a more established custom for determining inheritance than in medieval times, and this fact may be influential in the anonymous dramatist's portrayal of John as a king with a questionable title.

The first scene of the play involves the debate over the Falconbridge inheritance. John bases his decision concerning Falconbridge's heir on the concept of primogeniture. Robert says to John:

> Indeede the world reputes him [Philip] lawfull heire,
> My Father in his life did count him so,
> And here my Mother stands to proove him so. . . .
>
> (Part I, ll. 121-23)

In other words, Robert tells John to ignore the deceased Falconbridge's will because he is the rightful heir according to the laws of primogeniture. John agrees with Robert's argument, saying, "Prove this [that Philip is illegitimate], the land is thine by *Englands* law" (Part I, l. 130). The anonymous playwright includes this totally unhistorical scene so as to suggest a parallel with the main plot of John's dispute with Arthur. Both actions involve the question of legitimacy and the dispute over inheritances. John bases his decision concerning the Falconbridge inheritance solely on primogeniture, ignoring the will of the deceased man; but in respect to his own inheritance, which the playwright presents as an analogous situation, he disregards primogeniture and steadfastly claims to believe only in the will of his dead older brother. John's behavior may be contradictory because, as Virginia M. Vaughan points out, "Only with legal statutes passed under Henry VIII could a will disinherit a lineal heir."[7] According to medieval law, Arthur and not John was the rightful king. John's inconsistent decisions in the plot and subplot manifest his hypocritical behavior, and the anonymous playwright's invention of the Falconbridge inheritance becomes a subtle device to suggest the illegitimacy of John's claim to the throne. John apparently believes in primogeniture as the means of determining inheritances except when this principle, which would support the claims of his rival (Arthur), conflicts with his own interests.

Inasmuch as John has effectively established himself as king by the onset of the play and realizes the doubtfulness of his claim, he is no longer interested in the question of his legitimacy. When King Philip of France tells John that the alleged will is no proof that he is the rightful sovereign, the latter replies, "What wants, my sword shal more at large set down" (Part I, l. 547). Here the playwright implies that John intends to back up his title by force, not by law, since that is the only manner in which he can support his claim. Irving Ribner, Michael Manheim, Roy Battenhouse, David Bevington, and Marie Axton consider the play a conservative work in which John is the legitimate "hero king who vainly attempted to free his people from the yoke of Rome."[8] Axton says that "In the anonymous play the behaviour of Constance as well as that of Lewis of France and Blanche of Castile seems partly governed by the dramatist's desire to discredit any claims made through them."[9] We must comprehend, however, that the dramatist portrays John as the most sinister character in the play and treats his claim as questionable. These scholars, instead of judging it on its own qualities, perhaps compare it with Shakespeare's *King John*, a history in which John is clearly a tyrant and a usurper, and in which anti-papal propaganda is less of an issue. In *The Troublesome Raigne*, John is also a tyrant and possibly a usurper, but because the playwright is concerned with anti-clericism and to some extent with covert allusions to the Tudor monarchs (although not to the degree of Bale's comparison of John with

Henry VIII), he portrays John in a favorable light in the passages that
voice anti-Catholic polemics.

The above critics have also focused on the lecture of Philip the Bastard
to the rebellious nobles concerning the divine right of kings. The Bastard
defends John's actions, such as his exile of Chester and the murder of
Arthur:

> tis shame, and worthy all reproofe,
> To wrest such pettie wrongs in tearmes of right,
> Against a King annoynted by the Lord.
>   (Part II, ll. 461-63)

Philip's speech is quite impressive but in no way establishes that John is
God's anointed minister on earth. We cannot even be sure that he
sincerely means what he says since he attends the nobles at Saint
Edmund's Bury and defends John only after the embattled ruler commands
him to do so. John himself realizes that he is not a divinely sanctioned
sovereign; he claims, "The heaven, the earth, the sunne, the moone and all
/ Conspire with those confederates my decay" (Part II, ll. 205-06). If John
sincerely considered himself the legitimate heir to the throne, he would not
order his second coronation. As E.B. Everitt points out, "John's second
coronation is the perfect dilemma: either it is false, or the first one was;
if either is, the other presumably would be also."[10]

Perhaps related to his possible illegitimacy is John's evil and tyrannical
behavior. It was conceivable to many in Renaissance England that a
usurper would be a cruel and ineffectual ruler, especially in comparison
to a lawful sovereign. One example of John's evil behavior is his ill
treatment of his nephew Arthur. Although the anonymous playwright,
unlike Shakespeare, follows Holinshed by portraying Arthur as
presumptuous,[11] the character nonetheless manifests his innocent nature,
especially in his dialogue with Hubert de Burgh. Since Arthur is a
sympathetic character, audience members realize John's evil nature when
he cruelly orders Hubert to "put out the eyes of *Arthur Plantaginet*" (Part
I, ll. 1365-66), when he callously declares that "The brat shall dye" (Part
I, l. 654), and when he reacts apathetically and selfishly to Hubert's report
that Arthur is dead: John says, "Then with him dye my cares" (Part I, ll.
1668).

The first of these three quotations is especially telling. By using Arthur's
royal cognomen, Plantagenet, the playwright reminds the audience that
John heinously intends to mutilate a boy of royal blood, not a mere
common citizen; this emphasis magnifies the crime. Furthermore, John

wishes to blind Arthur, making him apparently unsuitable for leadership and hoping he will die as a result, but in his cowardice the king refuses to accept the blame for his nephew's death. Michael Manheim compares John's behavior to that of Cornwall and Regan in their horrifying blinding of Gloucester in *King Lear*; moreover, he points out that the adult duke would have a better chance of surviving the ordeal than a mere child such as Arthur. Manheim adds:

> The author of *TR* has thus introduced an element which for some makes John (here and in Shakespeare) more terrible than Richard Crookback, who orders his princes murdered, not tortured. Furthermore, the murder of the princes in *Richard III* is only reported to us by the murderer, not shown. John's attempt to avoid the accusation of murder only increases the implicit deceit and in no way mollifies the crime.[12]

Roy Battenhouse declares that the king feels remorse after the murder, that after his nobles "walk out on him, he soon awakes to torments of conscience."[13] I wish to argue, however, that although John later regrets ordering the attack, he is not sad that Arthur is dead; rather he is concerned that his nephew's death could lead to his own downfall. John experiences absolutely no compunction for the alleged murder, thus manifesting the cruelty of his nature. The king responds to his departing nobles:

> And are you gone? The divell be your guide:
> Proud Rebels as you are to brave me so:
> Saucie, uncivill, checkers of my will.
> Your tongues give edge unto the fatall knife:
> That shall have passage through your traitrous throats.
> (Part I, ll. 1680-84)

This passage certainly exhibits no remorse in John; in fact, Everitt's edition of the play uses exclamation points at the end of the first three lines of the passage, indicating uninhibited fury.[14] The king then proceeds to blame Hubert for following his orders, thus projecting his guilt onto his dutiful subject. John feels self-interest, not remorse; the two sentiments are in this case mutually exclusive.

John's ineffectiveness as a ruler becomes obvious in the scene in which he tries vainly to convince the citizens of Angiers to open their gates to him and his followers. After defying King Philip, Arthur, and Constance with valiant words, John asks that the townspeople of Angiers demonstrate their allegiance to him. When they refuse on grounds that his title to the throne is unsettled, he replies, "I shall not come in then? (Part I, l. 633). This response, from one who has declared himself king, appears feeble. John's meek submission to the authority of those he deems his subjects may perhaps be taken as an implicit acknowledgement of his own illegitimacy.

The anonymous author of *The Troublesome Raigne* also hints at King John's possible illegitimacy by portraying the decline of England under his rule. In the Renaissance, many believed that England--or any country for that matter--could not prosper under the governance of a usurping king. Shakespeare's *Hamlet* and *Richard III* are prominent examples of plays that dramatize such an attitude. We have already seen some evidence of John's ineffectiveness as king. Another instance is John's agreement with King Philip, a pact greatly to England's detriment. In an attempt to rid himself of Arthur as a rival for the throne, John relinquishes five English provinces (Volquesson, Poitiers, Anjou, Touraine, and Maine) to France. John does so even though he admits the foolhardiness of such an action:

> My brother [Richard I] got these lands
> With much effusion of our English bloud:
> And shall I give it all away at once?
> (Part I, ll. 832-34)

Although Saccio points out that the historical King John did not squander such extensive lands as his counterparts in *The Troublesome Raigne* and in Shakespeare's *King John*,[15] the fact that the king does trade English territories, those acquired with the loss of much life and bloodshed, in exchange for his personal security as ruler demonstrates his selfishness; and the action is disgraceful and politically injurious to the country.

John's bartering of England's interests for his own also reflects his ineptitude as a ruler because he cannot decide for himself whether he should make the bargain with France. When Philip demands the five provinces, John turns to Queen Elinor and meekly asks, "Mother what shall I doo?" (Part I, l. 832). After his mother advises him to relinquish the territories, he immediately does so. John here demonstrates his failure of leadership, his lack of an ability that was believed by some Renaissance thinkers to be an innate quality of divinely ordained monarchs. Furthermore, one of the main reasons why Arthur has few followers in his quest for the throne is that he is dominated too much by his mother, Constance. Yet the scene in which John consults his mother demonstrates that he too is maternally dominated.

But again, of foremost importance is John's squandering of English territories for his own personal profit--an example of his tyranny and its damaging effects upon England. John admits:

> O *England*, wert thou ever miserable,
> King *John* of *England* sees thee miserable:
> *John*, tis thy sinnes that makes it miserable. . . .
> (Part II, ll. 238-40)

What are these "sinnes" to which John refers? Could he be thinking of his usurpation of the throne? Such an inference is probable because his behavior in regard to Arthur (his possible usurpation of the child's right and his instructions to Hubert concerning his nephew) is his only major sin in the play, especially when we consider that he is unashamed and self-righteous in regard to his actions towards the Church of Rome and that the political bias of this drama is clearly pro-Reformation. Thus, if England is suffering because of John, it is plausible to conclude that he has illegally seized the crown.

Some scholars of this history play believe that John is portrayed as the legitimate heir to the throne because of the parallels to Tudor rulers in the character of King John and because of the anti-Catholic sentiment in the play. We should realize, however, that the anonymous playwright is not making a hero of John in an effort to flatter Queen Elizabeth, nor should we automatically assume that the author regards the two sovereigns as analogous. Battenhouse claims that the dramatist writes in the "apologetic tradition" of Reformation England with its stress on national duty:

> The *TR* prologue emphasizes nevertheless John's initial heroism. . . . The play as a whole appeals to patriotism by stressing the perfidy of John's enemies, his bravery in battle, and the unstinting loyalty he receives from King Richard's bastard son Philip, an invented character who serves also as the author's spokesman for Tudor political doctrine.[16]

The lines of the prologue to which Battenhouse refers describe King John as:

> A warlike Christian and your Countreyman.
> For Christs true faith indur'd he many a storme,
> And set himselfe against the Man of Rome,
> Untill base treason (by a damned wight)

Did all his former triumphs put to flight. . . .

                    (Prologue, ll. 5-9)

Battenhouse assumes that the author of *The Troublesome Raigne* also
wrote the prologue; prologues were, however, sometimes supplied by
writers other than the dramatist. This possibility is especially plausible
when we consider J. Dover Wilson's point that the prologue of *The
Troublesome Raigne* may have been written for the published version of
the play, which was probably printed at least two years after the drama was
first produced.[17] The passage quoted above is clearly incongruous with
the characterization of King John in the play and is much more suitable for
Bale's *King Johan* than for this anonymous play.

During the course of *The Troublesome Raigne* we recognize that John
is not the anti-Catholic martyr who three centuries earlier had anticipated
Tudor Reformation policies. When the sovereign orders Philip the
Bastard to plunder the monasteries, he does not make this request because
he is a Protestant reformer or an anti-clerical religious purist who despises
the avarice and lechery of the clergy but because he needs money to
finance his wars.[18] The anonymous play does not portray King John as a
firm and devout believer in Christianity but rather as an irreligious man
who uses religion as a political tool. We realize that John is undoubtedly
no anti-Catholic martyr when he unpatriotically capitulates and succumbs
to the demands of Pandulph, ingloriously and shamefully surrendering the
English crown to the Cardinal. John capitulates not because he realizes he
has comported himself irreligiously but rather because he may employ
Pandulph's power to legitimize and maintain his power. The king remarks:

> there is no way to keepe thy Crowne,
> But finely to dissemble with the Pope:
> That hand that gave the wound must give the salve.
> To cure the hurt, els quite incurable.

                    (Part II, ll. 274-77)

Since John lived centuries before the beginning of Lutheranism, when
England was a virtually undivided Catholic nation with few dissenters, his
dissembling with Pandulph and disdain for the Cardinal's religion signifies
that he is a worldly opportunist, not an early Protestant. Although one
may counter that the play contains anachronisms, John never mentions
Protestantism during the course of the drama and never embraces
Christianity. John R. Elliot notes that in the medieval chroniclers'
portrayals of King John, "the results of his defiance of the church were

held up as a warning to future rulers of the fruits of impiety. . . . He despised Christianity. . . ."[19] And the anonymous playwright portrays King John as just such an irreligious and deceitful sovereign.

The playwright's treatment of the royal adversary of the Church is quite negative despite the fact that *The Troublesome Raigne* is a pro-Reformation play in its portrayal of the Church of Rome. In fact, the title reflects King John's tyrannical rule because the king is chiefly responsible for the "troublesome" nature of his reign. John's imprisonment of Arthur and the subsequent death of his nephew, for which the monarch is largely responsible in the play, causes his nobles to rebel and compels him to seek a humiliating reconciliation with the Pope.

In the propagandistic sections of *The Troublesome Raigne*, however, the author breaks away from history and provides John with some prophetic political commentary applicable to the period in which the play was written. In a soliloquy, John despairs of his own incapacity to rid England of a corrupt foreign Church:

> Thy sinnes are farre too great to be the man
> T'abolish Pope, and Popery from thy Realme:
> But in thy Seate, if I may gesse at all,
> A King shall raigne that shall suppresse them all.
> (Part II, ll. 278-81)

Here the playwright clearly takes liberties with history. The term "popery," a Protestant term of abuse, clearly was not in use in King John's day. In the *Oxford English Dictionary*, the first recorded use of "popery" occurs in William Tyndale's *An exposicio vpon. . . Mathew* (c. 1534). The passage in *The Troublesome Raigne* obviously demonstrates John's anticipation of the Reformation centuries later; the reference to a king who will suppress Catholicism suggests the Tudors--that is, a composite of Henry VIII, Edward VI, and Elizabeth.

The play also acknowledges the king's sinful behavior. Yet John refers to his own evil nature by using the third person singular, as if he were talking to someone else. Thus he attempts to shift the blame by distancing himself from his sinful character, by pretending that he and the evils that he has caused may be separated. The anonymous dramatist, by acknowledging King John's evil deeds and his possibly illegitimate status, implies that it takes a great leader to guide the English people to the promised land (i.e., the Reformation). The Moses who does so must be virtuous, and John realizes his incapacity for the role, but he prophesies about the future sovereigns (Henry, Edward, and Elizabeth), virtuous rulers with what they considered legitimate claims to the throne, who led their people from the snares of "popery" to the "true" Christian religion. John is a valuable symbol in *The Troublesome Raigne* not only because he has defied the Pope three centuries before Henry, Edward, and Elizabeth but because his evil character makes a great contrast with the Tudor sovereigns to whom he compares himself. The dramatist, by portraying John as a tyrannical, irreligious, and possibly usurping king, implies that the Tudor rulers must be splendid by contrast and that they should consequently be appreciated for their vast superiority to John.

Even though King John is, for the most part, an unlikable character in *The Troublesome Raigne*, a Reformation audience, in contrast to a Catholic one, would have enjoyed his defiance of the Church of Rome. A prime illustration of this truth is the author's portrayal of the clergy in the monastery when Philip the Bastard arrives to plunder it. The friar whom Philip bullies speaks in Skeltonic verse (which makes him sound ridiculous). He shows the Bastard a chest allegedly full of gold but that actually harbors the abbot's sexual partner, the nun Fair Alice. Philip acts as a spokesperson for the propagandizing author when he declares:

> The Friers chest a hel for Nuns. How do these dolts deceive us!
> Is this the labour of their lives to feede and live at ease,
> To revell so lasciviously as often as they please.
> Ile mend the fault or fault my ayme, if I do misse amending,
> Tis better burn the cloisters down than leave them for offending.
>
> (Part 1, ll. 1269-73)

The anonymous dramatist wisely chooses Philip, the only brave and heroic character in the play, as the defender of Tudor Reformation politics. The Bastard, notes Axton, combats John's adversaries "to maintain English independence from foreign powers and later to assert independence from Rome."[20] Philip's words support not only the actions of King John but also the destruction of the monasteries by Henry VIII three centuries later.

The playwright later places more anti-Catholic propaganda and a prophesy of the Protestant Tudor dynasty in the mouth of the dying King John; his last words support the future Tudor policy in Renaissance England:

> Since *John* did yeeld unto the Priest of *Rome,*
> Nor he nor his have prospred on the earth:
> Curst are his blessings, and his curse is blisse.
> . . . .
> I am not he shall buyld the Lord a house,

Or roote these Locusts from the face of earth:
But if my dying heart deceave me not,
From out these loynes shall spring a Kingly braunch
Whose armes shall reach unto the gates of *Rome*,
And with his feete treade downe the Strumpets pride,
That sits upon the chaire of *Babylon*.

                                   (Part II, ll. 1075-87)

The concept of a dying man's ability to foretell the future was a prominent notion in the Renaissance. In *Hamlet*, the prince claims that "Conceit in weakest bodies strongest works" (III.iv.114), and the dying John of Gaunt in *Richard II* calls himself "a prophet new inspir'd" (II.i.31).[21] Hardin Craig confirms that this belief was widely held in Renaissance England, stating that "those near to death or weakened by old age, since they are less hindered by bodily sensitivity, are capable of divination."[22] King John is not a virtuous nor probably a legitimate sovereign, according to the anonymous dramatist's play, so he is unable to defeat the ambitious and corrupt Church of Rome. Nonetheless, he realizes the necessity of England's break with Roman Catholicism, and he attempts but fails to accomplish this separation. His desire to break with the Catholic Church, however, betokens self-interest, not the benefit of his subjects. Consequently, we see ambivalent portrayals of King John in Tudor chronicles. Some chroniclers are antipathetic; some are ambivalent; and some are favorable in their treatments of this brutal and tyrannical ruler who, like King Henry VIII and Queen Elizabeth, defied the Roman Church and was excommunicated.

Manheim correctly asserts that John is "a figure whose appeal to our sympathies shifts radically," for "the signals that the anti-papal hero speaks in *TR* are woefully out of harmony with what surrounds them."[23] Manheim attributes the ambivalent nature of John to the anonymous playwright's lack of skill and claims that Shakespeare, because of his superior talent, later constructs a more consistent character. But perhaps the unknown artist deals with an insoluble dilemma: he deals with two different King Johns and two different genres. The anonymous dramatist writes a history play in which he adheres to the chronicles he has read and faithfully portrays John by including the king's vices. Since the dramatist is concerned with anti-Catholic propaganda, he needs to provide King John with several heroic speeches, as when he defies the Church of Rome and prophesies the emergence of Tudor Reformation government. The playwright's inability to blend the two genres (history and political propaganda) causes him to present King John as a schizophrenic personality. Perhaps the problem is not the artist's lack of talent, for the playwright successfully conveys his anti-papal meaning to the audience while constructing a history play. Besides, we have no indication that the writer concerns himself with the consistency of John's character. Shakespeare later succeeds in drawing a more consistent King John, but in fairness to the unknown playwright, the Stratford artist only deals with one genre--that of dramatic history--and minimizes Reformation propaganda.

The political propaganda directed against the Church of Rome in *The Troublesome Raigne* teaches that the clergy are instrumental in severing the bond between ruler and subject and thus are responsible for ensuing civil wars. Like Henry and Elizabeth, John loses the allegiance of some of his nobles. Although King John is partly responsible for losing the loyalty of his subjects because of his murder of Arthur, he, like his Tudor descendants, faces a rebellion because of his breach with the Church of Rome. As John receives the holy curse (an oxymoron from a Protestant viewpoint) from the Cardinal, Pandulph damages the relationship between sovereign and subject: The legate says to John, "[I] pronounce thee accursed discharging every of thy subjects of all dutie and fealtie that they doo owe to thee, and pardon and forgivenes of sinne to those of them whatsoever, which shall carrie armes against thee, or murder thee: this I pronounce, and charge all good men to abhorre thee as an excommunicate person" (Part I, ll. 995-1000).

Essex later uses Pandulph's words as one excuse to raise arms against his king (Part II, ll. 415-19), but his reasoning is feeble: if the Cardinal's curse and excommunication of John are important to the nobles, why do they initially support their king in his struggle against the Church? Why do the nobles refuse to adhere to Pandulph's subsequent demand that they cease raising arms against their sovereign? Essex's defiance of King John because of the monarch's strife with the Church of Rome and the subsequent excommunication are ironic because shortly after the earl makes his comment, he and the other lords are themselves excommunicated by Pandulph (Part II, ll. 698-701) for disobeying the Cardinal's command. And why do they decide to rebel only after John refuses their request concerning Arthur, thus demonstrating his superior power?

The anonymous playwright, like Bale before him and Shakespeare after him, fails to mention the Magna Carta, an important document in its own time (the second decade of the thirteenth century) but then largely forgotten until the debates between the king and Parliament in seventeenth-century England made it relevant once more. The Magna Carta deals with the rights of subjects and the limitations of sovereign power. In a discussion of the document, J.C. Holt states that John's revolting nobles were

> the recalcitrant, the dissatisfied, and the rejected--men who had lost favour and fortune or who had struggled in vain to achieve them, men with real or imagined personal wrongs who now sougʰt restitution from the King and vengeance on his agents. . . . it also sprang from the nature of the rebellion, caused by the accumulation, as much as the abuse, of royal power.[24]

These nobles had lost rights under the rule of King John that their ancestors had acquired under Henry II, and they desired the restoration of their power. These feudal lords acquired their rights through the Magna Carta of 1215, forcing John to sign the document by raising armies and rebelling against him. This desire for rights and the concomitant limitation of the sovereign's power, rather than Pandulph's curse and excommunication of John and the king's murder of Arthur, were the real reasons for the civil war. Therefore, the anonymous playwright's plot (the nobles rebelling partly because of the Roman Catholic clergy) is historically inaccurate and exemplifies his anti-Catholic propaganda.

Rebellion is a complicated issue in *The Troublesome Raigne*. The civil war occurred in the second decade of the thirteenth century, but the dramatist writes from pro-Reformation and Renaissance perspectives. Holt says that in medieval England rebels were sometimes considered heroes and that "Rebellion incurred little social stigma."[25] Holt's statement is slightly reductive since some nobles disliked John for his treacherous actions against his brother when Richard was king, but his assertion that rebellion was considered a less heinous act in the twelfth century than in the Renaissance is correct. Such a conclusion is logical because feudal lords possessed great power during King John's reign. Civil war occurred frequently in his rule since, as Figgis notes, "the feudal idea, despite all the efforts of the central power, was still strong, and there is perhaps no more essential element in feudal theory, than the belief in the infinite divisibility of sovereign power."[26]

Not until the Tudor dynasty did authority became more centralized in the institution of monarchy. Although his setting is thirteenth-century feudal England, the anonymous playwright is also concerned with Elizabethan England. Since both John and Elizabeth dealt with rebellions of Catholic nobles, the theme of a subject's duty to his sovereign in *The Troublesome Raigne* is also important as regards the political situation of the late 1580s;

at this time support of the queen was especially stressed because of England's struggle with Spain and with the Pope, and because of the controversial issue of Mary of Scotland's imprisonment. The Elizabethan dramatist makes the allegiance to a monarch crucial in *The Troublesome Raigne* whereas it was less important in King John's reign because of the greater diffusion of political power.

Do subjects have the right to rebel? The anonymous dramatist raises this question and manifests that the answer is no. Elizabethan subjects, such as the unknown playwright, were compelled to attend church, where they heard propagandistic homilies that stated the need for obedience and the danger of rebellion. Arthur F. Kinney states that the homilies on obedience instruct that "rebellion--following Lucifer's model as anti-Christ, rather than the model of Christ Himself--was clearly a sin. No man had the right or capacity to judge rulers; his singular duty was one of obedience. It is important to recognize that this obedience was neither surrender nor impotence, but a loving submission to a higher force which is God."[27] The rebellious nobles look foolish when they transfer their allegiance from John and then later revert to him. They receive punishment for their disloyalty when Lewis betrays them; the Dauphin plans to assassinate them after receiving their aid. Meloun claims:

> they that infringe their oaths,
> And play the rebells gainst their native King,
> Will for as little cause revolt from you [i.e., Lewis],
> If ever opportunitie incite them so:
> For once forsworne, and never after sound,
> Theres no affiance after perjurie.
> (Part II, ll. 587-92)

Earlier, Philip the Bastard attends the lords at Saint Edmund's Bury and chastises them, telling them that even if John has transgressed, they have no warrant to rebel:

> admit the wrongs [of John] are true,
> Yet subjects may not take in hand revenge,
> And rob the heavens of their proper power,
> Where sitteth he to whom revenge belongs.
> And doth a Pope, a Priest, a man of pride
> Give charters for the lives of lawfull Kings?
> . . . .
> Ayd *Lewes,* leave God, kill *John*, please hell. . . .
> (Part II, ll. 464-75)

Therefore, the anonymous writer's dramatization of rebellious nobles, under the influence of the treacherous Church of Rome, is analogous to the situation in Elizabethan England; likewise, the dangerous consequences of the feudal lords' revolt in thirteenth-century England reminds the unknown artist's audience of the need to support the centralized monarchy of Queen Elizabeth.

CHAPTER 2: NOTES

1. See E.K. Chambers, *The Elizabethan Stage,* 4 vols. (Oxford: Clarendon Press, 1951) IV, 24; and John Dover Wilson, ed., Introduction, *King John* (Cambridge: Cambridge University Press, 1969), p. xix. They discuss the influence upon the play of the attack by the Spanish Armada in 1588 and note that the drama was written about that time. The text was later published in two parts in 1591, but the play was clearly performed before its publication.

2. Geoffrey Bullough, ed., *The Troublesome Raigne of King John,* in *Narrative and Dramatic Sources of Shakespeare,* 8 vols. (London: Routledge and Kegan Paul; New York: Columbia University Press, 1957-75), IV, 72-151. All quotations from *The Troublesome Raigne* are from this edition and are cited by part and line number in the text.

3. Raphael Holinshed, *Holinshed's Chronicles of England, Scotland, and Ireland,* 6 vols. (London: J. Johnson, et al., 1807-08), II, 270.

4. Peter Saccio, *Shakespeare's English Kings: History, Chronicle, and Drama* (New York: Oxford University Press, 1977), p. 190.

5. John Neville Figgis, *The Divine Right of Kings* (1914; rpt. New York: Harper & Row, 1965), p. 23.

6. Michel Foucault, *The Order of Things: An Archaeology of the Human Sciences* (New York: Vintage Books, 1973), p. 50.

7. Virginia M. Vaughan, "King John: Subversion and Containment," in *"King John": New Perspectives,* ed. Deborah T. Curren-Aquino (Newark: University of Delaware Press; London: Associated University Presses, 1989), p. 66.

8. Irving Ribner, *The English History Play in the Age of Shakespeare,* rev. ed. (New York: Barnes & Noble, 1965), p. 77. See also Michael Manheim's *The Weak King Dilemma in the Shakespearean History Play* (Syracuse: Syracuse University Press, 1973); Roy Battenhouse's "King John: Shakespeare's Perspective and Others," *Notre Dame English Journal,* 14 (1982), 191-215; David Bevington's *Tudor Drama and Politics: A Critical Approach to Topical Meaning* (Cambridge, Mass.: Harvard University Press, 1968); and Marie Axton's, *The Queen's Two Bodies: Drama and the Elizabethan Succession* (London: Royal Historical Society, 1977), p. 108.

9. Axton, p. 108.

10. E.B. Everitt, ed., Introduction, *The Troublesome Reign of John, King of England*. . ., in *Six Early Plays Related to the Shakespearean Canon* (Copenhagen: Rosenkilde and Bagger, 1965), p. 144.

11. Holinshed, II, 285.

12. Manheim, p. 122.

13. Battenhouse, p. 199.

14. Everitt, p. 174.

15. Saccio, p. 192.

16. Battenhouse, p. 189.

17. Wilson, p. xviii.

18. Henry's motives for plundering the monasteries were also far from pure.

19. John R. Elliot, "Shakespeare and the Double Image of King John," *Shakespeare Studies*, 1 (1965), 65.

20. Axton, p. 109.

21. David Bevington, ed., *The Complete Works of Shakespeare*, 3rd ed. (Glenview, Ill.: Scott, Foresman, 1980). These two quotations from Shakespeare are from this edition.

22. Hardin Craig, *The Enchanted Glass: The Elizabethan Mind in Literature* (New York: Oxford University Press, 1936), p. 45.

23. Manheim, pp. 118, 120.

24. J.C. Holt, *Magna Carta and Medieval Government* (London: Hambledon, 1985), p. 123.

25. Holt, p. 124.

26. Figgis, p. 30.

27. Arthur F. Kinney, "Introduction to 'Homily on Obedience,'" in *Elizabethan Backgrounds: Historical Documents of the Age of Elizabeth I, Newly Edited, With Introductions* (Hamden, Connecticut: Archon Books, 1975), p. 46.

CHAPTER 3

SHAKESPEARE'S *KING JOHN* AND THE DANGERS OF COMMODITY

King John (c. 1594) supports the Tudor dynasty, for, like *The Troublesome Raigne*, it manifests the dangers of foreign invasion and of the employment of commodity by the ambitious; the play also demonstrates the need for people to be true to their ruler in order for England to remain a powerful and unconquerable nation. Shakespeare's play may be viewed, following Virginia Vaughan, as potentially subversive in its omission of anti-Catholic propaganda, but the drama reflects the growing religious toleration that spread during the years separating the writing of *The Troublesome Raigne* and *King John*. Furthermore, Shakespeare, unlike his two predecessors, divorces political ideology from religious polemics. *King John* is more problematic than *The Troublesome Raigne*, for Shakespeare's John is a tyrannical king who has clearly stolen the throne from his innocent nephew and who is then indirectly responsible for the boy's death. Such an interpretation demonstrates the subversive nature of *King John* because the play undermines the parallel that Protestant martyrologists have made between the medieval King John and the contemporary Tudors rulers who also broke from the Catholic Church and were consequently excommunicated. Shakespeare's play, therefore, is more politically radical than Bale's since *King John* contradicts the polemics of the established Tudor government while *King Johan* vehemently and blindly defends these ideologies.

Shakespeare employed *The Troublesome Raigne* as his primary source for *King John*.[1] The plots of the two history plays are quite alike, one major difference being Shakespeare's exclusion of two comical anti-Catholic scenes. Bevington notes that *King John* "does in fact tone down the anti-Catholic virulence of its chief source, *The Troublesome Reign of King John*."[2] It is important to explore why Shakespeare refrained from employing the anti-Catholic polemics of his primary source, for such an analysis may illuminate trends in contemporary Elizabethan politics that occurred between the writing of *The Troublesome Raigne* (c. 1588-89) and *King John*. Unlike the play by the anonymous dramatist, Shakespeare's play is not a drama of anti-Catholic propaganda but rather a history play that attacks those who seek political power through the use of commodity (the compromising of ethical values and the breaking of promises out of motives of self-interest). The papal legate Pandulph, for instance, employs the Pope's authority to manipulate the political situation involving England and France. Laymen such as King John, King Philip, and Lewis, however, are equally guilty of abandoning their values for their own interests, so Shakespeare does not single out the Church of Rome as the villain of the play. Both secular and ecclesiastic leaders behave villainously in this dark history, which portrays a world in which ambition for power divorces morality from politics. Shakespeare concerns himself with the dangers of commodity and with the necessity of allegiance to an English sovereign, even if he is an evil usurper.

Shakespeare's omissions of the scene in which the Bastard encounters corrupt Roman clergymen while plundering their monastery and of the one involving their plot to murder John support the claim that the play contains little anti-Catholic sentiment. The anonymous dramatist of *The Troublesome Raigne* uses the former episode to satirize the hypocritical clergy of the Church of Rome: when the Bastard invades the monastery, he discovers the avarice, deceit, and lust of the monks. King Richard's illegitimate son also influences the audience with his anti-papal commentary concerning what he witnesses, such as the abbot's treasure chest that conceals the sexually promiscuous nun, Fair Alice. But in *King John*, the emphasis is quite different; the king orders the Bastard to pillage monasteries in order to acquire the money needed for his soldiers' pay, but Shakespeare chooses not to show the scene. Instead we merely hear the Bastard's report that he has accomplished his mission. Shakespeare is simply not very interested in promoting anti-clerical propaganda in his play.

The second major episode in *The Troublesome Raigne* that Shakespeare excludes involves a monk's plan to murder King John. The anonymous playwright slanders Roman Catholics in this ahistorical scene: as in John Bale's *King Johan*, *The Troublesome Raigne* indicates that a monk at Swinstead plots and performs the assassination of the king. The drama also implicates other ecclesiastics in the conspiracy, for they encourage and absolve the monk and also pray for his soul.

Shakespeare's approach is quite different. He is aware of the legend of Simon of Swinstead but does not portray the clergyman as being guilty. *King John* does not, for instance, show papists plotting nor does the drama present the alleged murder to the audience. When Hubert encounters the Bastard, he claims that "The King, I fear, is poison'd by a monk" (V.vi.23).[3] Hubert does not state that he is sure that a monk has poisoned John, only that he fears this is true. Roy Battenhouse, who believes that Shakespeare's play is not anti-Catholic, states that the phrase "'I fear' which begins the report leaves us wondering how much of Hubert's assertion rests on hearsay evidence only."[4] Since we receive the information second-hand and do not witness the act ourselves, the information may be erroneous. King John later says that he has been poisoned (V.vii.35, 46-48) but never says by whom; and since he acts deliriously, we should question whether to accept his words as truth. Shakespeare also omits the equivalent of Henry III's speech in *The Troublesome Raigne* in which the young king orders the Bastard to destroy Swinstead Abbey, for the monks "have kilde my Father and my King" (Part II, ll. 1142).[5] Battenhouse points out that Shakespeare fails to include this passage in his play because he "surely knew that Henry III never made any such request. Besides, it's not to Shakespeare's taste."[6]

Shakespeare provides us with an alternative cause of John's death-- namely, fever. Unlike the anonymous author of *The Troublesome Raigne*, Shakespeare indicates that John is quite feverish before he dies. In his last scene before the one in which he dies, John tells Hubert:

> Ay me, this tyrant fever burns me up,
> And will not let me welcome this good news
>   [of France's troubles in the war against England].
> Set on toward Swinstead. To my litter straight;
> Weakness possesseth me, and I am faint.
>   (V.iii.14-17)

Since John suffers from a severe illness before he ventures to Swinstead Abbey, it is unlikely that a monk poisons him; he probably dies of a fever. Battenhouse asks, "Could the poison be simply the 'tyrant fever' of earlier origin, here recognized as a deserved punishment? Curiously, no one in this scene lays blame on a villainous monk or on treachery by the abbey."[7] In fact, the play includes no monks at all, and it is doubtful that Shakespeare would write a drama in which a character who never appears onstage performs one of the major actions--unless he wanted to create suspicion in the minds of his audience. We cannot, therefore, be positive of the actual cause of the king's death in *King John* because Shakespeare purposely renders it unclear, but it is difficult to believe that a monk has actually murdered the king.

Most modern historians such as W.L. Warren agree that while John was feasting with the citizens of Lynn, he "contracted dysentery as a result of over-indulgence in their hospitality when fatigued by long days of hard riding."[8] John, shortly afterwards, travelled to Swinstead, where he suffered the grievous loss of his treasure. Roger of Wendover claims that King John "felt such anguish of mind about his property which was swallowed up by the waters, that he was seized with a violent fever and became ill."[9] This loss, combined with his sickness and fatigue, contributed to his death. Warren's claims that John died at Newark and not Swinstead, that the Abbot of Croxton nursed him, and that he possessed sufficient time and energy to dictate his will just prior to his death (a devoutly religious will that names five Roman ecclesiastics among its thirteen executors)[10] supports the theory that the king was not poisoned by a monk.

Warren and Holinshed reach similar conclusions. Holinshed, borrowing evidence from Matthew Paris, reports that after John suffered the loss of his treasure in the whirlpool:

> immediatlie therevpon he fell into an ague, the force and heat whereof, togither with his immoderate feeding on rawe peaches, and drinking of new sider, so increased his sicknesse, that he was not able to ride. . . . [Two days later, John,] with great paine, caused himselfe to be caried vnto Newarke, where in the castell through anguish of mind, rather than through force of sicknesse, he departed this life.[11]

Holinshed does list other accounts of the death of John, including the story of a monk who poisoned the king, for which he cites William Caxton as the source. The chronicler, however, does not place much faith in Caxton's account and merely mentions it as one of several possible alternatives with which he is familiar.

Shakespeare, unlike the anonymous playwright, adheres to Holinshed's account of John's death instead of following the propagandistic stories of anti-Catholic chroniclers. One possible reason for Shakespeare's break from the handling of John's death in the earlier play may be his alleged Roman Catholic sympathies.[12] Virginia M. Vaughan argues that Shakespeare's omission of anti-Catholic propaganda in *King John* is subversive, that "in deconstructing *The Troublesome Raigne* and reconstructing the events of John's reign into a new drama, Shakespeare subverted much of the Tudor ideology embedded in the original."[13] Vaughan, however, does not consider the growing religious toleration for Roman Catholicism that occurred in England between the writing of *The Troublesome Raigne* and *King John*. Anti-papal sentiment in England was high during the tension that existed between Protestant Britain and Catholic Spain in the late 1580s, the period of the Armada. The strife between the two countries was precipitated by Elizabeth's imprisonment of Mary Stuart, the English monarch's refusal to name an heir to the English throne, and Spain's desire for a Roman Catholic sovereign in England; the tension between the two powers led to war and the subsequent defeat of the attempted Spanish invasion in 1588.

Anti-papal feelings declined somewhat after the execution of Mary. Mary's imprisonment incited numerous romantic but unrealistic Catholic plots to overthrow Elizabeth and replace her with Mary Stuart. Consequently, before Mary died, Elizabeth's government regarded many English Catholics with suspicion. Lacey Baldwin Smith says that "For nineteen years Mary Stuart lived in England as an unwanted and embarrassing prisoner; but this did not prevent her from meddling in high treason. Surrounded by English spies, she went from one harebrained plot to the next."[14] The death of the Queen of Scots in 1587 obviously ended Catholic machinations to rescue her and in turn helped reduce anti-Catholic sentiment in England.

England's defeat of the Spanish Armada destroyed the enemy's navy and ruined her dreams of overpowering Elizabeth's Anglican settlement; Spain ceased to be so serious and so immediate a threat. Furthermore, the defeat of the Armada shattered the illusions of those Catholics who waited in vain for the papal curse on England and Elizabeth to take effect. Zealous Catholics, who regarded Protestants as heretics, began to realize that God perhaps was not against Queen Elizabeth and Protestant England. The Queen's ministers, such as Lord Burghley, wrote treatises expounding the well-being of England and the providential nature of the victory. In "The miraculous victory. . . upon the Armada," Emanuel van Meteren claims:

> God miraculously preserved the English nation. For the Lord Admirall [Howard] wrote unto her Majestie that in all humane reason, and according to the judgement of all men (every circumstance being duly considered) the Englishmen were not of any such force, whereby they might, without a miracle, dare once to approch within sight of the Spanish Fleet: insomuch that they freely ascribed all the honour of their victory unto God, who had confounded the enemy, and had brought his counsels to none effect.[15]

Even the Pope "expressed his admiration for the courage and bravery of the English queen."[16]

King Philip felt confident that Spain's invasion of England would succeed, partly because he expected the support of English Catholics. William Allen and Robert Persons, a zealous Catholic and a Jesuit respectively, erroneously informed King Philip that thousands of English Catholics were willing to aid Spain in their invasion of England. J.B. Black points out that "Both Allen and Persons held the view that to be a good catholic was synonymous with being pro-Spanish in politics. Of the intense patriotism which now surged through England they knew and cared nothing."[17] Most English Catholics, in fact, had no intention of helping the Spanish cause and were loyal to Elizabeth. Black points out:

> it had been demonstrated, not once but many times, that both the Catholic laity and the priests whom they supported were overwhelmingly loyal to the queen. Obviously the time had come to consider the question of extending some measure of toleration, with suitable safeguards, to the large body of non-political catholics in England.[18]

Consequently, English Protestants began to ease their fears and suspicions of members of the Church of Rome, and this change is apparent in *King John*.

Although I disagree with Vaughan's claim that the omission of anti-Catholic polemics in Shakespeare's play is subversive, I agree with her assertion that *King John* "is not the mirror of Elizabethan policy that Lily B. Campbell described in 1947; it is not a strict didactic representation of Tudor ideology."[19] Shakespeare's drama makes problematic and perhaps even undermines Tudor ideology by characterizing King John as an evil usurper. Medieval chroniclers such as Roger of Wendover and Matthew Paris portrayed King John in an extremely negative manner because of his defiance of Pope Innocent III and his impious behavior towards the Church of Rome and towards his barons. John R. Elliot notes that when Protestant polemicists attempted to restore John's reputation, the medieval king "became firmly identified with a set of religious-political doctrines that were at the heart of official Tudor policy."[20] If John were to be likened to Henry, Edward, or Elizabeth, his character must be portrayed in an unblemished and heroic manner. Carole Levin says that those in the sixteenth century who wrote about King John from a Tudor perspective neglected to mention Arthur because the "murder was probably the single event which most tarnished John's reputation and allowed him--then and now--to be considered by many to be a monster."[21]

Shakespeare not only includes Arthur as a character in his play but evokes pathos for the prince by presenting him as an innocent boy whom John cruelly imprisons and targets for death. John is indirectly responsible for Arthur's death, for his evil plot frightens the boy, causing him to jump from the Tower; after his body has smashed against the rocks, the dying prince says, "My uncle's spirit is in these stones" (IV.iii.9). Arthur behaves less ambitiously and more innocently in Shakespeare's play than in *The Troublesome Raigne* and in Holinshed's *Chronicles*. Unlike the Arthur of the anonymous playwright and of Holinshed, Shakespeare's character, while his uncle's captive, does not presumptuously declare himself and not John the rightful sovereign of England. The character in *King John* cares little for power, informing Hubert that he wishes he was his son instead of Geoffrey's, and "So I were out of prison and kept sheep, / I should be as merry as the day is long" (IV.i.17-18). Arthur's mentioning of tending sheep is noteworthy, for by doing so, he manifests his preference for the pastoral over court life and politics; it is but one of several quotations that leads us to believe that the attempt to place him on the throne reflects the ambition of Constance and King Philip, not that of the young prince. Charles R. Forker suggests the Christ-like innocence of Arthur by pointing out that the notion of a royal figure as innocent shepherd originated in "biblical tradition, for Christ was the prototype of the good shepherd (the *bonus pastor*) who was also king of the universe."[22]

Furthermore, Shakespeare's Arthur demonstrates an innocence absent from *The Troublesome Raigne* when he responds to Hubert's revelation that John has given orders to mutilate him. In the anonymous play, the outraged Duke of Brittany issues a vicious insult about John, describing the king as "a monstrous damned man" who poisons the world with the venom in his heart (Part I, ll. 1367-69); then he engages in a philosophical debate with his keeper about the duty to one's king versus that to one's God. In *King John*, Arthur does not become furious nor sophistical; he ingenuously reminds Hubert of his love for the man and how he nursed and cared for the jailer when the latter was ill.

The monarch in Shakespeare's play is slightly more cruel and calculating than the same character in *The Troublesome Raigne*. In *King John*, the king comports himself in a devious fashion throughout the play, hiding the possible illegitimacy of his birth, duping Hubert, and insisting upon a second coronation. Joseph Candido says:

The feeling of psychological enclosure that derives from being tainted by a corrupt, debased, or illegitimate stock--whether real or imagined--is one of the most strongly realized aspects of *King John* and does, quite clearly, haunt the title character. This anxiety manifests itself in John's case in an almost compulsive strategy of concealment and deception as regards the facts of his moral nature.[23]

One deceptive act instinctively begets another as John compounds his misdeeds during his attempts to cover them up.

In *King John*, the medieval ruler employs deception to coerce Hubert into executing his evil plans against Arthur. John inexplicably claims that he owes much to Hubert, never mentioning for what but promising to repay him generously. Hubert, perplexed but pleased, gratefully declares that he loves the king:

> So well, that what you bid me undertake,
> Though that my death were adjunct to my act,
> By heaven, I would do it.
> (III.iii.56-58)

Hubert, at this time, remains ignorant of John's plot. The monarch twice drops hints concerning Hubert's forthcoming task but craftily abstains from mentioning it until he has exacted the above oath from his faithful subject. John, for instance, tells Hubert:

> my good friend, thy voluntary oath
> Lives in this bosom, dearly cherished.
> Give me thy hand. I had a thing to say,
> But I will fit it with some better tune.
> (III.iii.23-26)

John's reference to Hubert's "voluntary oath" is confusing--he refers either to the duty a subject owes his sovereign or to Hubert's promise to carry out the king's plans regarding Arthur. But in this scene, Hubert has yet to speak at the time King John mentions the oath, so the latter possibility is questionable. When Arthur pleads to save his eyes, however, Hubert replies, "I have sworn to do it, / And with hot irons must I burn them out" (IV.i.58-59). Since Hubert claims that he has sworn to perform this specific act, he may indeed refer to the oath his king has (through manipulation) extracted from him. But the phrase "voluntary oath" is an oxymoron, for in medieval England, every subject owed his obedience to his sovereign. Edward Jenks says that the oath "could be imposed upon all subjects at all times; and, during periods of political and religious bitterness, it was often imposed in the most searching and vindictive manner. . . . the duty of allegiance is on every subject of the Crown, whether he has taken the oath or not."[24] However, subjects in medieval England who wished to limit monarchical power, such as the author of *Song of Lewes*, argue that monarchs must govern according to law and that subjects do not have to satisfy a king's request that conflicts with divine law.   Nevertheless, John coerces Hubert, an act that appears in Shakespeare's play but not in *The Troublesome Raigne*. By exacting a "voluntary oath," perhaps John attempts to justify his heinous deed by projecting his guilt onto another.

In both *The Troublesome Raigne* and *King John*, the English monarch wants Arthur to die, but the king of the earlier history is more ambiguous, telling Hubert:

> keepe him safe,
> For on his life doth hang thy Soveraignes crowne,
> But in his death consists thy Soveraignes blisse:
> (Part I, ll. 1119-21)

The king's words are purposely confusing, similar to Henry Bolingbroke's lament that led to Exton's murder of Richard II. The King John of Shakespeare's play is more explicit and uses the words "Death" and "A grave" (III.iii.65-66) when talking to Hubert about Arthur. In both histories, the ruler subsequently orders Hubert to blind the prince. Rather than believe that the unknown author and Shakespeare made a blatant mistake, we should believe that the king simply changes his mind because he worries about his reputation among the nobles; he decides therefore to incapacitate the boy for the role of monarch instead of murdering him. We may agree with Peter Saccio who "can only marvel at the scrupulosity of a conscience that will consent to such mutilation but baulk at murder."[25] We should question Elliot's assertion that since John's title is precarious because of "the thorns and dangers of this world" (IV.iii.141), "we are virtually forced by Shakespeare to recognize the political necessity of the act."[26] The heinous nature of John's order appears in the reluctance of the dutiful Hubert to obey his king, in the executioners who are "best pleas'd to be from such a deed" (IV.i.85), and in the innocence of Prince Arthur.[27]

In Shakespeare's play, unlike in *King Johan* and *The Troublesome Raigne*, John is clearly a usurper. In Bale's play, Arthur does not even exist, and in the work by the anonymous dramatist, we may possibly view John as the rightful king since Elinor mentions Richard's last will that named John as his successor. E.A.J. Honigmann is only partly correct in his assertion that "John's 'usurpation' is Shakespeare's fiction, for his 'right' is not seriously questioned in the chronicles."[28] John is the rightful king in the histories compiled by Protestant chroniclers but not in those written by Catholics. Polydore Vergil unquestionably portrays John as a usurper in *Anglica Historia*, which he wrote shortly before Henry's conflict with the Catholic Church led to the severance of England's religious and political ties with Rome. According to Vergil, Arthur, the son of John's older brother Geoffrey, deserves the crown because of lineal descent and because of Richard's initial will. Holinshed, who wrote during the reign of Elizabeth, includes the information (which Vergil omits) about Richard's last will that countermands the previous one by naming John as his successor. Marie Axton states that in *The Troublesome Raigne*, the "choice of scenes and characters combats historical arguments for Catholic Stuart and Catholic Spanish claims to Elizabeth's throne. Can the same be said of Shakespeare's play?"[29]

In *King John*, Shakespeare follows the historical perspective of the Catholic Vergil rather than that of the Protestant Holinshed when he presents the king as a usurper, thus undercutting the Tudor ideological perspective of John as a martyr-hero. In his discussion of John's usurpation, Elliot focuses on the first scene of *King John*. He claims:

> In stressing John's illegitimacy in this opening scene, Shakespeare diverges widely from *The Troublesome Reign*. That play opens not with Chatillon's challenge but with a speech by Elinor conferring the crown upon John in rightful succession to his brother, Richard, followed by a noble speech of acceptance by John. . . . In *TR*, even the French refrain from accusing John of usurpation.[30]

Furthermore, Elinor confides to her son in *King John* that he rules by

> strong possession much more than your right
> Or else it must go wrong with you and me--
> So much my conscience whispers in your ear. . . .
>   (I.i.40-42)

King John, unlike other Shakespearean histories, contains women who possess significant political influence and who subvert the patriarchal order. Phyllis Rackin says:

> As soon as Shakespeare attempts to incorporate those feminine forces, however, historiography itself becomes problematic, no longer speaking with the clear, univocal voice of unquestioned tradition but represented as a dubious construct, always provisional, always subject to erasure and

reconstruction. . . . An adulterous woman at any point could make a mockery of the entire story, and for that reason women were inevitably threatening to the historiographic enterprise.[31]

Elinor's declaration, which appears at the beginning of the drama, immediately informs the "audience that the play before them will not dramatize the familiar image of King John that they have learned from the 'Homily against disobedience' and its polemical progeny."[32]

Shakespeare's unique and ahistorical characterization of Arthur may be interpreted as an undermining of Tudor polemics, for the playwright portrays John, a medieval hero in Protestant polemics because Reformation propagandists compared him with Tudor monarchs, as a treacherous murderer of an innocent boy. Shakespeare's ill treatment of John may also be subversive since there are many similarities between the medieval king and Elizabeth. Both monarchs imprisoned a rival who arguably had a better claim to the throne and who died at their command.[33] John and Elizabeth also blamed scapegoats for the deaths of their adversaries, never admitting their guilt.[34] Popes labeled both rulers usurpers, excommunicated them for defying the Catholic Church, and persuaded Catholic nations to invade them.

Tyndale and other zealous Protestants of the Tudor dynasty advanced the belief that the Catholic clergy frequently defamed the medieval king: "Read the chronicles of England, (out of which yet they have put a great part of their wickedness,). . . Consider the story of king John where I doubt not but they have put the best and fairest for themselves, and the worst of king John: for I suppose they make the chronicles themselves."[35] Shakespeare questions the Protestant notion that Catholic chroniclers defamed the virtuous King John, and he presents the ruler in a manner contrary to that portrayed by Tudor polemicists.

Although *King John* refuses to adhere to Tudor ideology, Shakespeare does not refrain from portraying Cardinal Pandulph in a poor light, for the playwright wishes to demonstrate the dangers of commodity in politics. Pandulph, the papal legate, behaves in a hypocritical manner, yet he is a villain not because he is Catholic but because he practices commodity. Certainly Pandulph is guilty of abusing religion for political ends, but Shakespeare attacks the use of any ideology for the achievement of political gain. We should remember that secular individuals like John, Philip, and Lewis also sacrifice their integrity for political power and that Shakespeare does not single out papists for opprobrium but all who use commodity.

When Pandulph arrives in France in III.i, the play appears destined to end happily for all but Arthur and the grief-loving Constance. The marriage of Blanch and Lewis will presumably conclude the strife between England and France. King Philip declares:

> This blessed day
> Ever in France shall be kept festival.
> To solemnize this day the glorious sun
> Stays in his course and plays the alchemist. . . .
> . . . .
> The yearly course that brings this day about
> Shall never see it but a holy day.
>   (III.i.75-82)

At this point in the play, *King John* possesses the potential of a happy and comedic ending, as in the case of *Henry V*, which also ends with amity between England and France and concludes with a betrothal that unites the two nations. In *King John*, however, Pandulph causes the two nations to engage in war after the engagement of Blanch and Lewis and after the declaration of peace. The papal legate immediately causes a breach between the two sovereigns by making the following demand of King Philip:

> On peril of a curse,
> Let go the hand of that arch-heretic,
> And raise the power of France upon his head
> Unless he do submit himself to Rome.
>   (III.i.191-94)

Pandulph blackmails Philip by threatening him with excommunication. The papal legate enters with the Pope's authority to excommunicate John for his disobedience in refusing to permit Stephen Langton to occupy the position of Archbishop of Canterbury. The Church of Rome has a grievance with John and uses France as a pawn in its dispute with him. The Machiavellian Pope employs religion as a political tool to acquire an *The Troublesome Raigne*, Pandulph's desire that someone assassinate John appears as an extreme d maintain power by playing off one country against another. As in form of priestly hypocrisy. In Shakespeare's play, the papal legate declares to King John:

> And blessed shall he be that doth revolt
> From his allegiance to an heretic;

And meritorious shall that hand be call'd,
Canonized and worship'd as a saint,
That takes away by any secret course
Thy hateful life.

(III.i.174-79)

The hypocrisy of a clergyman who should be promoting brotherly love but who demands regicide and barters canonization and sainthood in exchange for murder would have been unmistakable to Shakespeare's Christian audience.

Pandulph's threat understandably creates a serious dilemma for Philip. The King of France fears excommunication by the Pope, but he has betrothed his son to John's niece and has recently sworn an oath of brotherhood and peace to the English king. By employing casuistical rhetoric, Pandulph convinces Philip that following the Church of Rome is his only logical choice. The Cardinal informs the French king that forswearing is not sinful if the swearer was wrong initially:

What since thou swor'st is sworn against thyself
And may not be performed by thyself,
For that which thou hast sworn to do amiss
Is not amiss when it is truly done,
And being not done, where doing tends to ill,
The truth is then most done not doing it.

(III.i.268-73)

Pandulph's style of rhetoric may be called equivocal. As Bevington points out in a footnote, equivocation was "much deplored by many Elizabethans and regarded as typical of Catholic duplicity."[36] And Herschel Baker notes, "for all his unctuous piety, Pandulph is a savage papal politician."[37]

Perhaps the most heinous of Pandulph's actions is his provision of Machiavellian advice to Lewis in III.iv. The Cardinal's words to the Dauphin are intelligent, but they are also coldly practical and smack of "policy." When the papal legate informs the Dauphin of his plan, he waits until the prince's politically experienced father, King Philip, leaves the stage. He then quickly implies that if the young man does not approve his plot, the prince is too young and naive (III.iv.125, 145). The papal legate preys on Lewis's ambition, informing the Dauphin that he expects and counts on John to murder Arthur. Instead of performing a Christian action such as rushing to King John and supplicating for mercy towards Arthur, Pandulph attempts to use the boy's misfortune as a means of precipitating the usurpation of John's kingdom. The papal legate wants the murder to occur so that Lewis will acquire the support necessary to overthrow the English king. The Cardinal says:

> This act so evilly borne shall cool the hearts
> Of all his people and freeze up their zeal,
> That none so small advantage shall step forth
> To check his reign but they will cherish it;
> . . . .
> when he shall hear of your approach,
> If that young Arthur be not gone already,
> Even at that news he dies; and then the hearts
> Of all his people shall revolt from him
> And kiss the lips of unacquainted change. . . .
> (III.iv.149-66)

Pandulph astutely recognizes that the English barons will revolt against King John after the monarch arranges Arthur's murder. The papal legate, however, reveals in this scene his willingness to precipitate the killing by goading Lewis to invade English territory and to demand the crown. By doing so, the Cardinal and the Dauphin agree to become accomplices in the murder.

The papal legate wants to punish King John for his disobedience to the Church of Rome, and he uses Lewis as his pawn to accomplish his goal. But Pandulph probably has an ulterior motive--the thirst for the heightening of the Church's political power. If Lewis conquered England, he would be indebted to the Cardinal for conceiving the plan that brought him to power. The Dauphin, like all sovereigns, would also realize (through the example of John's defeat) the danger of disobeying the Pope and the concomitant necessity of blind allegiance to the Catholic Church. Pandulph is eager to achieve the overthrow of King John because the king has exhibited no regard for the Pope's authority. When John reluctantly accepts the necessity of acceding to the Pope, the Cardinal immediately attempts to stop the war because he realizes that John would now become more subservient to Innocent III than would the Dauphin. John symbolically proves his subjugation to the Pope by relinquishing the crown to Pandulph, who then returns it to the king with the understanding that he is a vassal of Pope Innocent. Vaughan astutely points out that the conflict between John and Pandulph that ends in the former's submission:

> is a struggle between Church and State for control--the same struggle that led to civil war in the seventeenth century. By lessening the anti-papal discourse of his predecessors, Shakespeare stresses the venality of the established

church, whether Catholic or Protestant. It is the power to delegitimize John's rule and just as suddenly relegitimize it rather than particular religious doctrine that signifies.[38]

Pandulph concerns himself with political power under the guise of his religious purity. The papal legate's comportment in *King John* is similar to the deceitful behavior of Pope Alexander VI, which Nicholas Machiavelli describes in *The Prince*, a book with which Shakespeare may have been familiar. In his description of that clergyman, Machiavelli claims:

> There was never anie man woulde affirme a thinge with more substantiall reasons, or sweare it with more solempne religion, or perfoorme it with soe sleight regarde, yet did he reape commoditie with his craft, and fownde sownde proffytt by his subtile practises. . . ."[39]

Pandulph's questionable use of armies to achieve the ambitious goals of the Church prompts Lewis's angry speech to the Cardinal in V.ii. When the papal legate informs the French prince that John has meekly accepted the authority of the Church, the outraged Dauphin retorts:

> I am too high-born to be propertied,
> To be a secondary at control,
> Or useful servingman and instrument,
> To any sovereign state throughout the world.
> Your breath first kindled the dead coal of wars
> Between this chastis'd kingdom and myself,
> And brought in matter that should feed this fire;
> And now 'tis far too huge to be blown out
> With that same weak wind which enkindled it.
> . . . .
> [You] thrust that enterprise into my heart.
> And come ye now to tell me John hath made
> His peace with Rome? What is that peace to me?
>   (V.ii.79-92)

Lewis is justifiably furious that Pandulph has used him and his army to blackmail John into succumbing to the Church's demands in order to acquire power for the Pope. Here, again, we see an example of Pandulph employing religion as a political tool, inciting and stopping (or, in this instance, failing to stop) wars in which thousands of people die--merely to facilitate the Church's political gain.

Pandulph's remark to Lewis that John's subjects will revolt perhaps echoes the report spread by William Allen and Robert Persons that Elizabeth's Catholic subjects would undoubtedly rebel against her and join Philip of Spain's army. *King John* is, in many respects, a play about the importance of the loyalty of subjects to their sovereign. John needs the support of his feudal lords in order to defeat Lewis, especially since the action occurs in an era before the centralized monarchy, when land barons enjoyed a certain independence of the king in their own territories. Similarly, Elizabeth required the allegiance of English Catholics in order to unify her country against the Spanish invasion.

England's victory over the Armada was one of the most triumphant moments in English history, and it caused many to feel nationalistic sentiments intensely. The English government proved that it could withstand the forces of foreign armies and that it was one of the dominant powers in Europe. The nationalistic pride that characterized the era of the Armada appears in both *The Troublesome Raigne*[40] and *King John*. Hodgdon notes that "Elizabethan spectators would also recognize, in the Bastard's appeal to national integrity [in the concluding speech of the play], echoes of Armada pamphleteers who in turn are citing biblical watchwords."[41] The Bastard exclaims:

> This England never did, nor never shall,
> Lie at the proud foot of a conqueror
> But when it first did help to wound itself.
> Now these her princes are come home again,
> Come the three corners of the world in arms,
> And we shall shock them. Nought shall make us rue,
> If England to itself be true.
>
> (V.vii.112-18)

The Bastard's speech concerns England's triumph over the Dauphin's army after the disloyal English lords revert in allegiance to King John, but it also alludes to the necessity of English nobles maintaining their obedience to Queen Elizabeth so that the country may remain strong and prosperous.

The Bastard represents the ideal subject in the play, for he supports John even when the king's actions fail to warrant such loyalty. He suspects that John has murdered Arthur. When John responds to the news of Arthur's death by saying, "That villain Hubert told me he did live," the Bastard retorts, "So, on my soul, he did, for aught he knew" (V.i.42-43). William H. Matchett says that the latter "quotation, clearing Hubert, accuses John."[42] The Bastard, nonetheless, continues to serve John faithfully--in contrast to the traitorous behavior of the nobles who desert John not because of their alleged outrage over Arthur's death but because of commodity.

The Bastard also comprehends that Arthur has a better claim to the throne, but for the sake of England, he supports John anyway. England's enemies control Arthur.   Constance and Arthur enlist the aid of King Philip of France and that of the Duke of Austria, who has killed Richard the Lion-hearted, King of England and the uncle of the Duke of Brittany, and who wears the deceased man's lion skin. The Bastard follows John, for, as Matchett puts it, "Arthur is a pawn surrounded by an unscrupulous, self-seeking league. Were he to gain his right and become king, the results would presumably be disastrous for England."[43] We admire the Bastard for his allegiance to John and may accept the above speech as sincere since he has been loyal to his king throughout the play.

By demonstrating the dangers to the realm (such as dissension and civil war) for which commodity is responsible and by manifesting the virtues of honorable service to one's sovereign in the character of the Bastard, Shakespeare shows the essential need for allegiance to the monarch. The Bastard's last speech, however, is somewhat problematic, for it concludes the play rather abruptly and awkwardly. After the Bastard utters these Tudor homiletic words, members of the audience, according to Vaughan, "can leave the theatre on a burst of patriotism. But because this ideology has been subverted for four and a half acts, its imposition must be tenuous."[44] Her statement contains some truth but overlooks the fact that the Bastard has been a loyal subject throughout the play and is the hero of the drama. The political viewpoint of *King John* is ambivalent, for the play supports the established government of Queen Elizabeth and advocates allegiance to her while to some extent undermining Tudor propaganda.

CHAPTER 3: NOTES

1. There has been much dispute regarding the dates of The *Troublesome Raigne* and *King John* and involving the concomitant problem of which play is the main source for the other. E.A.J. Honigmann admits that "According to the large majority of critics, Shakespeare's *John* is based upon an anonymous play, The *Troublesome Raigne of John King of England*" (E.A.J. Honigmann, ed., Introduction, *King John* [London: Methuen, 1973], p. xi). Honigmann disagrees with the majority, however, and argues that Shakespeare's play precedes *The Troublesome Raigne*. (See William Matchett, ed., *King John* [New York: Signet, 1966] and L.A. Beaurline, ed., Appendix, *King John* [Cambridge: Cambridge University Press, 1990], pp. 194-210, for criticism of scholars who agree with Honigmann). Honigmann implies that Shakespeare's drama came first because it employs several sources, including Raphael Holinshed's *Chronicles*, John Foxe's *Acts and Monuments*, and Matthew Paris's *Historia Maior*. His evidence that Shakespeare used these works is neither conclusive nor persuasive. More importantly, the assumption of Honigmann that the playwright's usage of these works proves that Shakespeare's drama came before the anonymous work is illogical since the Stratford dramatist could have readily employed these works in addition to *The Troublesome Raigne* as sources when he constructed *King John*. It was quite common for a playwright to draw his information from a variety of sources.

Honigmann claims that "*John* must probably be dated back to the winter of 1590/1" (p. xix). We should remember, however, that *The Troublesome Raigne* was published in 1591 and that plays were usually not published until they were performed onstage and had acquired popularity. *The Troublesome Raigne*, therefore, must have been acted onstage before 1591, possibly as early as the Armada years (See E.K. Chambers, *The Elizabethan Stage* 4 vols. [Oxford: Clarendon Press, 1951], IV, 24; and John Dover Wilson, ed., Introduction, *King John* [Cambridge: Cambridge University Press, 1969], p. xix). Shakespeare's play consequently could not have preceded that of the anonymous dramatist if Honigmann is correct in his claim that the former is from the winter of 1590/1 because *The Troublesome Raigne* must be earlier still.

Honigmann also attempts to date Shakespeare's play by mentioning incidents such as the murder of Henry III of France by the zealous Roman Catholic Jacques Clement in 1589 (p. xlvi). There is a parallel occurrence in *King John* (that of John's death), but the king also dies in *The Troublesome Raigne*. In fact, the historical episode involving Clement resembles *The Troublesome Raigne* more than Shakespeare's play since a murderous monk appears only in the work by the anonymous playwright. Furthermore, there is no evidence that Shakespeare or the anonymous playwright was thinking of this incident when writing the dramas, and artists may write about an event many years and even centuries after it has occurred. Shakespeare, for example, wrote about John four centuries after the medieval king ruled England. Honigmann also provides the parallel of the Burbage-Brayne conflict: he likens Richard Burbage to the Bastard and Edward Alleyn to John (p. lii). It is quite unlikely that Shakespeare, in a drama about the battle for power in medieval Europe, would stoop to make allusions to a minor squabble over money. Honigmann's assertion that Shakespeare must have written *King John* immediately after such parallel contemporary historical events relies upon merely circumstantial evidence.

Shakespeare's *King John* was first published in the first folio of 1623. If the theory of Honigmann, Matchett, and Beaurline that Shakespeare's play precedes *The Troublesome Raigne* is correct, the unknown dramatist must have written the play after attending performances of *King John* since no evidence exists that he had access to a prompt book or a copy of the play in any form. The plays possess many similarities, so it is unlikely that someone could have echoed Shakespeare's play closely merely after attending it. It is more plausible that Shakespeare borrowed from *The Troublesome Raigne* after its publication in 1591. The reason for the similarities becomes less problematic when we realize that Shakespeare could have possessed a copy of the work by the unknown author.

The major reason why a few critics affirm that *King John* is the earlier work is because of bardolatry. Some scholars refuse to accept that other Renaissance playwrights were capable of writing quality dramas that were constructed as well as those by Shakespeare. Beaurline says that *The Troublesome Raigne* could not have been written first because "A greater dramatic artist conceived the design by which the scattered historical events were synthesised from the *Chronicles*. . . . Moreover, the ironies and the dilemmas that are built into the scenes of the two plays are too sophisticated to have been invented by the author of the dialogue and of the monastic episodes in *TR*" (pp. 197-98). Beaurline's reasoning is faulty since no correlation exists between a dramatist's skill in constructing plot and in writing dialogue. It is quite possible for a writer to be talented in one task, but not the other. A.R. Braunmuller, who believes that *The Troublesome Raigne* appeared prior to *King John*, contends that "there were several playwrights in the late 1580s and 1590s who could work up a plot from Holinshed and the other chroniclers with at least as much skill as Shakespeare shows in the first tetralogy, while there were few or none who could equal (with whatever difference) the quality of Shakespeare's dramatic verse" (A.R. Braunmuller, ed., Introduction, The Life and Death of *King John* [Oxford: Clarendon Press, 1989], p. 12). I dispute the contention that if a work is well constructed, it must be that of Shakespeare.

R.L. Smallwood claims that "At nearly all the points where it is suggested that *The Troublesome Reign*, through its author's inadequate grasp of Shakespeare's play, makes crude or muddled what is subtle or direct in *King John*, one can equally argue that we are observing Shakespeare's refining hand at work" (R.L. Smallwood, ed., Appendix, *King John* [Middlesex: Penguin, 1974], p. 367). It is quite conceivable that Shakespeare borrowed extensively from the plot of *The Troublesome Raigne*, omitted two anti-Catholic scenes, improved upon the anonymous playwright's dramatic verse, further developed the characterizations of the Bastard and Constance, and corrected various imperfections of the play.

Smallwood, who firmly believes that *King John* is the later of the two works, asks why the anonymous author, if his work did appear afterwards, would destroy the roles of the Bastard (omitting his soliloquies) and Constance (neglecting the presentation of her great sorrow). This "almost unfailing blindness to the powerful theatrical moments of Shakespeare's play," according to Smallwood, is impossible and contradicts the theory that the unknown dramatist borrowed from *King John* (p. 370). Shakespeare must simply have taken a published copy of *The Troublesome Raigne* and improved upon it.

In addition, Honigmann believes that *The Troublesome Raigne* was a hastily written play that the anonymous dramatist wrote in order to capitalize on the success of Shakespeare's play. This argument is illogical because *The Troublesome Raigne* contains two scenes in a monastery for which there is no equivalent in *King John*. *The Troublesome Raigne* is also a much longer play than *King John*. If a playwright were quickly to construct a play in which he borrowed from the work of a predecessor, his drama would most probably be shorter, not longer.

For all the above reasons, we should agree with John Dover Wilson, who believes that "the case for *King John* as the original version is a hopeless one" (p. xxxii).

2. David Bevington, *Tudor Drama and Politics: A Critical Approach to Topical Meaning* (Cambridge, Mass.: Harvard University Press, 1968), p. 18.

3. David Bevington, ed., *The Complete Works of Shakespeare*, 3rd ed. (Glenview, Ill.: Scott, Foresman, 1980). All quotations from Shakespeare throughout are taken from this edition.

4. Roy Battenhouse, "King John: Shakespeare's Perspective and Others," *Notre Dame English Journal*, 14 (1982), 195.

5. Geoffrey Bullough, ed., *The Troublesome Raigne of King John*, in *Narrative and Dramatic Sources of Shakespeare*, 8 vols. (London: Routledge and Kegan Paul; New York: Columbia University Press, 1957-75), IV, 72-151. All quotations from *The Troublesome Raigne* are from this edition and are cited by part and line number in the text.

6. Battenhouse, p. 194.

7. Battenhouse, p. 195.

8. W.L. Warren, *King John* (London: Eyre & Spottiswoode, 1961), p. 253.

9. Roger of Wendover, *Roger of Wendover's Flowers of History,* trans. J.A. Giles, 2 vols. (London: Henry G. Bohn, 1849), II, 378.

10. Warren, pp. 254-255.

11. Raphael Holinshed, *Holinshed's Chronicles of England, Scotland, and Ireland*, 6 vols. (London: J. Johnson, et al., 1807-08), II, 335-336.

12. Bevington, *Tudor Drama and Politics*, p. 18.

13. Virginia M. Vaughan, "*King John*: Subversion and Containment," in *"King John": New Perspectives*, ed. Deborah T. Curren-Aquino (Newark: University of Delaware Press, 1989), 65.

14. Lacey Baldwin Smith, *This Realm of England, 1399-1688*, 3rd ed. (Lexington, Mass.: D.C. Heath, 1976), p. 179.

15. Arthur Kinney, ed., *Elizabethan Backgrounds: Historical Documents of the Age of Elizabeth I, Newly Edited, With Introductions* (Hamden, Connecticut: Archon, 1975), p. 267.

16. J.B. Black, *The Reign of Elizabeth 1558-1603*, 2nd ed. (Oxford: Clarendon Press, 1959), p. 405.

17. Black, p. 393.

18. Black, pp. 452-53.

19. Vaughan, p. 63.

20. John R. Elliot, "Shakespeare and the Double Image of King John," *Shakespeare Studies*, 1 (1965), 68.

21. Carole Levin, *Propaganda in the English Reformation: Heroic and Villainous Images of King John*, Vol. 11. *Studies in British History* (Lewiston, New York: Edwin Mellen Press, 1988, p. 23.

22. Charles R. Forker, *Fancy's Images: Contexts, Settings, and Perspectives in Shakespeare and His Contemporaries* (Carbondale: Southern Illinois University Press, 1990), p. 83.

23. Joseph Candido, "Blots, Stains, and Adulteries: The Impurities in *King John*," in *"King John": New Perspectives*, ed. Deborah T. Curren-Aquino (Newark: University of Delaware Press, 1989), 117.

24. Edward Jenks, *The Book of English Law* (London: John Murray, 1928), p. 158.

25. Peter Saccio, *Shakespeare's English Kings: History, Chronicle, and Drama* (New York: Oxford University Press, 1977), p. 193.

26. Elliot, p. 79.

27. The story most modern historians believe appears in the chronicles of the abbey of Margam; this version claims that John, while "drunk and possessed with the devil, slew Arthur with his own hand, and tying a heavy stone to the body cast it into the Seine." Shakespeare most probably was unaware of this chronicle. I quote the translation of this episode in the abbey of Margam's annals, which appears in W.L. Warren's *King John* (p. 83).

28. Honigmann, p. xxvii.

29. Marie Axton, *The Queen's Two Bodies: Drama and the Elizabethan Succession* (London: Royal Historical Society, 1977), p. 109.

30. Elliot, p. 73.

31. Phyllis Rackin, "Patriarchal History and Female Subversion in *King John*," in *"King John": New Perspectives*, ed. Deborah T. Curren-Aquino (Newark: University of Delaware Press, 1989), 77.

32. Elliot, p. 72.

33. In *Danger to Elizabeth: The Catholics Under Queen Elizabeth I* (New York: Stein and Day, 1973), Alison Plowden says that "In the eyes of the Catholic world which, of course, had never recognised the King of England's famous divorce, Mary had a far better legal claim to the English throne than Henry's daughter, born during the lifetime of his first wife. Elizabeth had, after all, been bastardised and disinherited by her own father in a still unrepealed Act of Parliament, and her present title was based on another Act of 1544 restoring her to the succession" (p. 18).

34. Although Elizabeth never gave the command for Mary's execution and blamed Secretary William Davison, Lord Burghley, Francis Walsingham, Leicester, and others, she may have been responsible for the order. Black says that Elizabeth "signed the death-warrant. . . . She tried, in a moment of weakness, to get Paulet to play the executioner on his own responsibility. . . . At last Burghley took the intolerable situation in hand, and solved Elizabeth's dilemma for her . . . . Elizabeth took no part in the rejoicing. She grieved: she wept. . . . Whether

her emotions were real or simulated it is impossible to say. The most charitable explanation is that they were partly true and partly fictitious. Certainly the victims of her wrath had no illusions about the vigour with which it was expressed. . . . These punitive measures were necessary if Elizabeth desired to give substance to the legend that the execution of Mary was a 'deplorable accident,' for which she at least was not responsible" (pp. 386-87). It is quite possible that she used these politicians as scapegoats in order to retain a positive public image and to hinder negative propaganda that she knew would circulate after Mary's death. Although her mourning because of the Queen of Scots's death may have been genuine, she was relieved nonetheless that she no longer had a rival to the English throne.

35. William Tyndale, *The Obedience of a Christian Man,* in *Doctrinal Treatises and Introductions to Different Portions of The Holy Scriptures*, ed. Rev. Henry Walter (Cambridge: Cambridge University Press, 1848), p. 338.

36. David Bevington, ed. *Complete Works of Shakespeare*, p. 736, n. 271.

37. Herschel Baker, Introduction, *King John*, in *The Riverside Shakespeare*, gen. ed. G. Blakemore Evans (Boston: Houghton Mifflin, 1974), p. 767.

38. Vaughan, p. 70.

39. Nicholas Machiavelli, *Machiavelli's The Prince: An Elizabethan Translation*, ed. Hardin Craig (Chapel Hill: University of North Carolina Press, 1944), p. 76. John R. Elliot dates this anonymous translation of *The Prince* as c. 1584, approximately one decade before Shakespeare wrote *King John* (p. 83, n. 42).

40. See Chambers, IV, 24.

41. Barbara Hodgdon, *The End Crowns All: Closure and Contradiction in Shakespeare's History* (Princeton: Princeton University Press, 1991), p. 23.

42. William H. Matchett, "Richard's Divided Heritage in King John," in *Essays in Shakespearean Criticism*, eds. James L. Calderwood and Harold E. Toliver (Englewood Cliffs, N.J.: Prentice-Hall, 1970), p. 166.

43. Matchett, p. 156.

44. Vaughan, p. 73.

PART TWO

THE KING AND

HIS BASE FLATTERERS

CHAPTER 4

THE MUTABILITY OF POWER:

SKELTON'S *MAGNIFICENCE* AND THE EARTHLINESS OF KINGSHIP

I

The next four chapters analyze plays in which monarchs subjugate themselves to flatterers. In each of the four dramas, kings subvert their own authority by creating an upheaval of the sociopolitical hierarchy. Magnificence relegates power to the Vice characters; King Richard bestows authority upon his flatterers in *Woodstock* and in *Richard II*; and Edward II gratifies the ambition of Gaveston and Spencer Junior. Since kings maintain authority partly through the belief that they belong in power and atop the social order, the monarchs subvert the ideologies that legitimize their rule by granting great power to their subjects--predominantly to those of low birth such as Fancy, Tresilian, Gaveston, and Spencer Junior.

Because the monarchs demystify the ideologies that legitimize their power, they--and not their flatterers--are most blameworthy for their fall. In each of the four dramas, the kings not only bestow wealth and honors upon their sycophants but also shun and mistreat their trustworthy counselors--advisors capable of helping the monarchs to govern sagaciously.

The last three plays in part two are more subversive than *Magnificence*, for they question whether incompetent kings should be deposed. These later works characterize monarchs as ineffective rulers and portray rivals for the throne as having much more potential to govern well. The anonymous author of *Woodstock* distorts history in order to present the title character as a virtuous and unambitious person. Marlowe's Edward II is a complex character, for he is a heroic lover but an incompetent king. We admire him for his devotion to Gaveston and Spencer Junior, but we dislike his mistreatment of his nobles and his country. Edward, like Richard II in Shakespeare's play, badly misgoverns and is worthy to be deposed. *Richard II* also demonstrates the need for Richard's removal by demystifying the political and religious ideologies of kingship, such as divine right and the king's two bodies. Shakespeare's Richard learns about his earthly body and the limitations of his spiritual one.

As the monarchs lose power, they discover much about the nature of kingship; they realize, for instance, that a sovereign rules for the benefit of the nation, that the country does not exist for his own pleasure.[1] In Skelton's play, Magnificence recovers the throne. In the plays by Marlowe and Shakespeare, usurpers depose the kings, who are subsequently murdered. The outcomes of these three plays (the ending of the anonymous drama being lost) help us determine not only what the playwrights believe about kingship but also aid us in discerning the genre of the works. Magnificence's restoration to the throne (with the aid of the allegorical characters Good Hope, Redress, Sad Circumspection, and Perseverance) after he has learned about kingship reflects clearly the influence of the medieval morality play. These virtuous characters show mercy to the misguided king, who will govern more moderately in the future. Although we cannot know how *Woodstock* concludes, the drama is a moral history play that employs (and alters) chronicle history to demonstrate the need for monarchs to heed good counsel and to ignore flatterers. The drama, written during the reign of Queen Elizabeth, may have been commissioned by Robert Devereaux, Earl of Essex, who at that time engaged in a struggle with other courtiers for Elizabeth's favor. The plays by Marlowe and Shakespeare employ historical events but also include emotionally moving shifts in sympathy. Edward's love for Gaveston and Richard's obsession with the metaphysical ideologies of kingship allow the works to transcend the genre of the history play, creating a merger of history with tragedy.

The plays by Marlowe and Shakespeare include depositions and subsequent regicides, rendering both dramas tragic works involving English history. It would be reductive to label either play a history or a tragedy. *Edward II* also possesses tragic elements because of the heroic love story between Edward and Gaveston and Gaveston's murder that parts the two lovers forever. *Richard II* contains tragic aspects because of Richard's self-pity and his discoveries about the ideologies of kingship. Thus, the dramas in part two, from *Magnificence* to *Richard II,* become increasingly more subversive and more tragic.   In *Magnificence,* *Woodstock, Edward II,* and to some extent *Richard II,* monarchs lose power because they fall prey to self-interested parasites who corrupt them and cause them to refrain from governing their commonweal effectively.[2] The kings' relationships with sycophants lead to the abuse of monarchical power and the deterioration of the realm. Consequently, the audience may question whether these monarchs are suitable to govern. Such a question is quite radical in a society ruled by an absolute monarch.

The aforementioned plays also manifest subversive qualities by challenging political ideologies involving kingship. As in parts one and three, part two demonstrates a trend towards subversive ideas. Skelton, whose play is the most politically conservative of the four works in part two, portrays the monarch as well-meaning but gullible and pliant; yet the author allows him to retain power. The playwright also neglects to include another potential leader in his drama, forcing us to accept Magnificence as king. Furthermore, the drama, which is the earliest of the ten in this book, borrows from morality plays, which stress the virtues of forgiveness and mercy. In fact, the moral of the play, "Measure is treasure," (1. 125) is a line that appears in *Mankind.*[3] As Skelton's play concludes, we believe that Magnificence will learn from his mistakes and thus become an excellent and a moderate ruler.

II

Skelton's *Magnificence,* a moral drama written sometime between 1515 and 1523,[4] contains political and historical implications. The play, which the author labels an interlude, possesses many elements of a morality play but also includes political situations at court that provide secular, not spiritual, advice to rulers--perhaps to Henry VIII in particular. After plummeting into despair because of his fall, Magnificence learns the necessity of following honest and selfless counselors and of avoiding sycophantic courtiers who seek private wealth and self-aggrandizement.

Magnificence exhibits elements of the morality play in its didactic presentation of the meanings it conveys. The protagonist learns to value moderation and faithful counselors and to shun excess and parasitic courtiers. Paula Neuss, in fact, compares the work to morality plays such as *Mankind* in regard to theme and structure.[5]   Skelton's interlude, however, may not be classified strictly as a morality play because the lessons that Magnificence learns are predominantly worldly and political, not heavenly; the hero's enlightenment and repentance enable him to save his kingdom as well as his soul. The playwright's advice, says Neuss, may come from non-spiritual sources such as Aristotle's *Nicomachean Ethics*, Horace's *Odes*, or Lydgate's *Fall of Princes;*[6] the sovereign in the play discovers that reason should rule the will, that "Measure is treasure" (l. 125), and that political power on earth is fragile and temporary.

In the beginning of *Magnificence*, the king rules successfully; Wealthful Felicity, a restrained Liberty, and Measure dwell in his court. The monarch, however, quickly loses power because he foolishly entrusts his kingdom to deceitful counselors, abandons his trustworthy advisors, and permits his will to subjugate his reason; consequently he discovers the impermanence of worldly sovereignty. Magnificence errs initially by sending his wise counselor Measure from his presence with the task of monitoring Liberty. While Measure remains in court, the king governs sagaciously; Magnificence's faithful advisor ensures that the monarch's judgment will not go astray, that the king will rule moderately. Immediately prior to removing his trustworthy counselor from court, the ruler ironically declares to Wealthful Felicity and Liberty:

> That Measure be master us seemeth it is sitting.
> . . . .
> For by Measure, I warn you, we think to be guided;
> Wherein it is necessary my pleasure you know:
> Measure and I will never be divided
> For no discord that any man can sow,
> For measure is a mean, nother too high nor too low,
> In whose attemperance I have such delight
> That measure shall never depart from my sight.
> (ll. 176-90)

After Measure departs, the monarch no longer possesses the capacity to evaluate his courtiers effectively. When Fancy enters, assuming the alias of Largesse, Magnificence initially dislikes the parasite. The king then manifests his gullibility by foolishly giving credence to the forged letter the impostor has received from Counterfeit Countenance. Magnificence also hears the latter minion calling Fancy by name yet dismisses the fact that he has heard it. Perhaps these flaws in the ruler are minor. But as the play progresses and the flatterers dominate their king, his judgment becomes so impaired that ultimately the sycophants need not deceive him any longer, for he has become as corrupt as them. Magnificence's treatment of Measure, upon the advice of Courtly Abusion, is a prime example.[7]

The ruler whimsically decides to abuse Measure by feigning wrath towards the faithful advisor in an unprovoked and cruel attack. Magnificence's behavior in this episode is inexcusable, for he should be able to discern the hypocrisy of his flatterer, Cloaked Collusion, who has informed the king that he is Sober Sadness. Cloaked Collusion tells the ruler that he is tricking Measure by preventing the wise counselor from being reinstated in the king's favor while pretending to help him. The amused Magnificence fails to recognize the inconsistency between his flatterer's behavior and the alias, Sober Sadness. The monarch's ill judgment demonstrates that his will has clearly dominated his reason; this domination plunges him quickly into sin.

The scene in which Cloaked Collusion deceives Measure supports the notion that Magnificence has lost control of his realm. The deceitful sycophant initially kneels and begs for Measure's reinstatement to favor. The king declares that for Cloaked Collusion's sake "I will the rather / Do as much as for mine own father" (ll. 1642-43). The courtier then whispers that he disdains Measure and will dupe him. Consequently, Magnificence abuses Measure by playing on the advisor the practical joke that Courtly Abusion has taught him. Magnificence does the bidding of both sycophants: he mistreats a faithful counselor based on the corruptive influence of Cloaked Collusion and Courtly Abusion. He obeys them instead of following his own feelings for Measure.

Magnificence also foolishly delegates power to these flatterers rather than ruling on his own. The king should never be apart from Wealthful Felicity since he cannot govern effectively without him. Magnificence places Felicity under the guidance of Fancy, who claims that he cannot function without Liberty. The sovereign capitulates, allowing Fancy and Liberty to work together and demanding still another flatterer. He says to them, "get you hence then, and send me some other" (l. 1452). Magnificence does not ask for any courtier in particular; they are all alike to him. Fancy and Liberty will obviously destroy Wealthful Felicity, ultimately ruining Magnificence and the kingdom. Felicity laments, "Then waste must be welcome, and farewell thrift!" (l. 1445). Magnificence, by relegating his responsibilities to others and thus subjugating himself to his flatterers, blinds himself to the ensuing corruption in his government.

The subjugation of Magnificence's reason to his will after Measure's departure also manifests itself in the alteration of the king's conception of government. Although initially he governs with a genuine concern for the commonweal and his subjects, Magnificence becomes selfish and sensual, thinking only about gratifying his own desires while ignoring the welfare of his subjects. This transformation becomes apparent when he encounters the sycophant Courtly Abusion (Lusty Pleasure). The ruler, morally weak because of his lack of measure, immediately accepts the flatterer into favor. The courtier's elegant and flowery language entrances him. Magnificence declares:

> As I be saved, with pleasure I am surprised
> Of your language, it is so well devised;
> Polished and fresh is your ornacy.
>
> (ll. 1530-32)

Neuss observes that "surprised" has two objects, and the sentence could mean, "I am affected by your language."[8] The monarch's actions support the notion that Courtly Abusion's language influences him. Subsequent to the meeting between Magnificence and Courtly Abusion, the king delights in abusing Measure, destroying the faithful subject's political career exclusively for a joke, and he becomes enthralled by the desire for a mistress.

Courtly Abusion, appealing to the monarch's sensual desires, seduces the monarch with a blazon of a hypothetical mistress. Magnificence declares to Courtly Abusion that he will spend a thousand pounds to acquire a mistress who will satisfy his sexual appetite. The king readily agrees to use money belonging to the state for his private pleasure, and the money he would squander is not even for practical purposes but merely for lust. In this passage Magnificence unquestionably subjugates his reason to his will, and the power of the latter prevents him from governing capably.

After the sycophant entices Magnificence with his description of a mistress, the King asks, "Ah, cock's arms, where might such one be found?" (l. 1570). Here the alteration in Magnificence's language indicates his moral decline. Neuss says that the change from the high style of speech to the lower in the Tudor interlude "inevitably leads to assumptions about the moral qualities of the character speaking, and so variations in language can be used to indicate changes in the state of mind of the hero."[9] The king swears, using the name of God in vain, very much like the corrupt flatterers with whom he has surrounded himself. The language he adopts after he changes would have been considered representative of people of low birth, not of aristocrats or royalty. The increasing deterioration of Magnificence's language parallels his moral disintegration, and he emulates both the slang and the vices of his minions. The rhyme scheme of Magnificence's dialogue shifts from that of majestic rime royal earlier in the play to a simplistic aabbccdd.

While under the influence of the evil flatterers, Magnificence becomes extraordinarily proud--further proof of his loss of reasoning ability. In a soliloquy, the proud king irreligiously asserts his omnipotence and his ability to control Fortune:

> Fortune to her laws cannot abandon me,
> But I shall of Fortune rule the rein;
> I fear nothing Fortune's perplexity.
> All honour to me must needs stop and lean;
> I sing of two parts without a mean;
> I have wind and weather over all to sail,
> No stormy rage against me can prevail.
> (ll. 1460-66)

He then pompously declares his superiority to Alexander the Great, Cyrus, Cato, Hercules, and other heroes of renown. A.R. Heiserman compares Magnificence to ranting tyrants such as Herod and claims that the king's pride is "fed by sycophantic attendants."[10] The above passage manifests Magnificence's declining morality that will lead to his comeuppance and loss of power. After all, Skelton's play is a moral interlude with political implications, not a Marlovian drama with a glorious hero such as Tamburlaine who defies the gods and who "hold[s] the Fates bound fast in iron chains, / And with [his] hand turn[s] Fortune's wheel about. . . ."[11]

Fortune, in fact, has no role in the play since that concept deals with fate over which the hero has little or no control. Magnificence controls his own destiny and falls because of his willfulness and his poor choice of advisors. Adversity informs the king that he

> strike[s] lords of realms and lands
> That rule not by measure that they have in their hands,
> That sadly rule not their household men.
> (ll. 1939-41)

Magnificence's statement, "I sing of two parts without a mean" (l. 1464), contradicts the moral "Measure is treasure" and indicates how the willful aspect of his nature has conquered his reason and his desire to govern well. After Magnificence suffers, he discovers the sinfulness of his behavior and the necessity of altering his comportment in order to achieve grace.

A literal reading of the text forms the basis of the above interpretation of *Magnificence*. But we may further support the theory that the monarch is blameworthy for his downfall if we view the drama as an allegory. The evil minions (such as Fancy, Courtly Abusion, Folly, and Counterfeit Countenance) represent the Vice characters in morality plays. Although we may draw parallels between Magnificence and historical English kings such as Richard II and Edward II (because all three fall from power after subjugating themselves to court sycophants and disregarding their duties as sovereigns), we may also view the flatterers in Skelton's interlude as vices within the personality of the ruler. Characters like Courtly Abusion can be taken as extrapolations of the king's sinful nature. Magnificence, therefore, would be more responsible for his downfall than Richard and Edward, for others do not control him for their own personal gain. Rather the evil lies within himself. Magnificence behaves virtuously when his benevolent traits such as measure (moderation) dominate his consciousness, but in their absence, his vices control his mind, allowing his will to subjugate his reason and causing him to act malevolently. The monarch's inability to govern others well reflects his own failure to govern himself.

It would be an oversimplification to assert that Magnificence and the other characters in the interlude apply directly to historical figures in Tudor England, but Skelton does allude to actual people. If the play is indeed an allegory, we may notice characteristics of Cardinal Wolsey in Magnificence, as Neuss argues.[12] Animosity between Henry's chancellor and Skelton clearly existed; the playwright might conceivably attack his enemy the Cardinal in the guise of his fictitious character, the misguided and evil king. In 1519 the Venetian ambassador wrote that Wolsey

> ruled both the King and the entire kingdom. On Giustinian's first arrival in England he used to say to him, "His Majesty will do so and so." Subsequently, by degrees, he went forgetting himself, and commenced saying, "We shall do so and so." He had then reached such a pitch that he used to say, "I shall do so and so."[13]

Wolsey was notorious for his thirst for power and extraordinary wealth, which rivaled that of Henry. The Cardinal, Skelton notes, controlled the king's seal and took it with him to Calais.[14] He possessed two luxurious estates that were as extravagant as Henry's palaces. J.J. Scarisbrick says that Henry "had probably long envied Wolsey his magnificent London

residence, York Palace. . . , and his country residence, Hampton Court
. . . . [S]carcely had Wolsey fallen from grace than Henry seized both."[15]
When Courtly Abusion entices Magnificence with the description of a
woman, the monarch excitedly replies, "I would hawk whilst my head did
wark, / So I might hobby for such a lusty lark" (ll. 1564-65). This
quotation may be an allusion to Joan Lark, Wolsey's mistress. Courtly
Abusion's remark about "carnal delectation" (l. 1548) could be significant,
for "carnal" may be a pun on "cardinal."

We should, however, view the aforementioned evidence as circumstantial
and problematic. If Magnificence may be likened to Wolsey, as Neuss
believes, after whom are the Vice characters modeled? Skelton portrays
Magnificence as a well-meaning but gullible and impressionable king
whose minions corrupt him. This description does not match Wolsey's
personality, for Skelton views the cardinal as an ambitious man who
influences and perhaps even entrances Henry. If these characteristics of
Wolsey appear in *Magnificence*, they are not manifest in the protagonist
but in the Vice figures.

Skelton's only extant play may be viewed as somewhat dangerous: the
writer's portrayal of a flawed man who tyrannically and ineffectually rules
his kingdom, distributing power amongst evil flatterers who actually
despise him, could be interpreted as a thinly veiled attack on Henry VIII.
If Skelton alludes to Henry, not Wolsey, in his portrayal of Magnificence,
the playwright warns his former pupil of the dangers of sycophants like the
Cardinal and of the need for moderation. The interlude, as R.L. Ramsay,
A.R. Heiserman, H.L.R. Edwards, and Paula Neuss have noted, may
reflect the author's concern with Henry's lavish and wasteful spending,
especially in contrast to the king's excessively frugal father, Henry VII.

Henry VIII inherited a vast amount of wealth from his father but
squandered much of it. When the English king met Francis at the Field of
Cloth of Gold, the expense for this meeting between the two monarchs was
extraordinary, especially since, as Jasper Ridley notes, "Henry's escort
amounted in all to 3,997 persons and 2,087 horses, Catherine having an
additional escort of 1,175 persons and 778 horses." Henry's masons and
carpenters constructed a huge palace in which he resided for seventeen
days. The rooms were enormous and contained cloths of gold. Ridley
adds that "There was also a chapel, filled with priceless gold and jewelled
statues and crucifixes, and a cellar with three thousand butts of the most
expensive wines."[16]

Furthermore, Maximilian duped Henry out of much money. After Henry
paid Maximilian to invade Milan, the Holy Roman Emperor reached the

walls of the city and then inexplicably retreated and treacherously signed a peace treaty with Francis. Shortly thereafter, Henry, knowing full well that Maximilian could not be trusted, placed his faith in him anyway. Scarisbrick reports:

> The day on which, at Hagenau, Maximilian swore on the four Gospels to observe Wolsey's new league, he received a messenger from Francis offering him at least 60,000 florins if he would enter the treaty of Noyon--to which he soon agreed. He assured a Henry perplexed and "marvellously anguished" by news of his dealings that it was the French he was double-crossing. . . . He who had been paid by Henry to come as an avenging angel against France had been turned into a brother-in-law with prospects of a large French dowry; and, as a final insult, by the terms of his new engagement, he was to hand over Verona to the Venetians for the sum of 20,000 florins, having a few weeks before received 40,000 florins from Henry for the defence of that city against the same Venetians.[17]

Heiserman adds that in 1512 Ferdinand, the king's father-in-law, "perpetrated the first of what was to be a long series of betrayals of English interests, all paid for with magnificent quantities of English money. . . . England was the laughingstock of Europe; and it became the Continental habit to use English money, which seemed inexhaustible, for private adventures."[18] These are but two of many instances in which European leaders deceived Henry into squandering money from the English coffers, causing English citizens to pay heavy taxes.

If Skelton correlates Magnificence with Henry, we may also notice similarities between the evil counselors and Wolsey. Some scholars claim that during the time in which Skelton wrote *Magnificence*, two factions at court vied for power and the favor of Henry--the old aristocracy, led by the Howards (the Norfolks), and the rising middle class, such as Wolsey (the son of a butcher). The conservative Skelton sided unequivocally with the former. Scarisbrick notes:

> Skelton, a client of the Norfolks, had unleashed his outbursts against the cardinal, savaging him for allegedly ousting the aristocracy from their rightful place in the realm. This was the heart of their charge against him: that he had puffed himself up with splendid pomp, lived too gorgeously, thrust them from the king's table, ridden roughshod over them, made them and the whole kingdom his footstool, "accroaching" the royal authority (to use a medieval verb) and usurping the place which belonged to the king's "natural" councillors.[19]

Greg Walker, however, effectively refutes the aforementioned theory; he claims that Thomas Howard, the elder, and Wolsey were actually allies, not enemies; moreover he proves that no affiliation existed between Skelton and the Howards. It is odd that almost all critics of the play assume that the Howards were the laureate's patrons since very few of Skelton's poems mention the aristocratic family, and the author never dedicated any of his works to these nobles. Walker, furthermore, raises the logical point of "the obvious incongruity of a family as powerful as the Howards resting satisfied, if it was revenge they desired, with a few pieces of ribald verse."[20]

Although Skelton may have Wolsey in mind when he portrays the Vice characters, members of the old nobility are not comparable to the faithful but neglected advisors. Perhaps Skelton hopes his audience sees him as Measure, the worthy and essential counselor to the king who loses his place at court, much to the detriment of the monarch, the country, and himself. Skelton wished to be an influential courtier who could advise the king as does the trustworthy counselor at the beginning of *Magnificence*. Such a theory is plausible when we consider the author's tremendous ego, excited by the distinction of being both Henry's tutor and poet laureate. The writer, for instance, demonstrates his enlarged amour propre throughout "Garlande or Chapelet of Laurell," as in his Latin Epigraph, which claims that others will remember him as another Adonis. Skelton compares his skills to those of Orpheus, Quintillius, Theocritus, Cicero, Ovid, Virgil, Livy, Petrarch, Plutarch, and others; he also dreams that he receives praise from Gower, Chaucer, and Lydgate--gifted English poets who he considers almost as great as he: "Thei wantid nothynge but the laurell" (l. 397).[21]

Skelton, however, never achieved the notoriety that he craved. The writer perhaps lauded himself so highly because, pathetically, he waited in vain for others to extol what he believed was his extraordinary skill as an author and scholar. After Henry became king, he ignored his former tutor and failed to welcome him to court. The writer expected to rise in power with Henry's accession, just as Falstaff hopes to do after Prince Hal inherits the throne in Shakespeare's *2 Henry IV*. Instead Skelton fumed as the king selected the poet's enemies, such as Alexander Barclay and William Lily, for preferment. Contrary to popular belief, Skelton was not a court poet; he only functioned at court briefly in 1512 during the strife between England and France: Walker says that "if there was to be war with France, the strongly Francophobic poet might prove a useful propagandist for the cause. . . ."[22]

Henry also manifested his disrespect for Skelton during the Epiphany entertainments by ordering him to participate in a *flytyng* (a comic duel) with Christopher Garnesh, a courtier who lacked literary training. Walker believes that Henry listened to Skelton's flytyng only when he wished to take a break from refined entertainment. Walker adds, "That Skelton threw his considerable talent earnestly into the endeavour cannot, however, disguise the essential triviality of the contest, and thus what it reveals about the opinion held of Skelton by the King at whose 'commaundment' it was instigated."[23] Henry's disrespect for Skelton, combined with the laureate's high opinion of himself, caused the writer to long for fame and a place at court, and to express impatience with his former pupil.

Some critics of Skelton's interlude find the correspondence between Magnificence and Henry problematic, for they consider it unlikely that the author would portray Henry, the man whose favor he craved for many years, as a foolish and tyrannical king. These scholars doubt that Skelton would imply, especially in a public forum such as the performance of a play, that Henry comported himself in such a reprehensible fashion. Neuss, for instance, dismisses the possibility that the playwright alludes to Henry in the guise of Magnificence, assuming that "Skelton never wrote a word against Henry; on the contrary, he was always trying to ingratiate himself with the king. . . ."[24]

Neuss underestimates the dramatist's gumption and ambition. Bevington points out that "as former tutor to the Prince of Wales who became Henry VIII, Skelton evidently felt privileged to speak plainly concerning a monarch who savored too much of his youth. . . , a once-trusted counselor who saw his pupil turning to new masters."[25] Walker also notes that the laureate sent the king a copy of "Speculum Principis," his guide to royal comportment, with added sections in which he complains about Henry's failure to favor him; the work "is an almost insolent hint that he felt that it was time that the situation was changed."[26] Since Skelton, who believed his former duties to Henry provided him with special privileges, craved notoriety and became bitter, a subtle diatribe against his former pupil in an interlude would not be unlikely. The playwright demonstrates through his interlude the dangers and repercussions of shunning trustworthy people like himself and of rewarding courtiers whom he disdained.

The last part of *Magnificence* contains elements of a medieval morality play: Magnificence encounters stock allegorical characters such as Adversity, Despair, and Good Hope; he falls from grace, discovers that he has sinned, and subsequently experiences redemption. The play is nonetheless more political than religious, for Magnificence redeems his kingship, not his soul. The lessons he learns after his loss of power concern the government of his commonweal more than that of his soul.

The subversive nature of *Magnificence* lies in Skelton's portrayal of the king as a mere mortal being and as an incompetent ruler. Magnificence, who behaves no differently than any other person, suffers adversity like all human beings: Adversity claims to "pluck down king, prince, lord, and knight":

> Lo, sirs, thus I handle them all
> That follow their fancies in folly to fall;
> Man or woman, of what estate they be. . . .
> (ll. 1884-99)

Furthermore, while learning these lessons, he--as well as the audience-- realizes that although he is a king, he is also a mere mortal, far inferior to his Maker and no different from his subjects. Skelton demonstrates that a monarch's susceptibility to human failings (such as willfulness, pride, and ill judgment) equals that of anyone else. We realize that kings are mere human beings with a tenuous grasp on power when Crafty Conveyance, Cloaked Collusion, and Counterfeit Countenance fail to recognize Magnificence after the ruler has fallen. While it is possible that they choose not to acknowledge him because they may extend their parasitic relationship with him no farther, Magnificence's moral disintegration has perhaps resulted in a concomitant deterioration of his physical appearance, making him resemble a beggar. Magnificence's loss of reason and morality, not of power, have altered his appearance, rendering him spiritually and physically ugly. Without his kingly apparel, which Adversity removes from him (l. 1876), the monarch appears unrecognizable to his former subjects; he now looks no different from others. We may assume that the clothes do make the king, that Skelton implies that a king maintains power through appearances and the glamour of his cultural appurtenances.

Since, as we have noted, Magnificence may be held accountable for his downfall, he clearly rules incompetently. He loses power; no one attempts to usurp it from him. The portrayal of an ineffective monarch conflicted with the medieval-Renaissance ideology of divine right, for kings maintained power by perpetuating the myth of their physical, mental, and intellectual superiority to the capacities of the average human being. The questioning of the king's ability to govern is dangerous in Skelton's play, for similarities between Magnificence and Henry VIII clearly exist.

Skelton's interlude, performed in a London merchant's hall as a banquet entertainment, publicly enacted his wrath towards King Henry and manifested what the laureate considered His Majesty's inadequate skills of governing.[27]

CHAPTER 4: NOTES

1. Magnificence and Richard (in Shakespeare's play) learn a great deal about the role of a king. Edward stubbornly refuses, as we notice from his rhetorical question about his clemency (V.i.122-23), to admit that he has misgoverned. In *Woodstock*, we discern that Richard laments his mistreatment of his honest uncle, but we comprehend little about what he learns about monarchy since the conclusion of the drama is not extant.

2. We cannot determine whether Richard loses power at the end of *Woodstock* since the conclusion of the play is missing. The drama does foreshadow his deposition, however.

3. John Skelton, *Magnificence*, ed. Paula Neuss. (Manchester: Manchester University Press; Baltimore: The Johns Hopkins University Press, 1980). All quotations from *Magnificence* are from this edition and are cited parenthetically throughout the text by line number.
The line appears in: David Bevington, ed., *Mankind*, in *Medieval Drama* (Boston: Houghton Mifflin, 1975), p. 911, l. 237.

4. Fancy's comment that after King Louis XII "died, largesse was little used" (l. 282) indicates that Skelton wrote the play after the king's death on January 1, 1515. The laureate mentions *Magnificence* in "Garlande or Chapelet of Laurell" (1523), so Skelton must have written the interlude between 1515 and 1523. See Paula Neuss, ed., Introduction, *Magnificence*, by John Skelton, p. 17.
H.L.R. Edwards believes that the laureate wrote *Magnificence* in approximately 1516. (See H.L.R. Edwards, *Skelton: The Life and Times of an Early Tudor Poet* 1949; rpt. [Freeport, New York: Books for Libraries Press, 1971]). In regard to the remark concerning largesse after the death of King Louis, the scholar says that it is only "between Marignano, in September 1515, and Maximilian's treachery in January 1517--that Fancy's reference would apply" (p. 172). Edwards also implies that Skelton wrote *Magnificence* in 1516 after Wolsey's unpopular policies provoked the satirist, for they resulted in the depletion of the royal treasury, Maximilian's deceptions, France's prosperity and success at Marignano, and the Cardinal's mistreatment of noble courtiers. In order to justify the date of 1516, Edwards also notes Fancy's statement regarding the precarious situation of English citizens who travelled while their nation and France were enemies (see ll. 346-67); the relations between the two countries were strained at that time. For arguments that support Edwards's theory see R.L. Ramsay, ed., Introduction, *Magnyfycence*, in *Early English Text Society* ("*Extra Series*," Vol. XCVIII), 1908, pp. xxi-xxv; and A.R. Heiserman, *Skelton and Satire* (Chicago: University of Chicago Press, 1961), pp. 67-73.

Neuss considers Fancy's comment about the death of King Louis, but points out that the interlude could have been written several years after his death. Furthermore, Fancy lies often, so we cannot take his remarks seriously. We should note the irony of the statement in question: Louis XII rarely employed largesse; he was actually a miser like Henry VII. Neuss distrusts Fancy's claim about the dangers of traveling since he could make this claim in hope of receiving money from Magnificence. His remark, Neuss insists, cannot be employed to date the play in 1516 since England and France were oftentimes enemies. The critic believes that the drama possesses verbal and ideological similarities to "Why Come Ye Nat To Court?" (1522), "Speke, Parrot" (1521), and "Colyn Cloute" (1521-22); she therefore dates the play between 1520 and 1522 (p. 17).

Both Edwards and Neuss present reasonable explanations for their dating. Neither argument appears more convincing than the other. Since neither claim may be supported with concrete evidence, we should consider Edwards's and Neuss's positions inconclusive.

5. Neuss, p. 18.

6. Neuss, pp. 19-20.

7. See Skelton, *Magnificence*, ll. 1610 ff.

8. Neuss, p. 160, (see note on ll. 1530-31).

9. Neuss, p. 51.

10. Heiserman, p. 85.

11. Christopher Marlowe, *Tamburlaine: Part One, The Complete Plays of Christopher Marlowe*, ed. Irving Ribner. (Indianapolis: Bobbs-Merrill, 1963), p. 61, I.ii.173-74.

12. Neuss, pp. 31-42.

13. Rawdon Brown, ed. *Calendar of State Papers*, Venetian II, no. 1287, (1867-1869), p. 560.

14. See Skelton's "Speak, Parrot" in Alexander Dyce, ed. *The Poetical Works of John Skelton: With Notes, and Some Account of the Author and His Writings*, 2 vols. (1843; rpt. New York: AMS, 1965), II, 15 (l. 310).

15. J.J. Scarisbrick, *Henry VIII* (Berkeley: University of California Press), p. 502.

16. Jasper Ridley, *Henry VIII* (London: Constable, 1984), pp. 117, 118.

17. Scarisbrick, p. 65.

18. Heiserman, pp. 69-70.

19. Scarisbrick, p. 229.

20. Greg Walker, *John Skelton and the Politics of the 1520s* (Cambridge: Cambridge University Press, 1988), p. 6. See Walker's chapter one (pp. 5-34) for a convincing refutation of the popular theory that the Howards were Skelton's patrons.

21. Dyce, ed., *Poetical Works of John Skelton*, I, 361; I, 377 (l. 397).

22. Walker, p. 45.

23. Walker, p. 48.

24. Neuss, p. 36.

25. Bevington, p. 55.

26. Walker, p. 44.

27. That *Magnificence* played at a merchant's hall and not at court may be another reason why Skelton boldly criticizes Henry, further supporting my assertion that the laureate was unwelcome at court and craving favor.

CHAPTER 5

WOODSTOCK AND

THE (AB)USE OF HISTORY

Although *Woodstock: A Moral History* employs actual events and characters from fourteenth-century England, we should refrain from labeling it a chronicle play, for the anonymous dramatist alters the historical situations and characters greatly. The writer undoubtedly concerns himself more with the propaganda he wishes to convey to his audience than with a respect for historical truth. This statement implies not that the playwright writes poorly but rather that his motives in creating the drama are to portray King Richard as a cowardly and ineffectual monarch led by his flatterers, and to glorify Thomas of Woodstock, Duke of Gloucester. The word "moral" in the subtitle connotes the dramatist's distortion of actual events in order to demonstrate to his audience the necessity of deposing a monarch who fails to govern adequately and of replacing that ruler for the benefit of the country with a more patriotic, wise, and capable leader. In portraying the ruler as a weak monarch led by flatterers, the anonymous playwright could be drawing parallels between struggles for power in the courts of King Richard and the contemporary monarch, Queen Elizabeth: similarities exist between Richard and Elizabeth, between Richard's sycophants and the queen's favorites, and between the bluntly honest Woodstock and the Earl of Essex. The propagandistic drama, which lauds Woodstock while berating Richard for subjugating himself to flatterers, could have been written by an Essex supporter.

By the time King Richard first appears onstage in I.iii, the playwright has already established a negative image of him. In the opening scene, the innocent barons barely escape death when a Carmelite friar exposes the plot to poison them engineered by Richard's sycophants.   Richard apparently cannot be accused of personal involvement in the murder plot, but he has permitted his flatterers (the would-be perpetrators of the attempted assassination) to acquire great power and control over him. Woodstock laments, "King Richard's wounded with a wanton humour, / Lulled and secured by flattering sycophants" (I.i.144-45).[1] In the next scene we encounter the king's friends (Tresilian, Bagot, and Greene), who express their anger and fear because their plot has proven unsuccessful. The scene reveals that Richard's favorites are undoubtedly guilty of the murder attempt and that they control him. When Richard appears in I.iii, we realize already that he lacks the qualities essential to good government, and we sympathize with his uncles. The poison plot, absent from the chronicles, is the invention of the playwright and manifests his intention to manipulate his audience so that they disdain the king and his flatterers and respect the innocent nobles.

The dramatist characterizes Richard as a misguided king but not as an evil or a tyrannical ruler. His primary flaw is his subjugation to flatterers. The king's compulsion to please his friends results in his rejection of his uncles and in his incompetent government. Bagot informs Tresilian that he has coerced Richard into making the lawyer Lord Chief Justice of England (I.ii.23-28), thus demonstrating the monarch's pliant nature. Richard also agrees to farm the realm so that he may please Greene. The minion makes the preposterous threat to desert Richard if the latter fails to turn the kingdom over to him and the other sycophants: "Sfoot, an thou dost not and I do not join with thine uncles and turn traitor, would I might be turned to a toadstool" (IV.i.157-59). This whining speech may remind us of a spoiled child used to getting his own way--a child who threatens to hold his breath until he receives what he wishes. Such a threat, however, does not befit a true noble.

The monarch's curious response to Greene also requires scrutiny. Richard declares to him that the flatterers "did well to choose you for their orator, that has King Richard's love and heart in keeping. Your suit is granted, sir: let's see the writings" (IV.i.160-62). The king, ignorant that the Lord Chief Justice has plotted with his minions, hands the documents (that relinquish control of the kingdom) to Tresilian so that the lawyer may inspect them. Richard then signs and seals the papers without perusing them himself, manifesting his poor judgment and carelessness in a matter of the utmost gravity.

The king's answer to Greene, as quoted above, implies that the two men are engaged in an emotional and perhaps sexual relationship. Despite Richard's devotion to Anne of Bohemia in *Woodstock*, the dramatist portrays the king's relationship with Greene as possibly homosexual. The anonymous playwright's description of Richard's reaction to Greene's death further supports this interpretation: the king laments that by killing Greene, the barons "have murdered all [his] earthly joys!":

> O my dear Greene, were thou alive to see
> How I'll revenge thy timeless tragedy
> On all their heads that did but lift a hand
> To hurt this body, that I held so dear
> Even by this kiss and by my crown I swear--
> . . . .
> Each lend a hand to bear this load of woe
> That erst King Richard loved and tendered so.
> (V.iv.30-54)

Ian Robinson asserts that "The charge of homosexuality baselessly made in *Richard II* is pressed home in *Woodstock*, whose King is plainly infatuated with Greene, his lament over the dead minion being plainly that of a lover."[2] The homosexual element in the play is not as blatant as Robinson believes, yet it is clearly suggested nonetheless.

According to Holinshed's *Chronicles*, the *Woodstock* playwright's major source, Bolingbroke and other dukes seized Henry Greene at Bristol Castle and beheaded him.[3] The battle in which Greene dies in *Woodstock* never occurred. Writers of history plays sometimes alter events and telescope time but always with a purpose. Robinson believes that the anonymous dramatist manipulates his sources in *Woodstock* more than Shakespeare does in any of the histories, "going so far as to invent a whole war for the discomfiture of the King's favourites."[4] The playwright invents Greene's death in battle (as well as the king's reaction) to slander Richard by suggesting that he has divided the realm, sacrificing the prosperity of England, in order to please his homosexual lover.

The Duchess of Ireland labels the king a homosexual when she informs Queen Anne and the Duchess of Gloucester that Richard's sexual relationship with her husband "was the cause he left my bed" (II.iii.12) and destroyed their marriage. We understand that this line of dialogue represents the dramatist's conscious attempt to slander Richard since it was commonly known that Ireland "diuorsed from his lawfull wife. . . and tooke to wife one Lancegrone a Bohemer one of the queenes maids; by reason whereof, great occasion of slander and reproch grew."[5] DeVere did not desert his wife for the king but rather for one of the queen's maids. Holinshed's words indicate that Richard's relationship with DeVere was not homosexual, thus proving the falseness of the Duchess' comment. The *Woodstock* playwright, therefore, alters his sources by suggesting Richard's homosexuality in his effort to slander the king. The labeling of Richard as a homosexual is slanderous because of Renaissance attitudes towards homosexuals. Jonathan Goldberg says that "sodomy always was embedded in other discourses, those delineating anti-social behavior-- sedition, demonism, atheism. . . . In homosexuality so construed and so entangled with religious, political, and cosmic subversion, the most fundamental malaises of Elizabethan society were given expression."[6]

The Duchess also implies that Richard's homosexual feelings for his minions have caused him to discharge his uncles and other qualified men from their important governmental positions in order to bestow these jobs on men to whom he is sexually attracted. Richard banishes from court the middle-aged nobles Woodstock, Lancaster, York, Arundel, and Surrey, replacing them with Greene, Bushy, Bagot, Tresilian, and Scroope. After the lords leave, the king and the young, apparently beardless, flatterers mock them, proclaiming that men with beards, especially older men with gray ones, must avoid the court or perhaps be forced to shave (II.ii.170- 80). The sycophants are much younger than the former statesmen and presumably more attractive physically to the king. The *Woodstock* playwright characterizes the king and his young courtiers in an extremely negative manner, demonstrating how Richard's sexual needs and their political ambitions take precedence over England's necessities.

The king and his minions selfishly use their power for their own interests although their profit undoubtedly detracts from the prosperity of the nation. Their misgovernment stems not only from avarice but also from apathy, disregard for the common people, and immaturity. Richard immediately announces that he will "abridge the laws our late Protector made" (II.ii.184), not because he believes Woodstock's laws to be unfair but simply to spite his uncle. Cheyney informs Queen Anne that the king and his friends

> sit in council to devise strange fashions,
> And suit themselves in wild and antic habits
> Such as this kingdom never yet beheld:
> French hose, Italian cloaks, and Spanish hats,
> Polonian shoes with peaks a hand full long,
> Tied to their knees with chains of pearl and gold.

Their plumed tops fly waving in the air
A cubit high above their wanton heads.
Tresilian with King Richard likewise sits
Devising taxes, and strange shifts for money
To build again the hall at Westminster
To feast and revel in; and when abroad they come
Four hundred archers in a guard attend them.

(II.iii.88-100)

Cheyney's words accurately describe some of the problems that afflict Richard's government: the king cares more for ostentation and reveling than for competent rule, and he pitilessly taxes the commoners in order to support a lavish and pleasurable lifestyle for his minion, his friends, and himself. Rebecca W. Bushnell says that "a love of pleasure is seen to make a man 'effeminate'. . . . '[E]ffeminacy' in man matches the figure of the 'disorderly' woman, who is ruled by the lower powers of desire rather than the masculine principle of reason."[7] The portrayal of Richard as effeminate (and thus as someone governed by emotion rather than by reason) acquires further significance when we consider that the current monarch--Elizabeth--stated during precarious situations of her reign that despite her female gender, she possessed the capacity to think like a man.

After the playwright draws attention to the king's extravagant spending, Scroope, perturbed that the commons possess any material wealth whatsoever, exclaims "Hang 'em, codsheads, / Shall they spend money and King Richard lack it?" (IV.i.35-36). The audience's answer to this question should be an unequivocal yes, for the king lacks money because he wastes it at an alarming rate, boasting that chroniclers will immortalize him for being the most profligate monarch in history:

        every day I feast ten thousand men:
To furnish out which feast I daily spend
Thirty fat oxen and three hundred sheep,
With fish and fowl in numbers numberless.
Not all our chronicles shall point a king
To match our bounty, state, and royalty. . . .
. . . .
Let records say, Only King Richard did it.

(III.i.85-93)

The playwright effectively undercuts Richard's glorious words by portraying the commons' reactions to the blank charters--illegal documents implemented because of the king's lavish spending. The dramatization of the grazier's, farmer's, and butcher's fearful responses when being confronted with the blank charters, along with the buffoonery and stupidity of the king's officers, manifests the danger and the illegality of the papers. The comedy and the tragedy in the blank charter scene (III.iii) work effectively in conjunction with one another. The scene, which includes the "pestiferous" and illiterate bailiff Master Simon Ignorance (who arrests unsuspecting commoners for whistling treason), amuses us; but it cannot erase the fact that he and other of the king's officers arrest and intend to execute honest people who refuse to sign illegal documents that will provide ill-gotten pelf for the profligate monarch.

The actions of Richard and his minions, as reported by Cheyney, also connote a lack of patriotism and nationalism. Their expensive tastes are foreign; they have no interest in English products, so their fashions, which their subjects will presumably adopt, must be imported, costing English merchants and laborers money and jobs. The dramatist implies that Richard, born in Bordeaux, is himself a foreigner. A.P. Rossiter supports the aforementioned flaws in the leadership of Richard and his sycophants:

> Wrong is represented by beardless youth, political recklessness, luxury, contempt of tradition and respect, oppression of the people, with crooked law and scheming, treachery even among the upstarts, and a preparedness to back bad by worse, in seeking help from the traditional enemy across the Channel. The 'patriotic' aspect of the play depends on all these failings being regarded as un-English.[8]

When Anne (in this instance a kind of chorus) hears Cheyney's description of her husband's misgovernment, she laments:

> O certain ruin of this famous kingdom!
> Fond Richard! thou buildst a hall to feast in
> And starv'st thy wretched subjects to erect it.
> Woe to those men that thus incline thy soul
> To these remorseless acts and deeds so foul!
> (II.iii.101-05)

The playwright also denigrates the king's governing abilities by insinuating that the monarch disregards the sociopolitical order. The battle for Richard's affection and attention involves aristocrats of royal and noble blood such as the king's uncles, and upstart courtiers like Greene, Bushy, Bagot, Scroope, and Tresilian. The unknown playwright emphasizes Tresilian's low birth by inventing the common born fool Nimble, who informs us that he and Tresilian attended school together and that the Lord Chief Justice's "worshipful tail was whipped for stealing my dinner out of my satchel" (I.ii.106-07). Since Tresilian and Nimble, in the context of the play, originate from the same social class, we realize that the Lord Chief Justice has emerged from a much lower class than Richard's uncles, aristocrats whose power he supersedes because of the king's affection for him.

Furthermore, had Richard's plans to farm out the realm to his sycophants reached fruition, these men would have dominated the king's uncles and other important nobles since the lords would be under the flatterers' jurisdiction. We must remember that "The threat of the favourite is as much economic as political, in so far as the monarch's desire cannot be accommodated within the marital and kinship systems which guarantee the security of the state. . . . [T]he favourite who is personally desired thus gains a power base which did not come from inheritance."[9] Richard's supposed homosexuality, therefore, poses a threat to the sociopolitical hierarchy. The situation resembles that of *Edward II*, probably written less than two years after *Woodstock*, when Mortimer Junior and the other lords complain about the king's preferment of Gaveston and Spencer Junior. Contemporary audiences of *Woodstock* and *Edward II*, much more class-conscious and upper-class viewers than a twentieth-century group, would have sympathized with the nobles, who possess a right to partake in politics since royal blood flows through their veins. An early 1590s audience of *Woodstock* would probably have sided with Lancaster when he complains to his brothers, "Shall we that were great Edward's princely sons / Be thus outbraved by flattering sycophants?" (I.iii.210-11).

The playwright juxtaposes Richard and Woodstock in every respect. In *Woodstock*, the king is young, ignorant,[10] extravagant, profligate, and apathetic concerning England's prosperity and subjects; the writer portrays Plain Thomas as mature, intelligent, simple, and frugal--as a patriotic Englishman devoted to his country and her people. The duke appears as an altruistic, honest, and unambitious man loyal to his nephew. This characterization of Gloucester is intriguing, for it contradicts the descriptions of the man that appear in chronicles (the playwright's sources) and in modern historical scholarship. A history play need not dramatize every detail or character accurately, but the treatment of Woodstock is mainly fictitious and purposefully deviates from historical accuracy. This treatment renders the drama more of a propaganda play than a history.

Although the playwright portrays a largely fictional duke who cares not for power and who faithfully serves his king, he must have known of Woodstock's extremely ambitious nature from reading the chronicles.

Holinshed describes Woodstock as "a sore and a right seuere man, [who] might not by any meanes be remooued from his opinion and purpose, if he once resolued vpon any matter." Gloucester led the Lords Appellant, who defied their king and executed several of his closest friends and advisors. Holinshed reports that the bitter Richard reproved Gloucester and the other Appellants, asking, "by what meane or by what reason durst you so presumptuouslie take vpon within you this my land to rise thus against me? Did you think to feare me with such your presumptuous boldnesse? . . . I make no more account of you, than of the vilest skullions in my kitchen."[11]

Furthermore, the Lords Appellant, led by Gloucester, temporarily deposed Richard in December 1387. According to Holinshed, after the lords soundly defeated the Duke of Ireland's royalist forces at Radcot Bridge (V.vi in *Woodstock*), they entered London with a puissant army, forcing Richard to seek refuge in the Tower. Gloucester and the other barons ordered Richard to rid himself of his flatterers and travel the following day to Westminster to hear more of their demands; when the king refused, the Appellants said "they would suerlie choose another king, that would and ought to obeie the faithfull counsell of his lords."[12] Holinshed also implies (and modern historians support him) that the younger Appellants, Derby (Bolingbroke) and Nottingham (Mowbray), sympathized with Richard and were not as opposed to the monarch as was Gloucester,[13] the unofficial leader of the five lords who struggled to minimize the king's power and acquire some authority for themselves.

Woodstock and Arundel wished to depose Richard. Gloucester believed he had the perfect replacement--a man of royal blood, who he thought possessed the respect of the people, great intellect, and patriotism--namely, himself. The younger Appellants and perhaps Warwick objected, for they disapproved of Woodstock's choice. The Earl of Nottingham (later responsible for the duke's murder) and Derby disliked the proud and irascible Gloucester. Since the Appellants could not agree upon a successor or even whether Richard should be deposed, the king returned to power on January 1, 1388.

The historically ambitious nature of Woodstock contradicts the frequent assertions of the play's title character that he loyally supports Richard. The playwright, however, unwittingly permits Gloucester's true character to infiltrate the play briefly; the duke informs the masquers (the king, his minions, and four knights in disguise) that although Richard governs poorly because he subjugates himself to his flatterers,

he's our king: and God's great deputy;
And if ye hunt to have me second ye
In any rash attempt against his state,
Afore my God, I'll ne'er consent unto it.
I ever yet was just and true to him,
And so will still remain. . . .
                    (IV.ii.144-49)

The playwright invents this speech, which Woodstock delivers shortly before his kidnapping and subsequent murder, to demonstrate the duke's loyalty to Richard and the injustice of the monarch's actions. The dramatist must be unaware of the subtext of Gloucester's words, which actually betrays subversive thoughts. Woodstock refuses to partake in their rebellion, but the masquers never declare such intentions; they inform Cheyney that they wish to perform a masque for the duke's entertainment (IV.ii.85-87). The thoughts of usurping the throne originate in Gloucester's mind. The anonymous playwright, by attempting to manifest the duke's loyalty, unconsciously subverts his own propaganda by revealing Woodstock's historically documented ambition. After the masquers in the play kidnap Gloucester, royalist supporters remove him to Calais where LaPoole guards him. Significantly, the playwright omits Mowbray from the drama and deliberately assigns to LaPoole the position Mowbray historically occupied (as noted by Holinshed).[14] The anonymous dramatist alters this historical event to protect Woodstock's reputation. A vengeful enemy did not murder Gloucester, but rather one of the duke's own former confederates, an accomplice in his attempt to curb the king's authority, performed the deed. This fact may suggest the true extent of Woodstock's ambition: a major reason for the strife between the Appellants was Gloucester's overreaching and his ruthlessness.[15] The playwright conspicuously omits Derby and Warwick from the drama, and Arundel, who appears briefly, lacks the ambition and evil nature of the figure as historically described. The dramatist perhaps neglects the other four Appellants to prevent his audience from associating Gloucester with the treasonous actions that the duke performed while leader of the Lords Appellant and with his insidious executions of Richard's supporters during the Wonderful (from the nobles' perspective) or more aptly named Merciless Parliament of 1388.

The anonymous playwright undoubtedly alters his historical sources in order to portray Thomas of Woodstock as a patriotic hero whom his nephew cruelly and unjustly murders, and King Richard as a weak monarch who subjugates himself to flatterers, causing the potential ruination of England. The identity of the *Woodstock* dramatist is unknown and most probably will always remain so. But we may conjecture why the dramatist wrote the play if we correlate its ideology with the historical situation of the era in which he created it. The playwright is clearly not a strong royalist since his sympathies do not lie with Richard. We may not claim that he supports the Lords Appellant since only two of the five appear, nor may we assert that he sides with the nobles because of his ambivalent treatment of John of Gaunt. The dramatist supports only Woodstock. It is crucial to inquire why the creator of the play constructed a drama, sometime between 1591 and 1594, the primary goal of which was not to entertain his audience but rather to convince them of Gloucester's worthiness at a time in which the king subjugates himself to flatterers.

A battle for Queen Elizabeth's favor occurred between several of her courtiers in the early 1590s. Much strife ensued between the Earl of Essex (Robert Devereux) and several other of Elizabeth's favorites, especially Sir Walter Ralegh and the Cecils. Essex, debating with the queen about his rivalry with Ralegh, asked her

> whether I had cause to disdain his competition of love, or whether I could have comfort to give myself over to the service of a mistress that was in awe of such a man. I spake, what of grief and choler, as much against him as I could, and . . . [was] loth to be near about her, when I knew my affection so much thrown down, and such a wretch as Ralegh highly esteemed of her.[16]

Richard C. McCoy reports that a duel occurred because "When Charles Blount flaunted a token awarded by Elizabeth for his skill at jousting--a gold queen from a chess set--Essex angrily remarked, 'Now I perceive every fool must have a favour.'"[17] Essex's jealousy of a monarch's favor towards others parallels that of Gloucester in *Woodstock;* at Richard's wedding, the duke declares to the king's favorites seated at the ruler's side:

> Upstarts, come down, you have no places there:
> Here's better men to grace King Richard's chair,
> If't pleased him grace them so.
> (I.iii.118-20)

Woodstock and Essex, men of noble blood, expressed anger that monarchs whom they considered weak favored courtiers of common blood rather than themselves. The historical Woodstock and Essex (ambitious, stubborn, and self-righteous nobles) rebelled against their monarchs because others succeeded at court while they proved unable to acquire the status they craved. They claimed (and probably believed) that their actions were justifiable and that their attacks on the monarch's favorites (and thus indirectly against the monarch) were in their country's best interests.

We have already discerned how the historical Woodstock used the Merciless Parliament of 1388 to rid England of Richard's flatterers. Essex may also have attempted to employ his role as a politician to acquire greater authority and rid himself and England of the monarch's favorites. Mervyn James says that "Essex saw himself as chosen, both by lineage, and by his tenure of the office of lord marshal, to be the natural leader of a community of honour, 'the flower of the nobility and gentry of England', against a debased regime of upstarts."[18] Devereux campaigned vigorously for the important role of Earl Marshal and petulantly avoided the court until the queen granted him the office. The earl wished to use this position, which provided him with much authority, to destroy his numerous rivals for Elizabeth's favor, to install his friends such as Francis and Anthony Bacon in jobs of great eminence, and to become the most powerful man in England. McCoy believes that Essex, as Earl Marshal, would have been in charge of England's army and that he wished to "claim for the highest surviving feudal office a 'subaltern,' constitutional authority. As soon as he became Earl Marshal, he initiated extensive research on the status and privileges of the office, evidently determined to make full use of all its powers." McCoy quotes an anonymous tract supporting Devereux as Constable and stating that the powerful position should be combined with that of Earl Marshal. McCoy then quotes Francis Legh, who says that some believe "the constable of England by virtue of his office may arrest the king"; this authority may be the reason why Henry VIII failed to appoint a new Constable after he executed the Duke of Buckingham. Furthermore, McCoy notes that the Constable led the barons' rebellion against Edward II and that the *Modus Tenendi Parliamentum,* a document owned by Essex's step-father the Earl of Leicester, justifies their actions.[19] Since holders of either position acquired great authority, a person possessing both offices simultaneously would not only be enormously powerful but also might be extremely dangerous to the queen.

The anonymous tract mentioned above, which also declares that Elizabeth should bestow upon Devereux the office of Constable because of his noble descent and his virtue,[20] is but one of several that supports the Earl of Essex. After Devereux's faux pas in Cadiz threatened to harm his reputation and improve that of his rival Lord Admiral Charles Howard,

"Essex prepared a document setting out his own account of what had happened, how he personally distinguished himself. . . . The plan was to get it printed and distributed in London before anyone else had a chance to tell their own particular story."[21] Arthur Kinney claims that Devereux tried to publish *The True Relation of the Action at Cadiz*--"Essex's intended report glamorizing the expedition; and the Queen forbade all London printers to publish it without her approval on pain of death."[22] McCoy adds that one of the earl's chaplains delivered a sermon that praised Devereux and attributed the problems at Cadiz to the lord's envious rivals at court.[23] Essex's propaganda network, which employed the ideological writings of skilled anonymous authors, could also be responsible for the creation of *Woodstock*--a drama concerning a noble whose ambitions, temperament, and situation correlated well with that of Devereux.

These two vainglorious men possessed even more in common; Woodstock, in addition to being the Duke of Gloucester, also possessed the titles of Duke of Buckingham and the fourteenth Earl of Essex. The latter earldom is significant, for Robert Devereux, the twentieth Earl of Essex, proudly recognized his blood relationship to Thomas of Woodstock, the son of the great King Edward III. Devereux was the great-great-great-great-great-grandson of Woodstock.[24]   Possibly Devereux comprehended the similarities between his situation at court and that of his ancestor, and perhaps he hoped to acquire support by inviting others to understand the connection also. It may not be unlikely that Essex hired a supporter to write a play that sympathizes with an ancestor with whom he identifies and that demonstrates the dangers to England when a monarch unwisely surrounds herself or himself with sycophants instead of with deserving courtiers of noble blood.

We cannot prove that the Earl of Essex commissioned the writing of *Woodstock;* the absence of unimpeachable facts renders the possibility conjectural. But the play unequivocally lauds an Earl of Essex and defames a ruler who governs poorly when shunning the advice of the earl.[25] The drama also demonstrates the dangers that ensue when a monarch unwisely favors sycophants rather than nobly born courtiers. The anonymous dramatist purposefully alters his historical sources in order to portray King Richard in a negative manner and to glorify the king's uncle. In the play, Woodstock clearly would be a much better monarch than his nephew because he altruistically cares for the commons and not merely for himself. Gloucester's subordination to Richard, like the king's subjugation to his flatterers, is unquestionably detrimental to England's prosperity. By characterizing these historical figures as he does, the unknown playwright subversively calls into question whether the hereditary succession of rulers is more important than the safety of the commonwealth, whether an incompetent monarch who governs poorly should be replaced.

CHAPTER 5: NOTES

1. A.P. Rossiter, ed., *Woodstock: A Moral History* (London: Chatto and Windus, 1946). All quotations from the play are from this edition and are cited parenthetically throughout the text.

2. Ian Robinson, *"Richard II" & "Woodstock"* (Doncaster, Eng.: Brynmill, 1988), pp. 32-33.

3. Raphael Holinshed, *Holinshed's Chronicles of England, Scotland, and Ireland*, 6 vols. (London: J. Johnson, et al., 1807-08), II, 853-54.

4. Robinson, pp. 33-34.

5. Holinshed, II, 781. We understand that the Duchess of Ireland in *Woodstock* is DeVere's first wife since she speaks with the Duchess of Gloucester. Philippa, Ireland's first wife, was Gloucester's niece. Because of the enmity that ensued between Woodstock and DeVere as a consequence of the divorce, the playwright would not represent the Duchess of Gloucester conversing with Ireland's second wife. We should realize, therefore, that the accusation made by the Duchess of Ireland in *Woodstock* is false.

6. Jonathan Goldberg, "Sodomy and Society: The Case of Christopher Marlowe," in *Staging the Renaissance: Reinterpretations of Elizabethan and Jacobean Drama*, eds. David Scott Kastan and Peter Stallybrass (New York: Routledge, 1991), p. 75.

7. Rebecca W. Bushnell, *Tragedies of Tyrants: Political Thought and Theater in the English Renaissance* (Ithaca: Cornell University Press, 1990), pp. 67-68.

8. Rossiter, ed., Introduction, *Woodstock: A Moral History*, p. 26.

9. Simon Shepherd,"Shakespeare's Private Drawer: Shakespeare and Homosexuality," in *The Shakespeare Myth*, ed. Graham Holderness (Manchester: Manchester University Press, 1988), p. 102.

10. Richard does not know his age, the year of his nativity, or even the year in which he presently lives (II.i.97-114).

11. Holinshed, II, 794, 787.

12. Holinshed, II, 792-93.

13. Holinshed, II, 792.

14. The playwright must have known that La Poole, one of Richard's favorites who lost power during the Merciless Parliament, played no part in Gloucester's murder. Holinshed claims that La Poole escaped from England in 1388 (nine years before Gloucester's death), and the earl apparently never partook in politics again (II, 788-89). Holinshed also writes that "the king sent vnto Thomas Mowbraie earle marshall and of Notingham, to make the duke secretlie awaie . . . [Mowbray] caused his seruants to cast featherbeds vpon him [Gloucester], and so smoother him to death. . ." (II, 837).

15. During the Merciless Parliament, the Appellants disagreed upon the fate of vice-chamberlain Simon Burley, one of Richard's favorites. Derby and Nottingham desired leniency for Burley, but Gloucester insisted upon the sycophant's death. Richard H. Jones says that Woodstock acted so stubbornly that "The king's pusillanimous uncle, the Duke of York, mustered sufficient angry courage to offer to defend Burley's innocence on the field of combat against his brother, Gloucester. Yet Gloucester was implacable. When the queen humbled herself to kneel before him, he resisted her supplication with the curt comment that she had best save her prayers for her husband, who himself stood in great need of them. . . . As for the king, another threat of deposition was required to terminate his three weeks' refusal to give assent to the sentence" (Jones, *The Royal Policy of Richard II: Absolutism in the Later Middle Ages* [Oxford: Basil Blackwell, 1968], p. 55). Woodstock, furthermore, prevented Burley from receiving a fair trial. Holinshed claims that "Burley was without law or iustice, before any of the residue (as some hold) brought foorth and beheaded on the tower hill, by commandement of the duke of Gloster, and other of his faction, quite contrarie to the king's will or knowledge, insomuch that when he vnderstood it, he spake manie sore words against the duke, affirming that he was a wicked man, and worthie to be kept shorter, sith vnder a colour of dooing iustice, he went about to destroie euerie good and honest man" (II, 795).

16. Walter Bourchier Devereux, *Lives and Letters of the Devereux, Earls of Essex: In the Reigns of Elizabeth, James I., and Charles I., 1540-1646.* 2 vols. (London: John Murray, 1853), I, 188.

17. Richard C. McCoy, *The Rites of Knighthood: The Literature and Politics of Elizabethan Chivalry* (Berkeley: University of California Press, 1989), p. 83.

18. Mervyn James, *Society, Politics and Culture: Studies in Early Modern England* (Cambridge: Cambridge University Press, 1986), p. 423.

19. McCoy, pp. 90-93.

20. See McCoy, p. 92.

21. Robert Lacey, *Robert, Earl of Essex* (New York: Atheneum, 1971), p. 166.

22. Arthur Kinney, ed., Introduction, "The Honorable voyage unto Cadiz, 1596," in *Elizabethan Backgrounds: Historical Documents of the Age of Elizabeth I, Newly Edited, With Introductions* (Hamden, Connecticut: Archon, 1975), p. 281.

23. McCoy, p. 87. Furthermore, Essex's knighting of an enormous number of soldiers on his military expeditions worried the queen. She alone possessed the authority to confer such an honor upon soldiers, and she realized that Devereux's actions permitted him to transform the men's allegiances from her to the lord.

24. Robert Devereux's father, Walter (the nineteenth Earl of Essex), was the great-great-grandson of Henry Bourchier (the fifteenth Earl of Essex). Bourchier was the son of Thomas of Woodstock's daughter, Anne, and her second husband, Sir William Bourchier. The Earls of Essex in medieval and Renaissance England were mostly descendants of Woodstock. One exception was Thomas Cromwell, the seventeenth Earl of Essex. After Cromwell's death, the title reverted back to Woodstock's descendants (the Devereux family). *Handbook of British Chronology*, ed. E.B. Fryde, et al., 3rd ed. (London: Office of the Royal Historical Society, 1986), p. 461.

25. One may then wonder why the night before the Essex rebellion on February 8, 1601 a loyal supporter commissioned Shakespeare's *Richard II* instead of *Woodstock*. The most logical reason is that the anonymous play lacks a deposition scene, so the supporter may have felt Shakespeare's play would be more effective for Essex's purpose.

CHAPTER 6

FLATTERY AS SCAPEGOAT IN *EDWARD II*

In Christopher Marlowe's *Edward II*, proud and ambitious nobles overthrow their king. Edward loses his land barons' support after he subjugates himself to his flatterers, for he provides them with more power than his barons and neglects his monarchical duties. The nobles, initially subservient to Edward, wage war against their king after he overturns the sociopolitical hierarchy by advancing those who (in the context of the play) are of low birth while simultaneously preventing those of noble blood from increasing or even maintaining their high positions in society. By subverting the social order, the king jeopardizes his own authority. When the nobles attack Gaveston and Spencer Junior (spelled "Spenser" or "DeSpenser" by modern historians) in order to preserve their power, their actions threaten indirectly the monarch's position. While Edward possesses the throne, the playwright manipulates his audience so that it oftentimes favors the nobles, not the king, and may sympathize with their rebellion against their monarch. The ruler's love for his minions alienates the barons and his wife, ultimately leading to Edward's downfall and causing a merging of the history play with the tragic genre.

King Edward's subjugation to his flatterers is clear from the onset of the play. The king has recalled Piers Gaveston, whom the monarch's father had banished because of his corruptive influence over Edward. Gaveston, upon his return from exile, decides that he

> must have wanton poets, pleasant wits,
> Musicians, that with touching of a string
> May draw the pliant king which way I please;
>   (I.i.50-52)[1]

This quotation tells us immediately that this sycophant will threaten the nation's well-being and that if Edward behaves as pliantly and as hedonistically as Gaveston implies, the monarch will inevitably endanger the prosperity of the realm and his own political power. Edward quickly demonstrates the truth of his lover's words: for instance, he parrots Gaveston's language frequently, indicating that he merely follows his minion. When Gaveston states that the Bishop of Coventry "shall to prison and there die in bolts," Edward simply echoes his flatterer's words, "Ay, to the Tower, the Fleet, or where thou wilt" (I.i.196-97).

Furthermore, Spencer Junior (the king's favorite after the execution of Gaveston) rather than Edward orders Levune to France in order to bribe the French king, so that the latter will not aid Isabella. When Levune reports that his mission abroad has succeeded, he sends his message to Spencer Junior, not to King Edward. The king's submission to Gaveston and Spencer Junior implies his ineffectiveness as a ruler and his inevitable ruin of the commonweal; the sovereign cannot govern a nation well when he cannot even govern himself.[2] He allows those below him on the sociopolitical hierarchy to control him and to use flattery as a means of prospering at the expense of the country.

Edward's sycophants rule the monarch so completely that they achieve a status equal to his. Edward cares so much for Gaveston that the two men become as one. The king says to his minion, "knowest thou not who I am? / Thy friend, thy self, another Gaveston" (I.i.141-42). When the nobles wish to depose Edward's next flatterer, Spencer Junior, the king embraces his new sycophant and retorts defiantly, "see how I do divorce [Embraces Spencer] / Spencer from me" (III.ii.176-77). By openly refusing to divorce his minion, he equates their union with that of a marriage. The new flatterer, like his predecessor Gaveston, has supplanted Isabella in the heart of King Edward, thus becoming a sovereign and lover in her place.

King Edward's behavior towards his flatterers endangers his power for the following reasons: his actions hinder the prosperity of England and insult the nobles and his wife, Isabella. Edward prefers frolicking with his parasites to governing England; he informs the nobles that they may

Make several kingdoms of this monarchy
And share it equally amongst you all,
So I may have some nook or corner left
To frolic with my dearest Gaveston.
                    (I.iv.70-73)

The monarch's comment would have disturbed a Renaissance audience familiar with the dangers caused by the division of a kingdom. When Mortimer Junior informs the king that France has entered Normandy, Edward, thinking solely of Gaveston, responds, "A trifle; we'll expel him when we please" (II.ii.10). King Edward's love for Gaveston causes him to rule so ineffectually that foreign powers, including the one governed by his father-in-law, lose respect for England. W. Moelwyn Merchant believes that Edward's "shocking levity of the failure to care for the realm contrasts with the 'simple patriotism' of the barons."[3] England's weakness and vulnerability are macrocosms of the same characteristics present in its monarch.

England becomes a weak country since the king provides great wealth and a plethora of titles for his flatterers. The king tells Gaveston, "Want'st thou gold? go to my treasury" (I.i.166). Edward's generosity to Gaveston injures the nation, for the minion

> riot[s] it with the treasure of the realm,
> While soldiers mutiny for want of pay;
> He wears a lord's revenue on his back. . . .
> (I.iv.404-06)

The king also irresponsibly confers a wealth of titles upon Gaveston and Spencer Junior; when he encounters Gaveston in the play initially, Edward creates him Lord High Chamberlain, Chief Secretary to the state and the king, Earl of Cornwall, and King and Lord of Man. The audience must concur with the Earl of Kent's accurate but unheeded judgment that "the least of these [titles] may well suffice / For one of greater birth than Gaveston" (I.i.157-58).

In his construction of the play, Marlowe alters the socioeconomic statuses of the flatterers to whom Edward provides power. Holinshed describes Gaveston as "an esquire of Gascoine"[4] and never implies that the Spencers were commoners. Both favorites actually belonged to the second level of nobility. Marlowe purposely diminishes their class, characterizing Gaveston as an ordinary citizen and Spencer Junior as a servant. By increasing the initial disparity in social status between the nobles and the minions, the playwright magnifies Edward's improper conduct and provides greater validity to the barons' displeasure when the king "rewards" his flatterers.

Edward's lavish gifts to his minions are also detrimental to the nation because the sycophants basely abuse their undeserved power and wealth; their corruption ruins the country. Joel Hurstfield admits that he is unaware of any Renaissance politician "who was not believed to be corrupt,"[5] a contention that should hold true for medieval politicians; but he distinguishes between excusable corruption and evil, destructive corruption. Since these advisors, who oftentimes were not of the upper nobility, received little pay for their services, they compensated for their low income by accepting bribes or by somehow employing their positions to acquire wealth; such dealings were commonplace and even expected. If they fulfilled their duties well, alienated no one of great power, and stole moderately, their illegal doings were inconsequential. Gaveston and Spencer Junior, however, arouse the powerful barons' anger and envy, for the favorites control patronage, receive innumerable expensive presents, flaunt their power, and insult the hereditary nobles.[6] The jealous peers blame the sycophants for acquiring undeserved authority and their king for providing it.

Edward misgoverns because he neither fulfills the idealistic role of kingship nor even pretends to do so. To govern well, the monarch ideally must assume a sincere interest in the welfare of all his subjects and the prosperity of the realm; he must satisfy the needs of his nobles and his clergy so that they will help him govern the commons. Edward does not fulfill his obligations and rarely dissembles the performance of these duties. Even the semblance of performing his obligations would, to some extent, satisfy the nobles. He mistakenly believes that his political power and the possession of the crown enable him to behave as he wishes. Edward fails to learn that he rules for the benefit of the country, that England does not exist merely for his pleasure. The king refuses to allow the barons to acquire wealth and titles because he does not comprehend that his prosperity, especially in an era before the centralized monarchy, depends upon theirs.

The nobles, although perturbed by the manifold troubles England faces because of the king's misgovernment, mainly resent their own decline in power and reputation caused by Edward's preoccupation with his minions. Every financial reward and every title the monarch bestows upon his sycophants constitutes a concomitant loss for the barons. The lords fear that the basely born minions (according to Marlowe's play) will ultimately acquire enough power to destroy them. Mortimer Junior declares to the other barons that Gaveston, "swollen with venom of ambitious pride, / Will be the ruin of the realm and us" (I.ii.31-32).

Gaveston's success threatens the nobles' power, which they maintain partly through ideology. The barons possess power because their blood is "noble." What is noble blood and how does it differ from "normal" blood, such as Gaveston's? The difference lies in the myth of noble blood. The barons' blood is the same physically as anyone else's, and if one were to see a bloodstain, one could not discern whether the blood came from a land baron, a farmer, or a wild boar.[7] If one saw a noble and a peasant walking down a road together in the nude, one might have difficulty distinguishing between them--hence the need for sumptuary laws. The existence of sumptuary laws suggests that the concept of noble blood might have been created by those who benefitted from the ideology and who felt vulnerable without it.[8] Gaveston's success threatens the barons because the flatterer, whose birth the lords consider inferior to their own, has achieved dominance over them, causing a demystification of the ideology they perpetuate. Thomas Hobbes claims that "Nobility is Power, not in all places, but onely in those Common-wealths, where it has Priviledges: for in such priviledges consisteth their Power."[9] They have power not because they deserve it, but rather because their society expects them to have inherited it.

The feudal lords also dislike Gaveston because he is a parvenu. Aristocrats despise parvenus for climbing the societal ladder and demonstrating their success to ambitious people of lower classes. The nobility obviously benefitted from rigid class distinctions that permitted only limited social mobility, so Gaveston's good fortune, from their perspective, sets an ominous precedent. Mortimer Junior says that Gaveston possesses

> A jewel of more value than the crown;
> While others walk below, the king and he
> From out a window laugh at such as we
> And flout our train and jest at our attire.
> (I.iv.414-17)

It would be unfair to label Mortimer Junior's comment as snobbish because such a modern critique imposes a twentieth-century social criticism upon an attitude held by a fourteenth-century person. A Renaissance audience--especially members of the upper class who were accustomed to rather strict social classes--might well have agreed with him wholeheartedly.

In Marlowe's drama, Edward's obsession with his basely-born minions ultimately leads to his downfall, for it inverts the sociopolitical hierarchy. Bruce R. Smith says that "In the orthodox hierarchy of Elizabethan society, power was conceived as a force that properly operates in one direction only, from 'higher' to 'lower'--from god to mortal, from king to subject, from older to younger, from male to female."[10] The "Homily on Obedience" states that God

> hath assigned and appoynted kynges, prynces, with other governoures under them, all in good and necessarye order. . . . Some

are in hyghe degree, some in lowe, some kynges and prynces, some inferiors and subjectes, priestes, and layemenne. . . . For where there is no ryght ordre, there reigneth all abuse, carnal libertie, enormitie, synne, and Babilonical confusyon. Take away kinges, princes, rulers, magistrates, judges, and such estates of god's order,. . . there must nedes folowe all myschief and utter destruction both of soules, bodies, goodes and commonwealthes.[11]

Whenever the king provides a flatterer of low birth with a prestigious title, he disregards the political order. The sovereign cannot persuade the nobility that he rightfully sits upon the throne because of the sociopolitical hierarchy when he permits Gaveston, Spencer Junior, Spencer Senior, and Baldock to achieve statuses superior to that of the land barons and equal to his own. The nobles refuse to adhere to the hierarchy since the monarch does not do so, and consequently they believe they possess the right to challenge the king's authority. As Edward astutely realizes, "But what are kings when regiment is gone / But perfect shadows in a sunshine day?" (V.i.26-27). The king, sitting atop the sociopolitical ladder, destroys the rungs beneath him, causing the ladder and himself to fall.

The feudal lords, especially Mortimer Junior, initiate their rebellion against the king indirectly. Rather than threatening to seize his power, they claim (as Gloucester asserts to Richard II in *Woodstock*) to be helping their monarch--against his wishes--by ridding him of his flatterers. The barons' anger at the flatterers' domination of Edward incites attempts to acquire control of the kingdom. Initially, Mortimer Junior merely checks his king's power for purposes of justice and the benefit of the realm. He excuses his own rise to power on the ground that his ruler has delivered himself over to the thraldom of flatterers. Since Edward subverts the sociopolitical hierarchy that legitimizes his dominance, Mortimer Junior justifies overstepping his king's authority in order to punish the ruler's parasites by patriotically claiming he does so for the sake of England; his desire to exercise justice upon the parasites serves as a precedent for exceeding the king's authority. Once the baron supersedes the monarch's power in one instance, he may do so more easily in the future. Mortimer and the lords, having overruled the king by murdering Gaveston, no longer fear Edward or political ideologies grounded in the myth of mystical royalty. Their next step is open war against their sovereign.

The nobles exile their rival Gaveston by claiming that the minion has overstepped his bounds. In a meeting at The New Temple, Gaveston speculates what he would do if he were king, inciting the wrath of the nobles and the following dialogue:

> *Mortimer Junior*: Thou villain, wherefore talk'st thou of a king
>   That hardly art a gentleman by birth?
> *King Edward*: Were he a peasant being my minion,
>   I'll make the proudest of you stoop to him.
> *Lancaster*: My lord, you may not thus disparage us;
>   Away I say with hateful Gaveston.
>
> (I.iv.28-33)

The barons' attendants then remove Gaveston forcibly from the room, causing Edward to lament:

> Nay, then lay violent hands upon your king;
> Here Mortimer, sit thou in Edward's throne,
> Warwick and Lancaster, wear you my crown;
> Was ever king thus overruled as I?
>
> (I.iv.35-38)

In physical terms, the nobles attack the minion, but Edward clearly perceives the action as an indirect assault upon his power. The barons claim they respect the king's authority and merely desire to rid England of Gaveston; they say that they will follow their sovereign obediently once they have destroyed the minion, but after successfully removing the sycophant, they demand that Edward avoid Spencer Junior's company, proving the "politic" nature of their intentions. Edward's crisis involves confronting not merely the loss of his lover but also the loss of his control over his subordinates. The lords' insistence that King Edward avoid the company of flatterers is not as significant as the implication that neither the barons, nor anyone else, possesses the right to make demands of a monarch. If the king cannot compel his subjects to obey him, he cannot logically protect his flatterers, his power, or his life.

Although the lords disobey their king, they choose not to interpret their actions as treasonous, for they distinguish between the Crown (the ideology of kingship) and the king (the human being who possesses the title); they support the former but not the latter. The Articles of 1308, presented by the Earl of Lincoln to Edward during the 1308 Easter Parliament, state:

> Homage and the oath of allegiance are more in respect of the Crown than in
> respect of the king's person and are more closely related to the Crown than to

the king's person; and this is evident because, before the right to the Crown has descended to the person, no allegiance is due to him. And, therefore, if it should befall that the king is not guided by reason, then, in order that the dignity of the Crown may be preserved, the lieges are bound by the oath made to the Crown to reinstate the king in the dignity of the Crown or else they would not have kept their oath.[12]

The nobles created this document specifically to exile Gaveston; the last sentence of the quotation threatens Edward with a rebellion if he fails to banish his minion and justifies a revolt if he does not acquiesce to their demands. The sentence is clearly treasonous, for it permits the lords to judge their king and to decide which of the monarch's decisions are "guided by reason." They assert that they will behave as the king's loyal subjects only when he rules England to their satisfaction. Such power would permit the nobles to control and influence the king's comportment and decisions.

The barons also justified their actions by governmental law. Mortimer Junior was Lord Marshal and Lancaster, Steward; these positions provided them with great legal power. According to "Hic annotatur quis sit senescallus Angliae et quid ejus officium":

it is the steward's office [to intervene], if the king have evil counsellors about him who advise him to do such things as are plainly and publicly to his dishonour or disherison, and to the public hurt, and destruction of his people; . . . and if at the last neither the king nor such counsellor have regard to such missions and supplications [that request the advisor to leave the king's presence], but rather shall neglect to comply, then for the public good it is and shall be permissible for the steward and constable of England, the magnates and others of the commons of the realm, with banner raised in the name of the king and realm, to take such counsellor as the public enemy of the king and kingdom. . . .[13]

This passage provides the barons with power since it fails to specify the characteristics of an "evil counsellor," permitting the lords to judge for themselves the actions of the king's courtiers; moreover it states that they may disobey the king for the good of the public and the monarch himself. This document, like the previously quoted one, grants the magnates substantial freedom since they may decide what is best for the country and consequently supersede their king's authority. These treatises are relevant to Marlowe's play since the barons debate such issues and sign a legal document at I.iv.1-7 before the king, Gaveston, and Kent enter.

Although the nobles attempt to subvert Edward's power, Marlowe implies that the king's misgovernment and disdain for his barons precipitate and perhaps (in the context of the play) justify their rebellious actions. Our sympathies, which lie frequently (but not exclusively) with the barons early in the play, shift to Edward when Mortimer Junior attempts to commit regicide while he and the invaders from France defeat the king's army. As a monarch, Edward obviously behaves incompetently, but we pity him when Kent, referring to his reigning brother, cries out in soliloquy that "Mortimer aims at thy life" (IV.v.19) and expresses regret for taking up arms against the king. After Edward loses power, Marlowe causes us to feel pathos for the dethroned monarch rather than for the wronged nobles. The transformation in audience sympathies is significant, for we empathize more with Edward after he loses power than while he possesses control of the realm. We side with the barons initially, but our sympathies gradually shift towards Edward as the nobles become more ambitious and ultimately achieve success. Although Edward is clearly an incompetent king, when Matrevis and Gurney mistreat the former ruler, we may hope that Kent (as the challenger of Mortimer's newly acquired power) can rescue Edward and restore him to the throne--the seat from which we wished him removed initially.[14] Marlowe therefore manipulates us so that we disdain those with political power and support those who lack it.

When Mortimer succeeds in gaining control of England, we no longer empathize with him. His character loses its appeal, for the admirable pride he exhibits while still Edward's subject metamorphoses into intolerable arrogance. Once he achieves the authority we hoped he would acquire, we wish that he, in turn, will lose that power.[15]

Historically, Mortimer employed his newly acquired position to increase his wealth and titles, inciting the jealousy and anger of other nobles. Michael Packe reports:

> it was not so much Mortimer's by no means unique cupidity that set the tide against him. What mainly rankled, as with Gaveston and Despenser before him, was his presumption. His ancestors, the Monthermers, had been no more than a decent county family settled in the Marches by William the Conqueror. Yet this Roger Mortimer had dared to have three of his four sons knighted with the king at the coronation, and was now marrying his seven daughters one after another into the greatest households in the land. He treated Edward with step-fatherly familiarity, would remain seated in his presence, and sometimes preceded him in procession,. . . and required the king to create him earl of March.[16]

His actions created enemies who would destroy his power because they enviously coveted his authority and wealth, which in turn had been his motive for destroying Edward II, Gaveston, and the Spensers. We should discern history's cyclical nature in these events and recognize the difficulty of maintaining sovereignty when many desire political power and the concomitant material wealth. Hobbes insists that human beings behave according to their natural passions and "are continually in competition for Honour and Dignity, . . . and consequently amongst men there ariseth on that ground, Envy and Hatred, and finally Warre."[17]

Packe claims above that Mortimer was of ordinary lineage, not of the prestigious noble blood with which Marlowe provides him as he rises to power. Marlowe's mistake is understandable because Mortimer ultimately held the title of Earl of March, possessed much wealth and land, and his family became closely related to that of medieval English kings.[18] We should realize, as Marlowe apparently did not, that these signs of prestige occurred after his meteoric rise to power and his subsequent fall. The passage demonstrates that Mortimer, during the time of his rebellion, was of only a slightly higher social class than Gaveston and the Spensers. Perhaps the nobles' jealousy and the minions' ostentation--not the social hierarchy--were the most important causes of the usurpation. As we have noticed, Marlowe, by increasing the disparity between the social classes of the noble lords and the sycophants in the history play, heaps blame on Edward for permitting his flatterers to rise unnaturally.[19]

When Marlowe characterizes the barons who oppose Edward, he focuses on Mortimer even though other magnates (such as the Earls of Lincoln, Lancaster, and Warwick) historically behaved in a more adversarial manner towards their king during most of the monarch's reign. Mortimer, in fact, played no role in the six-year struggle (1308-13) between the king and the barons over Gaveston.[20]   J.R.S. Phillips claims that Roger Mortimer of Chirk and Roger Mortimer of Wigmore comported themselves loyally towards Edward until the rebellion of 1321.[21] Marlowe concentrates on Mortimer Junior because of two interrelated events: the noble's sexual affair with Queen Isabella and the couple's successful usurpation of Edward's power.

Edward's inadequacies as a husband result in his loss of the throne since Mortimer cannot seize power without the queen's help, and the king's adulterous relationship with Gaveston (and more importantly, the power the monarch bestows upon the minion) angers the feudal lords. Isabella deserts Edward since he neglects her by spending much of his treasure and attention on Gaveston and Spencer Junior. The king, for instance, angered his nobles, Isabella, and her uncles (brothers of the King of France) during his coronation: J.S. Hamilton notes that Gaveston's

> ostentation coupled with the king's typical attention to him so infuriated one earl that he reportedly wished to kill the favorite then and there. Philip the Fair's brothers were allegedly thoroughly disgusted and insulted by Edward's preference for Piers's couch rather than Isabella's, and left the banquet in indignation.   Only the king and his favorite seem to have enjoyed the festivities.[22]

Edward's behavior at the coronation resulted in perhaps the first breach between Gaveston and the barons, and between Edward and Isabella-- wounds that never healed.

Furthermore, Edward endangered his nation's line of succession because of his love for Gaveston. When Lancaster, Percy, and Clifford pursued the king, Isabella, and Gaveston in 1312, the monarch risked capture by spending three weeks in Newcastle with his lover since the minion was not feeling well. When Gaveston felt better, they departed immediately, but Edward abandoned the queen to his enemies, fearing that she would slow them down since she was pregnant (with England's heir to the throne).[23]

Despite Edward's neglect of Isabella and her indifference towards her husband, she remained faithful to the king during the early years of their marriage. Packe believes that "The rivals that Isabella noticed were not sexual but financial."[24] Marlowe ahistorically portrays her as possibly having an affair with Mortimer during Gaveston's lifetime. She apparently fell in love with Mortimer in 1322 (one decade after Gaveston's murder) while he remained a prisoner in the Tower of London, and she twice used her influence to commute death sentences against him.   Because of Edward's mistreatment of her, Isabella ultimately turned against her husband and fell into the arms of his rival, while she and Mortimer lived in France.

When she purposely delayed returning to England, Hugh Spencer persuaded Edward to seize Isabella's extensive financial assets. Spencer's and Edward's decision proved a fatal mistake, for it enraged the avaricious queen, causing her to seek vengeance and evoking pathos for her in the hearts of many English citizens. Edward also foolishly sent his eldest son to France to pay homage to Charles of Valois, thereby separating himself from his heir forever. Afterwards, Isabella, Prince Edward, Mortimer, Edmund of Kent (Edward's half-brother), the Earl of Richmond (Edward's cousin), John of Hainault, and others invaded England, where they found widespread support. Many of Edward's subjects fought against their rightful king since they must have realized his weakness in this instance: they may have found it difficult to be loyal to a monarch whose own wife waged open war against him.[25] From a medieval and a Renaissance perspective, a man who could not control his wife and who begged the Pope to force her to return to him could not be expected to govern a nation effectively.

After capturing London, Mortimer and Isabella essentially controlled the country. Despite having the commoners' sympathies and despite Edward's unpopularity, the rebels probably could not have succeeded without including the king's son in their retinue. His presence--whether willingly or not--lent credibility to their rebellion (IV.ii.69-70, IV.iv.17-20). The commoners accepted the replacement of Edward II by his son, but they most probably would not have approved of Mortimer as their king and would have interpreted his attempt to seize the throne as a usurpation.[26]

Mortimer fell from power in 1330. Marlowe may have labeled the noble's death as tragic since the title page of the 1598 quarto mentions "the tragicall fall of proud Mortimer."[27] We begin to despise Mortimer after he acquires power, for the reversal of Edward's fortune carries with it a concomitant transference of our sympathies and because the newly acquired authority corrupts the usurper--as it does many. We feel no pity for the remorseless magnate when he quickly loses the power he has recently gained. As the First Lord and attendants lead Mortimer away to his execution, he triumphantly declares:

> Base fortune, now I see, that in thy wheel
> There is a point to which when men aspire
> They tumble headlong down; that point I touched
> And seeing there was no place to mount up higher
> Why should I grieve at my declining fall?
> (V.vi.59-63)

Mortimer's comments are in line with the *de casibus* tradition, but the noble perhaps misses the point. The challenge and the difficulty, as Machiavelli realized, lie not in attaining great power but rather in maintaining it. Mortimer is more like Marlowe's Barabas than Tamburlaine: he successfully acquires the power he seeks, yet he rapidly loses it without enjoying the fruits of his struggle, leaving us to doubt whether his effort was worthwhile. Mortimer claims he has succeeded. He has actually failed, and therein lies his tragedy.

Edward's deposition and murder are definitely tragic--not because of Fortune but because of the romantic relationship between the king and his minion. Holinshed's *Chronicles* never describes Edward in a manner that would indicate that he is a homosexual; Marlowe reaches that conclusion based on his interpretation of certain passages in the *Chronicles*. Holinshed reports that while in Gaveston's company, Edward

> gaue himselfe to wantonnes, passing his time in voluptuous pleasure, and riotous excesse: and to helpe them forward in that kind of life, the aforesaid Peers, who (as it may be thought, he had sworne to make the king forget himselfe, and the state, to which he was called) furnished his court with companies of iesters, ruffians, flattering parasites, musicians, and other vile and naughtie ribalds, that the king might spend both daies and nights in iesting, plaieng, [banketing], and in other such filthie and dishonorable exercises.[28]

Although this passage never explicitly states that the king's relationship with Gaveston is sexual, Marlowe's interpretation is plausible. Smith says that Holinshed's words, such as "filthie and dishonorable exercises," "come straight out of moral polemics against sodomy."[29] Holinshed's decorous employment of the term "plaieng" may refer to a homosexual union. The Oxford English Dictionary defines "plaieng" [sic] as "amorous disport; dalliance; sexual indulgence"; the Renaissance example the dictionary provides for the word (the quotation of Randolph in 1565 that appears in Tytler's *History of Scotland* [1864]) describes a homosexual relationship. Holinshed's report that Edward's murderers placed a red hot spit into his entrails through his fundament may also be important;[30] Claude J. Summers believes that Holinshed's description of Edward's death, "symbolically suggesting homosexual intercourse, inspired Marlowe to make Edward a deviate."[31] Modern historians concur with Marlowe in regard to the homosexual nature of Edward's relationship with Gaveston, but the playwright was one of the first to make this claim.

The sexual nature of the relationship is significant to aspects of Edward's kingship and of the play--not because the bond is homosexual but because his adulterous affairs cause the monarch to neglect his kingly responsibilities and the prosperity of his nation. Edward was notoriously generous to those for whom he cared deeply.[32] The obsessiveness of the king's love caused Edward to squander money and jewels on Gaveston, depleting the country's treasury. If Edward's extramarital relationship had been with a woman, his obsessive love and loyalty would have still caused him to shirk his monarchical duties and his wife, consequently destroying his reign, marriage, and life; the only difference would have been in the manner in which his murderers killed him.

If we focus on the homosexual nature of the relationship between Edward and Gaveston and read the first three acts of the drama as the tragic story of two "star-cross'd" lovers, we may read Marlowe's play not only as a history but also as a tragedy. Marlowe appropriates the political events in chronicles such as Holinshed's *Chronicles* and Stow's *Annales*, combining these incidents with the sexual and emotional relationships of the protagonists; this blending of politics with romance creates a concomitant merging of genres. Harry Levin believes that in *Edward II,* Marlowe's "unique contribution was to bring the chronicle within the perspective of tragedy, to adapt the most public of forms to the most private of emotions."[33] In *Romeo and Juliet,* Juliet must choose between love and duty--her love for Romeo and her duty to her family; the play ends tragically because the two are irreconcilable. The same dilemma exists in Marlowe's play. Smith says:

> If Hegel is right that the essence of tragedy is to play out the conflict, not of right against wrong, but of two irreconcilable rights against each other, *Edward II* is a tragedy of the highest mark. On the one hand we see the needs of England as a society and the necessity of right rulership; on the other, the needs of Edward as a man and the necessity of love and companionship.[34]

Edward loses power and dies because he cannot balance his love for his minion with his duties as king.

Edward's affection for Gaveston exists both as the strongest and the weakest aspects of his character. The behavior of Edward towards Gaveston would be heroic and admirable if he were not king. The monarch defies his powerful, ambitious barons and his queen, risking his crown and his life for the sake of the person he loves. In fact, the only times in the play in which Edward appears noble concern his romantic relationship with Gaveston. Mortimer Senior compares him to heroes who had homosexual relationships,[35] such as Alexander the Great, Hercules, Achilles, and Socrates (I.iv.390-400). Edward's realization that Warwick has murdered Gaveston is one of the few times in the first four acts of the play that the audience sympathizes with the monarch. Marlowe also portrays the nobility of Edward's love when the king bravely avenges Gaveston's murder in III.iii. In this tragic history, Edward's hamartia may not be merely a weakness but also a strength. We should consider Edward's loyalty to his friend admirable--perhaps even in its excess. The playwright may have portrayed Gaveston and Spencer Junior as minions of low birth, thus widening the sociopolitical distance between them and the king, partly as a way of glorifying Edward's love, demonstrating that the monarch ignores important social conventions such as class distinctions. We may even forgive Edward his neglect of his wife, for instead he devotes his time and wealth to the one he truly loves. As king, he must marry a woman of royal blood and father an heir. No historical information supports the notion that he married her because of some emotional bond between them, and Isabella's love for her husband in Marlowe's play clearly deviates from historical truth. Edward's devotion to Gaveston is the only genuine love in the drama.[36]

Marlowe demonstrates, however, that strong attachments to lovers are poor traits in a political leader.[37] A monarch must always think and behave objectively, and he must avoid strong emotional ties to others in order to govern well and maintain power. Edward's inability to do so leads to his downfall. Marlowe portrays Edward as a benevolent person and a wonderful lover but as a neglectful king who does not deserve to rule and whose deposition is justifiable. The blending of a character who is a great man but an ineffective ruler, containing the transference of sympathies *after* the usurpation, renders Marlowe's play a subversive historical tragedy.

CHAPTER 6: NOTES

1. Christopher Marlowe, *Edward the Second*, ed. W. Moelwyn Merchant (1967; rpt. London: A.& C. Black; New York: W.W. Norton, 1989). All quotations from Marlowe's *Edward II* are from this edition and are cited parenthetically throughout the text.

2. Historically, Gaveston and Hugh Despenser, unlike their king, were quite competent leaders. J.S. Hamilton claims that Gaveston's "administrative acts show him to have been actively involved in the governance of Ireland. With the major exception of the murage dispute, his acts were in accord with the desires of his Irish subjects. His restraint and deference to the crown on major appointments and grants demonstrates a tactfulness he had not displayed in England" (J.S. Hamilton, *Piers Gaveston, Earl of Cornwall, 1307-1312: Politics and Patronage in the Reign of Edward II* [Detroit: Wayne State University Press; London: Harvester-Wheatsheaf, 1988], p. 66). Although most medieval and Renaissance historians, such as Holinshed, portray Despenser in a completely negative manner, he was a talented administrator. Michael Packe says that despite his avarice, Despenser ruled England rather efficiently, and Edward ultimately allowed him to lead the country himself. See Michael Packe, *King Edward III* (London: Ark Paperbacks, 1985), pp. 13, 14, 32.

3. W. Moelwyn Merchant, ed., *Edward the Second* by Christopher Marlowe, p. 21 (n. 49).

4. Raphael Holinshed, *Holinshed's Chronicles of England, Scotland, and Ireland*, 6 vols. (London: J. Johnson, et al., 1807-08, II, 539.

5. Joel Hurstfield, "The Politics of Corruption in Shakespeare's England," *Shakespeare Survey*, 28 (1975), 16.

6. Gaveston and Spenser also duped and cheated the lords occasionally. Holinshed claims that William de Bruce wished to sell land that lay adjacent to property owned by the Mortimers and the Earl of Hereford. The Mortimers and Hereford wanted to purchase the land, but Spenser "found such means through the kings furtherance and helpe, that he went awaie with the purchase, to the great displeasure of the other lords that had been in hand to buie it" (II, 559).

7. The king makes a similar comment to Bertram in Shakespeare's *All's Well That Ends Well*:

Strange is it that our bloods,
Of color, weight, and heat, pour'd together,
Would quite confound distinction, yet stands off
In differences so mighty.

David Bevington, ed., *The Complete Works of Shakespeare*, 3rd ed. (Glenview, Ill.: Scott, Foresman, 1980), II.iii.118-21.

8. Even if playwrights believed that God instituted the social hierarchy, sumptuary laws were social laws conceived by those in power.

9. Thomas Hobbes, *Leviathan*, ed. C.B. Macpherson (1968; rpt. Harmondsworth, Eng.: Penguin, 1983), p. 151.

10. Bruce R. Smith, *Homosexual Desire in Shakespeare's England: A Cultural Poetics* (Chicago: University of Chicago Press, 1991), p. 216.

11. Arthur Kinney, ed., *Elizabethan Backgrounds: Historical Documents of the Age of Elizabeth I, Newly Edited, With Introductions* (Hamden, Connecticut: Archon, 1975), pp. 60-61.

12. The English translation of "The Alleged Articles of 1308" appears in H.G. Richardson and G.O. Sayles, *The Governance of Mediaeval England from the Conquest to Magna Carta*, trans. H.G. Richardson and G.O. Sayles (Edinburgh: Edinburgh University Press, 1963), p. 468.

13. Quoted from L.W. Vernon-Harcourt, *His Grace The Steward and Trial of Peers: A Novel Inquiry into a Special Branch of Constitutional Government: Founded Entirely upon Original Sources of Information, And Extensively upon Hitherto Unprinted Materials* (London: Longmans, Green, 1907), pp. 149-50. The translation is that of Vernon-Harcourt; the first interpolation in brackets is the translator's; the second is my own.

14. According to Michael Packe, the historical Earl of Kent attempted to rescue his half-brother more than two years after the king's death:

Kent, unreliable and impetuous as ever, having been party to Edward of Caernarvon's deposition, and having attended his official though not his actual funeral, had become so stricken with remorse that he allowed himself to be convinced that his half-brother was not really dead, and he engaged in a conspiracy for his rescue. . . . To disclose a real plot, Mortimer had planted a sham one of Gordian cunning.

Mortimer spread the false rumor that Edward still lived and resided at Corfe castle in Dorset. Kent attempted to rescue his half-brother, but Mortimer arrested him, along with his conspirators (who were Mortimer's enemies), on the first day of the parliament held in Winchester. See Packe, p. 45.

15. Mortimer lost power because he committed the same mistakes that he complained about during Edward's reign. Michael Packe says that Mortimer permitted Edward III's "Council [of Regency] to bear full responsibility while he, in the way of favourites, ruled obliquely through the queen. The ruin of so many enemies made possible the distribution of rewards to those who had shared in the risky enterprise. The efficient fiscal machinery developed by Despenser continued to run smoothly and. . . there was plenty of money to hand. Even so, Mortimer's disbursements were so lavish that scarcely a third of the crown revenues were left for the use of the Council" (p. 32). Mortimer clearly did not learn from Edward II's errors: he ruled through his sycophants and provided them with large financial rewards that depleted the treasury and that were thus detrimental to the commonweal.

16. Packe, pp. 40-41.

17. Hobbes, pp. 225-26. Hobbes uses this idea to justify his belief that the monarchy is the most efficient form of government. Although he may be correct, the ambition, pride, and covetousness of human beings cause a king's position to be quite precarious and unstable. Hobbes's comment appears fifty-nine years after Marlowe's play, but the idea existed in people's minds well before the philosopher published *Leviathan* in 1651.

18. Roger Mortimer, the fifth Earl of March and great-grandson of Mortimer Junior, was Richard II's heir apparent until his death in July 1398.

19. The playwright's motive, however, may be to glorify Edward's love for Gaveston and Spencer Junior.

20. The political battle stemming from Gaveston's preferment began one year into Edward's reign and concluded one year after his death in 1312.

21. J.R.S. Phillips, *Aymer de Valence, Earl of Pembroke 1307-1324: Baronial Politics in the Reign of Edward II* (Oxford: Clarendon, 1972), p. 12.

22. Hamilton, p. 48.

23. Hamilton, pp. 48, 95. See also Holinshed, II, 551.

24. Packe, p. 18.

25. A similar situation occurred during the reign of Henry II; his wife, Eleanor of Aquitaine, went to war with her husband and persuaded her children to do so.

26. Mortimer, however, did not attempt to become king himself, for he enjoyed ruling through Edward III and the young king's Council of Regency. Mortimer and Isabella may have later attempted to control the line of succession; if they did, their plot failed. Edward III married his cousin Philippa on January 24, 1328, but Isabella continually refused to allow her to be crowned. Two years passed, yet the queen steadfastly declined to crown Edward III's bride. Finally, in February of 1330, Isabella reluctantly agreed to crown her daughter-in-law; she could stall no longer since Philippa was five months pregnant with the baby who was to be Edward the Black Prince. Perhaps she waited such a long time because she and Mortimer were planning to assume full control of England. At approximately the same time that Philippa was pregnant, Isabella, Holinshed claims, "was found to be pregnant by [Mortimer]" (II, 599). Isabella possibly delayed crowning Philippa since she herself carried a child and Mortimer hoped their baby, not Philippa's, would succeed Edward III. Their baby's claim to the throne would garner more credibility if its mother were England's queen. Philippa was not officially queen during the first five months of her pregnancy since Isabella would not crown her; perhaps Mortimer's lover did so only after suffering a miscarriage. In an age of an enormously high infant mortality rate, poor medical care, and numerous wars, Mortimer may have felt he could sire England's next king after Edward III, especially if his baby were male and Philippa's female.

We realize that the rate of early mortality was high since Edward II became heir to the throne after his three eldest brothers died. King John (nicknamed Lackland by his father Henry II because he was the youngest of eight children) survived his five elder brothers, who died young. Packe, furthermore, mentions that the papal dispensation permitting the cousins Edward and Philippa to marry declares that the prince would marry one of the Count of Hainault's daughters; Isabella did not wish to specify which daughter because, if Philippa died and Edward married another of the count's daughters, the queen would require a second papal dispensation (p. 27).

Mortimer's plot may have been inspired by the similar situation in France involving Isabella and the end of the Capetian line. Packe notes that after the death of King Philip, his three sons struggled in vain to produce a male heir that would enable the Capetian line to continue (pp. 20-21).

27. Merchant, p. 1; see also pp. 2-3. My argument depends on the admittedly questionable assumption that the title-page wording derives from a Marlovian manuscript and was not a Renaissance printer's invention.

28. Holinshed, II, 547. I place the word "banketing" in brackets because the reprint incorrectly uses the word "blanketing."

29. Smith, p. 216.

30. Holinshed, II, 587.

31. Claude J. Summers, *Christopher Marlowe and the Politics of Power*, *Salzburg Studies in English Literature: Elizabethan and Renaissance Studies*, ed. James Hogg. (Salzburg: Institut Fur Englische Sprache und Literatur, 1974), p. 159 (n. 8).

32. Edward's extraordinary generosity led to Gaveston's first exile. According to Walter of Guisborough, Edward asked Bishop Walter Langton to convince Edward I to make Gaveston the Count of Ponthieu. The furious king, realizing the Gascon knight's influence on his son, banished the prince's friend. (See Walter of Guisborough, *Chronicle of Walter of Guisborough*, ed. H. Rothwell, 3rd ser., 89 [London, 1957], pp. 382-83). Although Edward I exiled Gaveston, the banishment was actually a means of punishing the prince and not the knight.

33. Harry Levin, *The Overreacher: A Study of Christopher Marlowe* (1952; rpt. Gloucester, Mass.: Peter Smith, 1974), p. 88.

34. Smith, p. 221.

35. These heroes, like Edward, probably were bisexual since they also had heterosexual relationships. Edward fathered four children by Isabella. Although he may have impregnated his wife because of his responsibilities as king and not because of an interest in heterosexual sex, he also fathered an illegitimate son named Adam who went to war with him in Scotland in 1321 (Hamilton, p. 17).

36. Spencer Junior represents, in some respects, a surrogate Gaveston.

37. Shakespeare makes a similar implication in *Antony and Cleopatra*.

CHAPTER 7

THE BATTLE BETWEEN WORDS AND SWORDS:

BREAKING IDEOLOGICAL BARRIERS IN

SHAKESPEARE'S *RICHARD THE SECOND*

Shakespeare's *Tragedy of King Richard the Second* subverts the notion of the metaphysical nature of kingship by exposing the hypocritical cultural aspects of the ideologies that legitimize a sovereign's title to power. King Richard's preoccupation with and reliance upon the concepts of the divine right of kings, the king's two bodies, and the teleological design of the sociopolitical hierarchy ultimately leads to his downfall. Ronald R. MacDonald says that because of "an apparently incorrigible tendency of the human mind to confound culture and nature, it [kingship] will be understood not as a collective fabrication of the social order with discernible historical origins, but as a part of the metaphysical order handed down from on high at the creation."[1] John Milton claims that "People, exorbitant and excessive in all thir motions, are prone ofttimes not to a religious onely, but to a civil kinde of Idolatry in idolizing thir Kings; though never more mistak'n in the object of thir worship."[2] Bolingbroke, however, does not permit the aforementioned myths to dupe him, for he comprehends the historical and cultural bases for these beliefs. Shakespeare illuminates these myths by portraying Richard as an incompetent monarch, a much worse ruler than the chronicles indicate.

As this history play progresses and the fortune of King Richard declines, Shakespeare exposes the fictional nature of the ideologies those in power employed to justify their authority. The audience recognizes, and Shakespeare's title character discovers, that the aforementioned beliefs exist "as an amalgam of religious belief, aesthetic idealism and ideological myth."[3]   The ruling class perpetuated these concepts, which deceive Richard but not Bolingbroke, to maintain power without the questioning of the ambitious nobility and the disgruntled multitude. According to J.W. Lever, those in power employed these myths as a "creed of absolutism [serving] chiefly to bolster up a precarious monarchy which lacked a standing army or an efficient police force."[4] During the course of the play, Richard learns gradually that he cannot rely upon these ideologies, that angels will not fight with him against Bolingbroke; consequently, he relinquishes the crown passively to Henry.

A medieval king such as Richard II relied on ideology in order to maintain his power because he governed in an era before that of the centralized monarchy.   Medieval land barons, who governed their territories as though they themselves were kings, controlled the nation's armies. MacDonald comments:

> the language of sacred kingship arises in response to a fundamental contradiction in the feudal system as Shakespeare understood it.   That contradiction may be brought to the surface by wondering why a feudal system should have a king at all, for feudal society is marked by the formation of *many* centers of power, independent families with bands of retainers, each internally bound together by blood ties and *comitatus* loyalty. To speak of a centralized monarchy in a situation that yields, in effect, a number of private armies verges on paradox.[5]

In the drama, Richard attempts in vain to check the power of feudalism. During the confrontation between Bolingbroke and Mowbray, the opponents defend themselves by employing chivalric discourse while Richard resorts to absolutist language.   Graham Holderness says that the language indicates:

> in this conflict king's man and opposition baron have both broken away from royal authority, into the realm of knighthood.   Honour has become more absolute than allegiance; loyalty to kin has superseded duty to sovereign; chivalric personal dignity has exceeded civil obligation. Monarchy has failed to control the power of feudalism.[6]

Feudal lords, not the monarch, possessed much of the actual power in medieval England. A king remained in power as long as his magnates acknowledged him as the monarch. As we have seen in the segment on *Edward II*, when a ruler governed so poorly that his barons withdrew their support, he might lose his political authority. The king, therefore, required the approval of his barons in order to retain power and attempted to maintain their support through ideological means since the soldiers were under their command. The demystification of the myths concerning a sovereign's right to govern, which Shakespeare's play clearly manifests, resulted in Richard's deposition.

Although kings in the Middle Ages promoted (and perhaps actually believed in) myths such as divine right and the teleological hierarchy in order to legitimize their power, some of their subjects understood that these beliefs were fictitious. The subjects in Shakespeare's play discern the mythical nature of the ideologies that support kingship because Richard subverts these concepts. Phyllis Rackin notes, for instance:

> When Richard stops the trial by combat he interferes with a symbolic embodiment of his own authority. Trial by combat is a ritual based upon the assumption that right makes might, an assumption that underlies the authority of the whole feudal system, including the authority of God's anointed king. In preventing the symbolic ritual of chivalry, Richard attacks the source of the only authority that makes him king.[7]

Richard's demystification of the concepts that legitimize sovereignty results eventually in his loss of power and his death. He becomes obsessed with the myth of kingship that he perpetuates and allows it to dupe him when it no longer deceives his adversary, the Duke of Hereford.

Upon arriving at Berkeley Castle, King Richard declares that Bolingbroke's rebellion will undoubtedly fail:

> Not all the water in the rough rude sea
> Can wash the balm off from an anointed king;
> The breath of worldly men cannot depose
> The deputy elected by the Lord.
> For every man that Bolingbroke hath press'd
> To lift shrewd steel against our golden crown,
> God for his Richard hath in heavenly pay
> A glorious angel. Then, if angels fight,
> Weak men must fall, for heaven still guards the right.
> (III.ii.54-62)[8]

This passage consists of some of the most beautiful lines of Richard's poetry in the play. The imagery that describes divine right is heroic and triumphant but also pathetic because it demonstrates the king's impracticality. His poetry evokes pathos in the audience because his religious ideology cannot protect him from Bolingbroke's armed soldiers;

the king resorts unwisely to theory instead of practical necessity. In a battle between those armed with words of religious ideology and those with swords, the outcome is clear; everyone comprehends this truism except for the poet-king himself. Even after the king's rhetoric ceases to control the actions of Bolingbroke, Northumberland, Percy, Ross, Willoughby, and others, he continues to rely upon it.

The passage above regarding Richard's belief in the divine right of kings connotes the monarch's self-delusion since he relies upon the ideology that God protects divinely ordained kings, and subsequently he is deposed and murdered. Bolingbroke, who, according to the theory, sins against God by revolting against His viceroy, by indirectly ordering a regicide, and by breaking his religious oath to Richard that he would fulfill his term of banishment, succeeds to the throne, as if he has been rewarded. Bolingbroke, a worldly man, deposes successfully "The deputy elected by the Lord." Angels do not fight for Richard, thus challenging, in the context of Shakespeare's play, the king's assertion that "heaven still guards the right." Richard's unfortunate fate in the drama undermines his speech advocating divine right.

Aumerle, one of Richard's few loyal subjects in the play, thinks much more pragmatically than his king. He feels compelled to goad his too passive sovereign into acting:

> we are too remiss,
> Whilst Bolingbroke, through our security,
> Grows strong and great in substance and in power.
> (III.ii.33-35)

Bolingbroke gains an advantage over his cousin Richard, for the latter relies more on metaphysical ideology than on practical concerns such as the preparation for battle and the search for military allies.

Richard also manifests the earthliness of kingship by comporting himself in a manner unbecoming of a sovereign. As in *Magnificence, Woodstock*, and *Edward II*, the monarch in Shakespeare's play "is not himself, but basely led / By flatterers" (II.i.241-42). In all four dramas the king subjugates himself to his friends, elevating them to a status equal to or above his own. We must question the theory of divine right when Richard admits:

> And, for our coffers, with too great a court
> And liberal largess, are grown somewhat light,

We are enforc'd to farm our royal realm. . . .
                    (I.iv.43-45)

Because Richard has been profligate (like Magnificence), he finds himself at the mercy of his favorites, who possess economic power over him. He intends to relinquish his full control over England to Bushy, Bagot, and Greene in exchange for large sums of money. Richard claims to have been divinely selected to rule but undermines this ideology by distributing his authority to his subjects. Several characters in the play lament Richard's subjugation to his flatterers; the dying John of Gaunt says the king's

> death-bed is no lesser than thy land,
> Wherein thou liest in reputation sick;
> And thou, too careless patient as thou art,
> Commit'st thy anointed body to the cure
> Of those physicians that first wounded thee.
> A thousand flatterers sit within thy crown,
> Whose compass is no bigger than thy head;
> And yet, incaged in so small a verge,
> The waste is no whit lesser than thy land.
>   (II.i.95-103)

Although Gaunt, York, Bolingbroke, and Northumberland claim that sycophants dominate the king, the play does not fully corroborate their statements. We may accept their viewpoints as truth, nonetheless, for Shakespeare relies upon his audience's familiarity with the anonymous *Woodstock* and perhaps does not wish to repeat the plot of the earlier play. A.P. Rossiter provides convincing evidence that Shakespeare borrows frequently from *Woodstock*, and Peter Ure, Robert Potter, and Ian Robinson support the scholar's position.[9] The dramatist assumes his audience's understanding, because of their knowledge of *Woodstock*, that Richard permits his flatterers to govern him. Bearing this point in mind, the words of Gaunt, York, Bolingbroke, and Northumberland are truthful; the king does govern poorly by subjugating himself to his sycophants; consequently, he leads his country on the path to ruin, and he undercuts the concept of divine right by being his flatterers' subject.

Shakespeare demystifies the ideologies that legitimize kingship by portraying Richard as an incompetent ruler. Even though all kings may possess flaws and weaknesses because of their mortal body, few demonstrate these imperfections more than Richard. We may label the king's behavior upon his arrival at Berkeley Castle in III.ii as schizophrenia. Richard alternates between acting like a dignified,

confident ruler and a scared, despairing child. Upon hearing from
Salisbury that the Welsh army has deserted his cause, King Richard falls
into despair and orders his followers to leave him. Aumerle soothes him
by saying, "Comfort, my liege. Remember who you are" (III.ii.82). The
comment, which refers to the theory of divine right, immediately restores
the king's confidence. Richard declares:

> I had forgot myself. Am I not king?
> Awake, thou coward majesty, thou sleepest!
> Is not the king's name twenty thousand names?
> Arm, arm, my name! A puny subject strikes
> At thy great glory.
>   (III.ii.83-87)

The speech contains dramatic irony, for Shakespeare's audience, knowing
Richard's destiny, realizes the king's name is not equal to twenty thousand
names--merely one. Ernst H. Kantorowicz says that "A curious change in
Richard's attitude--as it were, a metamorphosis from 'Realism' to
'Nominalism'--now takes place. The Universal called 'Kingship' begins to
disintegrate; its transcendental 'Reality,' its objective truth and god-like
existence, so brilliant shortly before, pales into a nothing, a *nomen*."[10] The
comfort that Aumerle gives Richard merely provides the king with a false
sense of hope, as the monarch eventually realizes. The ruler finally
comprehends that he has deluded himself and has permitted others to
deceive him when Scroop informs him that York, the king's regent, has
joined Bolingbroke's side.

   Richard refuses subsequently to hear any more flattering words, and he
questions too late the power of divine right;[11] he also begins to recognize
the existence of the king's human and imperfect body:

> Cover your heads, and mock not flesh and blood
> With solemn reverence. Throw away respect,
> Tradition, form, and ceremonious duty,
> For you have but mistook me all this while.
> I live with bread like you, feel want,
> Taste grief, need friends. Subjected thus,
> How can you say to me I am a king?
>   (III.ii.171-77)

The words of the ruler challenge the ideologies of kingship he has
believed in and has relied upon to maintain power. When Richard claims
that he is "subjected" to human needs like all mortal beings, he puns on the

word: Richard acknowledges that although he possesses the title of king, he is actually no different from his subjects, and he wonders how others may "say to me I am a king." In this passage Richard fails to mention his spiritual body, focusing exclusively upon his earthly body. The statement foreshadows his deposition, for "the collapse of kingship seems to be confirmed in the discovery of the physical body of the ruler."[12] This passage is also noteworthy because it indicates that Shakespeare, who places these words into the mouth of King Richard, demystifies the ideological concepts that legitimize royal authority.

Richard challenges the beliefs that justify sovereignty, but he attempts nevertheless to employ these ideologies as weapons in his struggle with Bolingbroke for power. While trapped at Flint Castle, Richard demands that Northumberland, Bolingbroke's mediator, genuflect to him. By kneeling, a subject acknowledges his allegiance and sociopolitical inferiority to the person to whom he bends his knee. When a subject kneels submissively, he rests close to the earth while the monarch remains higher and thus greater; the subject indirectly acknowledges his earthliness and mortality while the king stands closer to the sun (a symbol of power) and the heavens.

Richard tries to reassert his authority over Bolingbroke, through Northumberland, by inducing the earl to kneel to him; he says to Bolingbroke's ally, employing the royal "we":

> We are amaz'd; and thus long have we stood
> To watch the fearful bending of thy knee,
> Because we thought ourself thy lawful king.
> And if we be, how dare thy joints forget
> To pay their aweful duty to our presence?
> If we be not, show us the hand of God
> That hath dismiss'd us from our stewardship;
> For well we know, no hand of blood and bone
> Can gripe the sacred handle of our scepter. . . .
> . . . .
> Yet know, my master, God omnipotent,
> Is mustering in his clouds on our behalf
> Armies of pestilence;
>
> (III.iii.72-87)[13]

No stage direction indicates that the earl kneels, so we may assume he remains standing. Richard's rhetoric deceives neither Northumberland nor Shakespeare's audience. We comprehend that Richard does not believe in the truthfulness of his own words since he watches impotently and says nothing when Northumberland refuses to genuflect. When Bolingbroke bends his knee to his cousin later in the scene, Richard and the audience realize immediately that the insincere act mocks the king's lack of power.[14] We must also question whether Richard believes in the truthfulness of his own words since he hides from his enemies within the castle walls while saying that "no hand of blood and bone / Can gripe the sacred handle of our scepter. . . . ," and then he surrenders meekly.

Raphael Holinshed notes that Northumberland promised Richard safe passage as the monarch left the castle but then ambushed him as he departed and took him prisoner:

> The king keeping on his waie, had not ridden past foure miles, where he came to the place where the ambushes were lodged, and being entred within danger of them, before he was aware, shewed himselfe to be sore abashed. But now there was no remedie: for the earle being there with his men, would not suffer him to returne, . . . but being inclosed with the sea on the one side, and the rocks on the other, hauing his aduersaries so neere at hand before him, he could not shift awaie by any meanes. . . .[15]

Such an event possesses many excellent dramatic possibilities, none of which Shakespeare employs; the playwright's dramatization of the event would have created more sympathy for Richard. Instead, Shakespeare's Richard willingly and cowardly permits Bolingbroke to take him prisoner. Shakespeare omits Northumberland's devious tactics, which undoubtedly conflict with the laws of arms, perhaps to portray the king as weak and pusillanimous.

In *Richard II,* the monarch relinquishes power without a struggle, after Bolingbroke declares that he merely wishes to recover the property that he believes rightfully belongs to him. The king perceives Bolingbroke's true intention but fails to struggle to retain his authority. S.C. Sen Gupta astutely remarks that "Richard surrenders the crown more than Bolingbroke snatches it from him." The king could have restored his cousin's land and possibly maintained his authority. Yet, argues Sen Gupta, "Richard says that he is Bolingbroke's and all, calls the latter his heir, and proceeds to surrender the crown which even then he might have tried to retain."[16] Instead of confronting Lancaster, the resigned king says to Aumerle:

> What must the King do now? Must he submit?
> The King shall do it. Must he be depos'd?
> The King shall be contented. Must he lose

The name of king? A' God's name, let it go.
(III.iii.143-46)

Instead of using the royal "we" to call attention to his authority (as he does approximately seventy lines earlier), Richard speaks of himself now in the third person, as if to distance himself from the power he has enjoyed heretofore. The alteration in his language implies a self-deposition. Shakespeare's decision to allow Richard to encounter Bolingbroke at Flint Castle creates a symbolic abdication, further demonstrating ahistorically that the king meekly relinquishes political power. When Northumberland approaches the castle, the stage direction reads that "Richard appeareth on the wall" (III.iii.61); in other words, he appears in the gallery above the stage.[17] Bolingbroke and Northumberland are on the stage platform below while King Richard, standing in the gallery, towers above them as the sun hovers over the earth. The king legally retains power and Hereford is his subject. Northumberland informs the monarch that Henry awaits him in the base court. The king must walk downwards to meet Bolingbroke, for the latter will not come to him. Richard for the first time in the play (and in his life) follows orders. When Richard descends, he no longer stands above Hereford spatially, and the altered position indicates his loss of political dominance. Historically, the king had to submit since the Machiavellian Northumberland ambushed him. In Shakespeare's play, however, Richard voluntarily submits and laments his cowardice:

Down, down I come, like glist'ring Phaethon,
Wanting the manage of unruly jades.
In the base court? Base court, where kings grow base,
To come at traitors' calls and do them grace.
In the base court? Come down? Down court! down king!
(III.iii.178-82)

Misguided Phaethon attempted to assert his divine birth by borrowing the chariot from his father Apollo, the Sun God, but he handled the horses incompetently; the chariot plummeted towards the earth, so Zeus responded by thrusting the presumptuous Phaethon into the waters of the Eridanus. Similarly, the irresponsible King Richard (Phaethon) employs ideology (the chariot) to assert his divine position but cannot control his subjects (the unruly jades). King Richard descends the steps of Flint Castle as Phaethon fell to earth, indicating a loss of power and control. Bolingbroke (Zeus) then destroys him.

Shakespeare continues to undermine the ideologies that authorize sovereignty by indicating that Richard is not only incompetent and cowardly but also cruel, for the monarch has ordered the murder of his uncle, the Duke of Gloucester. We recognize Richard's involvement when Gaunt says to the king:

> O, spare me not, my brother Edward's son,
> For that I was his father Edward's son!
> That blood already, like the pelican,
> Hast thou tapp'd out and drunkenly carous'd.
> My brother Gloucester, plain well-meaning soul--
> Whom fair befall in heaven 'mongst happy souls!--
> May be a precedent and witness good
> That thou respect'st not spilling Edward's blood.
>
> (II.i.124-31)

When the Duchess of Gloucester demands justice from John of Gaunt for the murder of her husband, he claims that he cannot do so:

> God's is the quarrel, for God's substitute,
> His deputy anointed in His sight,
> Hath caus'd his death, the which if wrongfully,
> Let heaven revenge;
>
> (I.ii.37-40)

Gaunt's statement, which connotes a firm belief in the divine right of kings, is unwittingly ironic. If Richard were truly God's "deputy anointed," he would not have arranged for the murder of his uncle; a divinely ordained viceroy is theoretically incapable of committing such a heinous deed. Sir William Blackstone writes that "Besides the attribute of sovereignty, the law also ascribes to the king, in his political capacity, absolute *perfection*. The king can do no wrong; . . . [t]he king, moreover, is not only incapable of *doing* wrong, but even of *thinking* wrong: he can never mean to do an improper thing: in him is no folly or weakness."[18] Once again Shakespeare undermines the notion of the ideology of sovereignty, implying that a king is simply a human being, no different from any other.

Shakespeare portrays Richard as a worse king than he was historically. No historical information exists to justify Shakespeare's inclusion of Richard's callous words about Gaunt's illness: "Now put it, God, in the physician's mind / To help him to his grave immediately!" (I.IV.59-60). After Gaunt's death, Richard seizes his uncle's property, an action that

Holinshed claims "was much misliked of all the nobilitie, and cried out against of the meaner sort."[19]   Holinshed's account may be true, but Shakespeare's play defames Richard by inaccurately characterizing the Duke of Lancaster as a loyal and "time-honour'd" subject who has unwaveringly supported his nephew, thereby making the king's appropriation of the property appear illegal. Gaunt's refusal to question Richard's authority, exemplified in the quotation in the previous paragraph, deviates from historical truth and is the playwright's fabrication. Gaunt in fact behaved in an adversarial manner towards his nephew on several occasions and once even raised an army against him.[20] Since Shakespeare purposefully begins his plot with actions in 1398, he omits the treacherous deeds of Lancaster and the part of Hereford (Gaunt's heir) in the unlawful deposition of Richard in December 1387--actions with which Shakespeare was familiar from his reading of Holinshed's *Chronicles*.

Bolingbroke was one of the five Lords Appellant who captured the king in the Tower, forced him from power for three days yet who could not agree upon an acceptable successor. We may consider Henry's behavior unequivocally traitorous. Richard's confiscation of Gaunt's property in the play appears unjustified, but a king could lawfully impound the possessions of traitors. Even before Richard's seizure of the property, we comprehend Bolingbroke's ambition, as does the king. A bitter Richard of Bordeaux complains to Aumerle, Bagot, and Greene that he may never recall Hereford from exile since the duke dangerously courts the support of Richard's loyal subjects:

> Ourself and Bushy, Bagot here, and Green
> Observ'd his courtship to the common people;
> How he did seem to dive into their hearts
> With humble and familiar courtesy,
> . . . .
> Off goes his bonnet to an oyster-wench;
> A brace of draymen bid God speed him well
> And had the tribute of his supple knee,
> With "Thanks, my countrymen, my loving friends,"
> As were our England in reversion his,
> And he our subjects' next degree in hope.
>   (I.iv.23-36)

Gaunt's great wealth made him arguably the most powerful person in England, perhaps more authoritative than the king, so Richard understood that the transfer of this wealth to the even more ambitious Bolingbroke would cause some serious political problems for himself. Richard's motives for confiscating the property included self-preservation and revenge for Hereford's treachery. The king's action, which provided Bolingbroke with a ruse to return to England, was politically foolish but not illegal. The king's deed seems illegal in the context of Shakespeare's play because the playwright dramatizes Richard's seizure of the property but purposefully omits the monarch's reason and justification for doing so, causing the king to appear evil.

Shakespeare also implicates Richard in Gloucester's murder--and correctly so. Although the playwright implies some degree of responsibility on Richard's part, he fails again to include the king's motivation for his actions. The ambitious Gloucester coveted the throne and deposed King Richard briefly during the last three days of 1387. Harold F. Hutchison reports that the Lords Appellant, led by Woodstock, confined the king in the Tower and made demands:

> only after Derby had taken him to a window, and shown him the threatening besiegers outside, did Richard consent [to the nobles' demands]. The darkest and perhaps the true story is that a reckless Gloucester actually proclaimed Richard deposed "for two dayes or thre," and that so crude a usurpation was only circumvented because of the opposition of Derby, Nottingham, and possibly of Warwick, and hushed up so that posterity might be unaware both of Richard's degradation and of Gloucester's treason.[21]

Derby, Nottingham (Mowbray), and Warwick permitted Richard to resume power not because they favored his rule but rather because they disapproved of Woodstock as an alternative. Shakespeare must have been familiar with the Lord Appellants' treasonous acts in the Tower, for Holinshed mentions them in the *Chronicles*.[22] The playwright ignores this information, rendering Gloucester an innocent victim and Richard a cruel murderer of his uncle.

Shakespeare omits the facts regarding Gloucester's executions of Richard's friends and the duke's attempt to imprison the king, himself. During the Merciless Parliament, Woodstock executed several of Richard's advisors without a trial and stubbornly refused pleas for mercy from his allies, his relatives, and his enemies. Holinshed reports that Richard, York, and Derby strove diligently to convince Gloucester to spare the life of Simon Burley;[23] yet the implacable and cruel Woodstock executed the king's advisor and former tutor. Gloucester's refusal to heed his monarch's pleas definitely constituted treason, especially since he threatened again to depose Richard when the nephew attempted to delay Burley's execution.[24]

The duke also plotted in August 1397 to imprison and depose Richard. Holinshed notes that Woodstock met with a group of conspirators to plan the fall of the king but that Mowbray, one of the nobles Gloucester invited, immediately informed the ruler. Richard then rode to Pleshy and arrested his uncle; realizing that he could not rule peacefully while such a dangerous noble lived, he arranged his uncle's death.[25]   Gloucester's treasonous actions clearly warranted his execution.   Shakespeare, undoubtedly familiar with the information that Holinshed provided, chooses again to ignore the duke's evil behavior, yet he suggests the king's role in the noble's death, causing the monarch's actions to appear unjustified.

By choosing not to telescope time (as he does without restraint in his other histories), Shakespeare omits the treasonous behavior of Derby and Mowbray during the brief deposition and at Radcot Bridge, thus depriving the audience of the king's reasons for interrupting the duel in I.iii and for exiling the two knights. Since Hereford and Mowbray committed treason and both nobles were ambitious and dangerous, Richard needed to rid himself of them. A trial by combat would have dispatched one lord, but the victor would remain at court and be as powerful and dangerous as ever. By throwing down his warder and exiling the two combatants, he intended to protect himself from both nobles.[26]

The subversion in *Richard II* appears not only in the dramatist's portrayal of the monarch as a man who foolishly dupes himself by ideological rhetoric, who cruelly murders his youngest uncle, and who unjustifiably steals his cousin's rightful property; the playwright also chooses to write a drama about the deposition of a king with an undisputed title to the throne. No king in Shakespeare's histories possesses a better claim to power than Richard, yet the playwright dramatizes this king's loss of authority. Because of Richard's undisputed title, the portrayal of his deposition demystifies the ideologies of kingship more than does the dramatization of Henry VI's decline and fall. We may consider *Richard II* subversive, especially since Queen Elizabeth's claim to the crown was far inferior to that of Richard;[27] if a monarch who rightfully succeeds to the throne may be deposed, the same unhappy fortune could occur to a ruler whose title is questionable.

Shakespeare also includes a deposition scene in *Richard II*. Queen Elizabeth and her advisors must have realized how potentially subversive the dramatization of that act could be, for they ordered that scene removed from the printed text of the play.[28]   The subversion lies not only in the portrayal of the act, but also in the demystification of the symbols that legitimize kingship.   Hodgdon claims that during the deposition scene, Richard "disenfranchise[s] Bolingbroke's right to the crown by making his own stunningly visible. . . .   In a ritual that takes form as a transcendent instance of festival inversion, Richard evokes the symbols of majesty--the crown, the sceptre, the balm, the sacred state and duteous oaths belonging to kings--and strips them away. . . ."[29]   If dramatic art mirrors life and if all the world is a stage, a deposition onstage could later be re-enacted in real life in the Elizabethan court.   Even if Shakespeare's intent in dramatizing this scene was not subversive, the fact that the deposition occurs onstage in front of many witnesses renders it dangerous.   Margot Heinemann says:

> Fundamental changes in accepted ways of seeing the world and one's place in it take a long time to mature and to spread widely through society. Yet without such slow changes in mentalities over a long period the rapid transformations of the revolutionary years would have been unthinkable. Indeed the greatest political drama--*Richard II, King Lear*--often seems strangely to prefigure what was to become real material history a generation later.[30]

When audiences witness action onstage, especially in a history play that supposedly recounts the lives and actions of real people, they may believe that history can and perhaps should repeat itself.

One may argue that Shakespeare opposes Richard's deposition and portrays it as an evil act since the Bishop of Carlisle prophesies that if Bolingbroke acquires the throne:

> The blood of English shall manure the ground,
> And future ages groan for this foul act;
> Peace shall go sleep with Turks and infidels,
> And in this seat of peace tumultuous wars
> Shall kin with kin and kind with kind confound;
> . . . .
> O, if you raise this house against this house,
> It will the woefullest division prove
> That ever fell upon this cursed earth.
>   (IV.i.138-48)

We must remember that Richard II lacked an heir to the throne and that his second wife, Isabella of France, was only a child at the time of his death; she was therefore several years too young to bear offspring.   Had he not been deposed and murdered, Richard still might never have fathered an heir. John Hardyng says that John of Gaunt, understanding that

> kyng Rychard, in his greate excellence,
> None yssue had, he would haue been his heire
> Apparaunt then, by act in perlyament feire.[31]

The belief that Richard's maintenance of authority would have permitted a smooth succession of power to his rightful heir is but speculation. Furthermore, Shakespeare knew from reading Holinshed's *Chronicles* that Roger Mortimer, the Earl of March and Richard's heir apparent, had been murdered in Ireland.[32] England could have lacked an heir after the king's death even if Richard had retained power. Consequently, if Bolingbroke had not usurped the crown, he might have battled other nobles for the vacant throne, so a civil war could have ensued anyway. We must also consider the possibility that if Bolingbroke had not seized the throne, Elizabeth might never have become queen.

We should also not disregard the possibility that Shakespeare includes Carlisle's prophecy as a practical means of linking the plot of *Richard II* with that of *1 Henry IV* since the Lord Chamberlain's Men may have performed the plays in the second tetralogy on successive nights. Evidence exists of Shakespeare's intention to connect the plays, such as the fact that both the conclusion of *Richard II* and the opening of *1 Henry IV* refer to Bolingbroke's intention of making a crusade.

The last drama in the tetralogy, *Henry V*, contradicts the Bishop of Carlisle's assertion that Bolingbroke's usurpation will result in divine punishment. Shakespeare glorifies Henry V as the ideal, model king. If the playwright believed that Bolingbroke's deposition of Richard incurred God's wrath, he would not have portrayed the usurper's son as an almost perfect hero who emerges victorious against overwhelming odds at Agincourt.[33] After the battle, Henry V declares:

> O God, thy arm was here!
> And not to us, but to thy arm alone,
> Ascribe we all!
> . . . .
> God fought for us.
> (IV.viii.106-20)

The fact that the outnumbered English in *Henry V* slay ten thousand French soldiers while losing only twenty-nine of their own is important:

it demonstrates that Shakespeare supports Henry's words and undermines Carlisle's prophecy of the evil ramifications of usurpation. One may argue that the triumph at Agincourt was but one victory during a turbulent and bloody era from Richard's deposition (1399) to the ascension of Henry VII (1485) and thus does not prove the fallacy of Carlisle's prophecy; the successful reign of Henry V, however, lasted for ten glorious years (1413-22), seven years longer than the troublesome reign of Richard III (1483-85). One may argue that the rebellions and the War of the Roses during the eighty-six year period prove the accuracy of the prophecy. We should remember, however, that Henry II, Richard the Lion-hearted, John, Elizabeth, James I, Charles I, Charles II, and other monarchs before and after this eighty-six year interval faced rebellions. English history is notoriously bloody and full of civil strife. It is an oversimplification, therefore, to argue that the years between Richard's deposition and the Battle of Bosworth Field were turbulent because of Bolingbroke's usurpation and Richard's death.   Henry Ansgar Kelly adds that Shakespeare undercuts Richard's providential remarks so that "The force of his prediction of future divine discomfiture for Henry and his allies is therefore somewhat weakened."[34] Lastly, we realize that depositions and regicides do not necessarily result in civil war since the tragedy of Edward II initiated the long reign of Edward III, perhaps the most successful of medieval kings.

One may also argue that Shakespeare opposes the king's deposition since he clearly wishes his audience to sympathize with the ruler. But, as we have noted in the segment on *Edward II*, we only feel pity for the monarch after he loses power. We empathize with the human being but not with the king. Although we pity his tribulations, we take comfort in the realization that England will no longer suffer under the rule of an incompetent king, which is how Shakespeare portrays Richard.

King Richard II was not the worst of rulers. He comported himself courageously during the Peasant's Revolt of 1381, was a man of peace and a patron of poets such as Chaucer and Gower, and assumed the throne at the age of nine during an extremely turbulent era. Although Richard was not an admirable king, he was not as terrible as Shakespeare's play indicates. Shakespeare's dramatization of Richard as incompetent (as opposed to his characterization of Bolingbroke as efficient) is subversive, for the playwright demonstrates the necessity of his removal in order for England to thrive. As in Marlowe's play and the anonymous *Woodstock*, *Richard II* demonstrates that political necessity takes precedence over lawful succession: if a king fails to govern wisely, these playwrights suggest, a usurper may justifiably depose him.

Shakespeare entitled his play *The Tragedy of King Richard the Second* because the monarch's fall from power and subsequent murder are indeed tragic. Irving Ribner says that in his "fall [Richard] carries the sympathies of the audience with him. . . . Richard in his suffering, moreover, comes to even more of an understanding of himself, both as man and king, than does Marlowe's Edward, and in his death he attains something of a tragic stature."[35]   Part of the tragedy lies in Richard's questioning of the metaphysics of kingship and his comprehension that he has misgoverned England; unfortunately for the ruler, he thinks introspectively only after his deposition is probable.   We realize from Edward II's rhetorical question while in captivity, "how have I transgressed / Unless it be with too much clemency?", that he fails to learn that he has governed poorly and has badly mistreated his nobles.[36] Richard's self-awareness allows him to mature as the play progresses, but Edward's refusal to accept the blame for his misfortunes causes the audience to feel less sympathy for him; Shakespeare's history play is more tragic than Marlowe's.

CHAPTER 7: NOTES

1. Ronald R. MacDonald, "Uneasy Lies: Language and History in Shakespeare's Lancastrian Histories," *Shakespeare Quarterly*, 35 (1984), 24.

2. John Milton, "Eikonoklastes," in *Complete Prose Works of John Milton*, ed. Don M. Wolfe, 8 vols (New Haven: Yale University Press, 1953-82), III, 343.

3. Jonathan Dollimore, *Radical Tragedy: Religion, Ideology and Power in the Drama of Shakespeare and his Contemporaries* (Chicago: University of Chicago Press, 1984), p. 6.

4. J.W. Lever, *The Tragedy of State* (London: Methuen, 1971), p. 5.

5. MacDonald, p. 23.

6. Graham Holderness, *Shakespeare's History* (Dublin: Gill and Macmillan; New York: St. Martin's, 1985), pp. 50-51.

7. Phyllis Rackin, *Stages of History: Shakespeare's English Chronicles* (Ithaca: Cornell University Press, 1990), p. 49.

8. David Bevington, ed., *The Complete Works of Shakespeare*, 3rd ed. (Glenview, Ill.: Scott, Foresman, 1980) All quotations from Shakespeare throughout are taken from this edition.

9. See A.P. Rossiter, ed., Introduction, *Woodstock: A Moral History* (London: Chatto and Windus, 1946), pp. 47-53; Peter Ure, ed., *King Richard II* (1961; rpt. London: Methuen, 1969), pp. 58-59 (n. 128); Robert Potter, *The English Morality Play: Origins, History and Influence of a Dramatic Tradition* (London: Routledge & Kegan Paul, 1975), p. 130; and Ian Robinson, *"Richard II" & "Woodstock"* (Doncaster, Eng.: Brynmill, 1988), pp. 31-36.

10. Ernst H. Kantorowicz, *The King's Two Bodies: A Study in Medieval Political Theology* (1957; rpt. Princeton: Princeton University Press, 1981), p. 29.

11. Perhaps Richard does not abandon his belief in divine right because he mentions it again in the deposition scene (IV.i.233-43) and in his death scene (V.v.107-10).

12.   Stephen Greenblatt, "Invisible Bullets: Renaissance Authority and its Subversion, *Henry IV* and *Henry V*," in *Political Shakespeare: New Essays in Cultural Materialism*, eds. Jonathan Dollimore and Alan Sinfield. (Ithaca: Cornell University Press, 1985), p. 40.

13.   The deposition of Edward II seventy years earlier sets a dangerous precedent and undercuts Richard's speech about divine right.

14.   Bolingbroke's mockery becomes readily apparent when we contrast his kneeling to Richard in III.iii.188 with that in I.iii.46-47, shortly before the trial by combat is about to begin.

15.   Raphael Holinshed, *Holinshed's Chronicles of England, Scotland, and Ireland*, 6 vols. (London: J. Johnson, et al., 1807-08), II, 857.

16.   S.C. Sen Gupta, *Shakespeare's Historical Plays* (London: Oxford University Press, 1964), p. 22.

17.   See Richard Hosley, "Shakespeare's Use of a Gallery over the Stage," *Shakespeare Survey*, 10 (1957), 77-78.

18.   Sir William Blackstone, *Commentaries on The Laws of England: in Four Books; With an Analysis of the Work*, 2 vols. (New York: W.E. Dean, 1836), I, 184-85.

19.   Holinshed, II, 849.

20.   Holinshed, II, 838.

21.   Harold F. Hutchison, *The Hollow Crown: A Life of Richard II* (London: Eyre and Spottiswoode, 1961), p. 115.

22.   See Holinshed, II, 787, 792-93, 795.

23.   Holinshed, II, 794-95.

24.   Hutchison, p. 120.

25.   Holinshed, II, 835-36.

26.   One may argue that Richard acts upon the advice of Gaunt, but the king manipulates him in order to exile Bolingbroke and Mowbray.

27. Elizabeth's legitimacy was in doubt for the following five reasons:

1) The claim of her father (Henry VIII) was questionable since he descended from the union of Gaunt and his mistress Catherine Swynford, a match that some considered illegitimate. Henry's great-great-grandfather, John Beaufort, was born in approximately 1373, but according to Hutchison, Gaunt (Beaufort's father) married his third wife in January 1396 (after she bore him four children). Hutchison adds that during "the January Parliament of 1397, Richard had granted by letters patent, full legitimization to the offspring of Gaunt and his new wife Catherine Swynford" (pp. 162-63, 171). After the deposition of Richard II and the subsequent War of the Roses, no leader possessed an undisputed claim to the throne.

2) Henry VIII disinherited Elizabeth in an act of Parliament.

3) Jasper Ridley says that Ann Boleyn's "execution was postponed for forty-eight hours so that she could be divorced before she died. Henry wished his marriage to her to be declared a nullity so that their daughter Elizabeth would be a bastard   . . . . [T]he child of the marriage, whom the people had sworn to accept as the lawful heiress to the crown, was to be pronounced illegitimate." Thomas Cranmer's main argument for the divorce was the incestuous nature of the marriage (Boleyn's sister Mary was one of the king's mistresses). Henry executed Ann Boleyn on the charges of adultery and incest: she was charged with sleeping with her brother, Lord Rochford, and some believed that Sir Henry Norris was Elizabeth's true father, which further called into question Elizabeth's title to the throne. See Jasper Ridley, *Henry VIII* (London: Constable, 1984), pp. 269-70, 270, 268.

4) The Reformation in England rendered Elizabeth's claim problematic since some Catholics wanted Mary Stuart to be queen. The pope's excommunication of Elizabeth granted people the right (from a Roman Catholic perspective) to break their allegiance to Elizabeth.

5) The fact that Elizabeth was female called into question her legitimate right to govern since some believed that monarchs should be male.

28. The deposition scene, however, was still performed onstage; the inclusion of the deposition in the production of *Richard II* provided the false impression that the scene was not politically subversive. Leah Marcus indicates that "a play licensed for production is officially declared free of a whole range of potentially subversive significations." Leah Marcus, *Puzzling Shakespeare: Local Reading and Its Discontents* (Berkeley: University of California Press, 1988), p. 28.

29. Barbara Hodgdon, *The End Crowns All: Closure and Contradiction in Shakespeare's History* (Princeton: Princeton University Press, 1991), p. 133.

30. Margot Heinemann, "Political Drama," in *The Cambridge Companion to English Renaissance Drama*, ed. A.R. Braunmuller and Michael Hattaway (Cambridge: Cambridge University Press, 1990), p. 162.

31. John Hardyng, *The Chronicle of Iohn Hardyng. Containing an Account of Public Transactions from the Earliest Period of English History to the Beginning of the Reign of King Edward the Fourth. Together with The Continuation by Richard Grafton, To the Thirty Fourth Year of King Henry the Eighth.*, ed. Henry Ellis (1812; rpt. New York: AMS, 1974), p. 290. According to Hardyng, Gaunt attempted to become heir apparent to Richard by producing a falsified chronicle that stated that Edmund Crookback (Lancaster) and not Edward was actually the eldest son of Henry III (pp. 290-91, note on p. 353).

32. Holinshed, II, 768.

33. It is true that Henry does pray before the battle of Agincourt, for he fears that Richard's death will have a negative effect upon the outcome of the battle. The death of the deposed king, however, has no evil ramifications for the English.

34. Henry Ansgar Kelly, *Divine Providence in the England of Shakespeare's Histories* (Cambridge, Mass.: Harvard University Press, 1970), p. 209.

35. Irving Ribner, *The English History Play in the Age of Shakespeare,* rev. ed. (New York: Barnes & Noble, 1965), pp. 152-53.

36. Christopher Marlowe, *Edward the Second*, ed. W. Moelwyn Merchant (1967; rpt. London: A. & C. Black; New York: W.W. Norton, 1989), V.i.122-23.

PART THREE

ABDICATED KINGDOMS AND

MERGING GENRES

CHAPTER 8

THE MIRROR FOR MONARCHS

Scholars have almost universally considered Thomas Norton's and Thomas Sackville's *Gorboduc, or Ferrex and Porrex* and Shakespeare's *King Lear* to be tragedies, and the anonymous *King Leir* a comedy or a romance. The playwrights, however, base these dramas on chronicles of pre-Christian English history. The pre-Christian historical accounts found in the first volume of Holinshed's *Chronicles* and in Geoffrey of Monmouth's *Historia Regum Britanniae* are clearly legends, if not fictions. But this fact may not be very significant in determining the genre of these three plays, for many Elizabethans and Jacobeans believed in the historical accuracy of these stories. Felix E. Schelling says that "The Elizabethan conception of history accepted such tales and gave them the credence which we accord to historical fact."[1] Thomas Nashe says that history plays are "borrowed out of our English Chronicles, wherein our forefathers valiant acts (that have line long buried in rustie brasse and wormeeaten books) are revived, and they themselves raised from the Grace of Oblivion."[2] History is a series of events that people believe to have happened; the contemporary audience's acceptance of these occurrences as truth carries more significance than whether the events are factual. The first two dramas cannot be completely tragic nor the third comedic or romantic, for their authors and audiences believed in the veracity of these chronicled accounts involving their supposed ancestors. If we categorize *Gorboduc* and *King Lear* exclusively as tragedies and *King Leir* strictly as a comedy or a romance, we overlook the effects of the plays upon their audiences: the historical past may be employed as a mirror for the contemporary audiences since history is a cyclical phenomenon. The effects of a dramatization of historical accounts upon theatre audiences are important in these dramas, especially in *Gorboduc*, as we shall discover in this chapter.

Let us begin by analyzing the tragic elements of *Gorboduc* that have historical and political significance. The first dumb show of the play, which precedes the first scene, portrays six savage men attempting in vain to break a fagot; the savages then divide the bundle into individual sticks and subsequently break them easily.[3] The dumb show symbolizes unequivocally, and then states explicitly, the playwrights' belief that a kingdom united by the governance of a monarch is strong but that a divided nation becomes susceptible to dissension and civil war.[4]

The first act of Norton's and Sackville's play dramatizes the theme of the aforementioned dumb show. In the first scene, Videna laments to her eldest and favorite son, Ferrex, that Gorboduc has committed a most unnatural act: the king has bequeathed to Ferrex only half the inheritance to which he is entitled:

> But thee of thy birthright and heritage,
> Causeless, unkindly, and in wrongful wise,
> Against all law and right, he will bereave.
> Half of his kingdom he will give away.
> $\qquad$ (I.i.26-29)[5]

Videna claims that her husband's foolish decision conflicts with the laws of political succession and of primogeniture.[6] A strong correlation exists between political and familial inheritance;[7] the word "unkindly" means not only that Gorboduc has been unfair to Ferrex politically but also that he has disregarded his familial responsibility to his eldest son, to one of his kind. Videna's assertion that Gorboduc's action will "bereave" Ferrex of the boy's inheritance connotes the unlawfulness and irregularity of the decision.

Ferrex's response is also telling: when the queen complains that Gorboduc will "give away" (as in squander) half the kingdom, Ferrex replies, "To whom?" (I.i.30). His failure to consider his younger brother as a political rival for the throne indicates the extremely unusual nature of the king's decision. This scene in which Videna issues her vehement diatribe against her husband's action, combined with the dumb show that characterizes the evils of dividing a nation, sets the stage for Gorboduc's discussion before Parliament of his wish to abdicate in favor of his sons.

Monarchs ordinarily possess the throne until their deaths. In upsetting that principle by abdicating, Gorboduc creates a potentially dangerous precedent, for his action informs his subjects that reasons exist for a king to relinquish power during his lifetime. If a king may create circumstances in which he loses power while he lives, his subjects may also wish to devise reasons to replace a monarch before his death.

The audience should question Gorboduc's motives for abdicating. The legitimacy of Gorboduc's reasons for deposing himself appears questionable and requires careful scrutiny. Gorboduc resigns for both personal and public reasons. He wishes to relinquish power so that he may live the remaining years of his life in tranquility: the king declares that his age calls him to a life of "greater ease" (I.ii.57); he also wants to transfer his power to his sons so that he "may joy to see their ruling well" (I.ii.67). Both of Gorboduc's personal reasons are quite selfish and conflict with his regal responsibilities, for the king ignores a monarch's duties to his subjects, who rely on his experienced government. A king has the obligation to govern his people until his death; peaceful retirement and abdication because of parental fondness amount to nothing so much as dereliction of royal duty.

Gorboduc's political reasons for abdicating appear plausible on the surface. The king informs his counselors that he wishes to allow his sons to become rulers for the good of the commonweal:

> That, when by death my life and rule shall cease,
> The kingdom yet may with unbroken course
> Have certain prince by whose undoubted right
> Your wealth and peace may stand in quiet stay;
> And eke that they whom nature hath prepared
> In time to take my place in princely seat,
> While in their father's time their pliant youth
> Yields to the frame of skilful governance,
> May so be taught and trained in noble arts,
> . . . .
> And not be thought, for their unworthy life
> And for their lawless swerving out of kind,
> Worthy to lose what law and kind them gave;
>   (I.ii.7-21)

The import in this passage is illogical. Gorboduc predicts a smooth transition after his death ends his rule, yet he is in the process of abdicating. The king implies that his relinquishment of the crown will prevent a change in power since his sons will already be kings when he dies, but a transitional period ensues after he vacates the throne in favor of Ferrex and Porrex; Gorboduc cannot prevent the inevitable change in authority. The monarch wishes to yield to a leader with an "undoubted right," but he foolishly divides the kingdom in half, creating a potential dispute regarding his sons' right to govern.

The king's decision to depose himself while his sons are in their "pliant youth" is illogical since their acquisition of power will supersede their pliancy. Sons obey their parents since the latter are the authority figures in the relationship, but "When fathers cease to know that they should rule, / The children cease to know they should obey. . ." (I.ii.207-08). In Norton's and Sackville's drama, Gorboduc fails to realize that when he transfers his political power to Ferrex and Porrex, he greatly diminishes his role as a parental authority: political power subjugates and mutes parental dominance. When Dordan and Philander advise Ferrex and Porrex, respectively, to discuss with their father their antagonism, both kings dismiss immediately the idea of confiding in Gorboduc. Furthermore, the latter's statement that he wishes that his sons not "lose what law and kind them gave" falsely asserts that his division of the realm conforms to law and kindliness (i.e., nature); we have already witnessed the lawlessness and unkindliness of the monarch's failure to leave his kingdom solely to Ferrex.

Gorboduc also informs Parliament:

> that they may better rule their charge,
> I mean forthwith to place them in the same,
> That in my life they may both learn to rule. . . .
>   (I.ii.64-66)

The king may have noble intentions, but he exhibits faulty reasoning in the statement just quoted; furthermore, he denies the importance of Parliament. We have seen in the previous paragraph that Gorboduc's abdication results in his loss of political and parental power, so his sons will not learn from him how to rule now that he has relinquished the crown. They could learn, however, if he taught by example, but this possibility does not occur to him. His claim that "in my life they may both learn to rule" is also problematic because when Ferrex and Porrex discuss their precarious situations with their advisors, Gorboduc is notable for his absence. Audience members should wonder where the former king is during this turbulent transition and why he remains completely ignorant of the political rivalry between his royal sons.[8] Norton and Sackville manifest the king's unfamiliarity with political events subsequent to his retirement by dramatizing the problem for the audience before Gorboduc comprehends it; the playwrights also include messengers to the former monarch who relay information of which we are already aware.

Furthermore, Gorboduc asserts that his sons will govern well since he will provide them with an advisor

> whose long approved faith
> And wisdom tried may well assure my heart
> That mining fraud shall find no way to creep
> Into their fenced ears with grave advice.
>   (I.ii.361-64)

The outcome of the drama manifests unequivocally the monarch's naivete. As I shall argue in the following paragraph, a king does not have to heed the advice of his counselors; ironically, Gorboduc declares that his sons need trustworthy advisors in the same speech in which he decides to ignore the sagacious counsel of his Parliament.

We may regard the king's faith in Parliament as specious. Gorboduc's wish to be present when his sons begin their rule denies the importance of Parliament; that organization's function, according to the playwrights, is to guide leaders. Gorboduc manifests his wish to abdicate immediately and divide the kingdom in two, bestowing one half upon each of his two sons; but he declares that he requires the advice of his trusty counselors in Parliament:

> Now more importeth me than erst to use
> Your faith and wisdom, whereby yet I reign . . . .
> . . . .
> Thus do I mean to use your wonted faith
> To me and mine and to your native land.
> My lords, be plain without all wry respect
> Or poisonous craft to speak in pleasing wise.
>   (I.ii.5-30)

We realize from Videna, however, that Gorboduc has already decided to divide the realm; if the counselors possess the ability to prevent Gorboduc from implementing his plan, the queen would not have behaved in such a distraught manner when informing Ferrex of the news. The elderly king, therefore, disregards his advisors' counsel.

We also recognize that Gorboduc has decided to divide the kingdom regardless of his counselors' opinions because the latter two of the three advisors disapprove of his plan. The order of the three Parliamentarians-- Arostus ("flabby and weak"), Philander ("friend of mankind"), and Eubulus ("wise counselor")--is significant.[9] The first is a sycophant; Philander flatters the king somewhat but also disagrees with his plan; and the last speaks his mind honestly. The advice becomes progressively more critical of the king's decision, and Eubulus's view, which strongly opposes that of Gorboduc, stands out most prominently to the audience since it is the last and is eighty-nine lines long. Nonetheless, Gorboduc responds by shunning Eubulus's criticism, barely attempting to refute it. The audience must wonder why the king asks for his counselors' advice yet pays no attention to it.

Perhaps Gorboduc expects that Parliament will approve his plan wholeheartedly. Since the king intends to have his will, the reasonable objections of Eubulus and Philander fail to influence him. Franco Moretti believes that the king's refusal to heed his counselors' advice carries more significance than the issue of abdication; Gorboduc's insistence on carrying out his plan

> manifests itself as a sovereign decision, an act of free will. In Elizabethan terms, the conflict in the abdication scene (I.ii) occurs between the *will* of Gorboduc and the *reason* of his counsellors. Both terms are crucial in sixteenth-century ethical-political treatises, which locate the difference between king and tyrant precisely in the relationship that is instituted between will and reason.[10]

Reason dictates that the division of the kingdom may harm the realm, yet Gorboduc's will to live the remaining years of his life restfully and to enjoy watching his sons rule supersedes it. As he says, "In one self purpose do I still abide" (I.ii.342). The monarch's will is so strong that he ignores Eubulus's fear that Ferrex and Porrex will fight amongst themselves. Gorboduc, like his historical predecessor King Lear, cannot understand the true natures of his children because his will dominates his reason.

Since the king's will dominates his reason, it also dominates the voices in Parliament. Despite Eubulus's and Philander's reasonable objections, the monarch emerges triumphant. Gorboduc's behavior in Parliament resembles that of a tyrant. The king asks for and permits opposing viewpoints, but the counselors' lack of power renders their voices impotent. Only the monarch's words have importance, for the king possesses complete political power. Moretti raises the intriguing question of whether a king may be considered a tyrant when he abdicates. We usually interpret tyranny as the abuse of power by ambitious leaders who quest insatiably for greater authority, not as the relinquishment of one's position. Gorboduc, however, comports himself tyrannically since "the force that the king manifests in his decision proclaims him not only a tyrant, but incapable of governing as well. As a consequence, the exercise of sovereignty leads to complete anarchy, as though the two were one and the same."[11] The king's imposition of his will upon Parliament and the disastrous ramifications of his foolhardy plan render Gorboduc a tyrant.

Although the second dumb show explicates occurrences in Act II, it applies to the previously discussed scene as well. A king encounters two cup bearers: the first, "a grave and aged gentleman," brings him wine in a glass, which the monarch refuses; then "a brave and lusty young gentleman" brings him a cup of gold filled with poison, from which the king drinks, resulting in his death (II.5, 7). The dramatists' meaning is clear:

> as glass by nature holdeth no poison, but is clear and may easily be seen through, ne boweth by any art; so a faithful counselor holdeth no treason, but is plain and open, ne yieldeth to any undiscreet affection, but giveth wholesome counsel, which the ill-advised prince refuseth. The delightful gold filled with poison betokeneth flattery, which under fair seeming of pleasant words beareth deadly poison, which destroyed the prince that receiveth it.[12]

The clear cup may refer to Eubulus's wise counsel that Gorboduc refuses to heed, and the gold cup of poison may apply to Arostus's sycophantic acceptance of the king's foolhardy plan to divide the kingdom. The gold vessel signifies the flatterer's artful support of his ruler, and the poison indicates the deadly ramifications of that support. If Arostus--and all the counselors--had expressed disapproval of the monarch's plan, Gorboduc might not have foolhardily proceeded with it; since the advisors disagree with one another, Gorboduc employs their dissenting opinions as an excuse to dismiss the ideas of those who dislike his decision to abdicate.

David Bevington claims that "Monarchs like Gorboduc are (somewhat condescendingly) expected to come up with erratic decisions; . . . With a majority catering to his whim, of a divided kingdom, however, Gorboduc is largely exculpated for proceeding as he does."[13] Bevington implies correctly that Norton and Sackville emphasize the importance of counselors providing loyal and honest advice to princes, but we cannot condone the monarch's refusal to heed Eubulus's trustworthy advice nor his initial concoction of the foolish plan. Two-thirds of Gorboduc's counselors express dissatisfaction with the king's plan to abdicate. We should fault Gorboduc more than Arostus, who supports the king's plan, since the monarch has already made up his mind before he hears the sycophant's advice.

The concepts of age and experience play an integral role in the second dumb show but refer directly to the events of Act II. The dramatists characterize the trustworthy advisor as elderly, and the flatterer as youthful; these descriptions of counselors that Norton and Sackville advance adhere to commonly held beliefs in the Renaissance regarding courtiers and intelligence. Renaissance philosophers such as Baldesar Castiglione and Sir Thomas Elyot associate age with wisdom and honesty. In Castiglione's *Book of the Courtier* signor Gaspare suggests that "the courtier who must introduce the prince to virtue through his own merits and authority must of necessity be an elderly man, for only rarely does wisdom not wait upon age, and especially as regards what we learn from experience."[14] Although *Gorboduc* never states Hermon's and Tyndar's ages, these parasites appear much younger than the loyal Dordan and Philander.

The sycophants are not the only characters whose youth may lead the country to ruin; the second dumb show foreshadows the dramatists' characterization of Ferrex and Porrex as boys who are too young and inexperienced to rule England effectively. Gorboduc's decision to depose himself is unwise not only because he divides the kingdom but also because he relegates power to boys presently incapable of governing properly. Norton and Sackville compare Ferrex and Porrex several times to Phaeton, the ambitious youth who attempted to drive his father's chariot, although he was too young and inexperienced to do so. Eubulus pleads with Gorboduc:

> Arm not unskilfulness with princely power.
> But you, that long have wisely ruled the reins
> Of royalty within your noble realm,
> So hold them, while the gods for our avails
> Shall stretch the thread of your prolonged days.
> Too soon he clamb into the flaming car
> Whose want of skill did set the earth on fire.
> (I.ii.325-31)

Phaeton's unfortunate voyage across the earth acts as a metaphor for the two brothers' short and tragic reign. Phaeton and the young kings assume their father's task of ruling their respective realms before they are ready, and their inexperience leads to tragedy. One major difference exists: Phaeton commandeers Apollo's chariot without permission, but Gorboduc hands the reins of the kingdom to his sons; the elderly monarch must bear much of the responsibility for the tragic results of his division of the realm. Ferrex and Porrex, however, share the rest of the blame almost equally.

Ferrex and Porrex behave as tyrannically as their father. Both ignore their trustworthy advisor but heed the counsel of their flatterer, who tells them what they wish to hear. In II.i, Hermon, Ferrex's parasitic advisor, exploits his master's sibling jealousy by concurring with the ruler's assertion regarding Porrex's alleged pride and ambition:

> Was this not wrong, yea, ill-advised wrong,
> To give so mad a man so sharp a sword,
> To so great peril of so great mishap,
> Wide open thus to set so large a way?
> (II.i.64-67)

After Hermon reinforces Ferrex's distrust of his younger brother, the older brother decides to defend himself from a possible invasion. Ferrex refuses to contact Porrex or Gorboduc concerning the precarious situation because he wishes to war with his brother, hoping to gain control of the entire realm. Consequently, he ignores Dordan's defense of Porrex's character.

Although Ferrex insists that he wishes his brother no harm and does not covet the other half of the kingdom, his actions and inactions belie his words. His failure to communicate with his brother and father manifest his attempt to avoid a peaceful resolution to the conflict. Hermon advises Ferrex to murder Porrex:

> lust of kingdom hath no law.
> The gods do bear and well allow in kings
> The things that they abhor in rascal routs.
> (II.i.143-45)

When Dordan vehemently condemns this wicked counsel, Ferrex claims that he will not commit fratricide, but he prepares his army against Porrex nonetheless. Since Ferrex possesses no reason to assume that Porrex will attack him, his decision to arm himself for war manifests his ambitious and treacherous intentions.[15] The elder brother, furthermore, departs with the sycophant who has suggested the murder, leaving the faithful Dordan onstage by himself. The stage direction indicating that Ferrex exits solely with Hermon implies that the ruler supports the flatterer's mischievous plot. The older brother has received excellent advice from Dordan but ignores it, for it conflicts with his imperialistic wishes, just as Gorboduc disregards Philander's and Eubulus's counsel since it contradicts his own.

When Ferrex shuns Dordan and listens only to Hermon, he behaves as tyrannically as Gorboduc.

II.ii occurs in Porrex's court shortly thereafter and parallels the scene in which Ferrex consults with his advisors. Tyndar, Porrex's parasite, reports to the younger king that he has witnessed Ferrex's preparation for war; he also mentions unsubstantiated rumors, from unnamed friends, asserting that Ferrex's counselors are goading the older brother into war with Porrex. Choosing to ignore Philander's counsel that he communicate with Ferrex or Gorboduc, Porrex decides to launch an offensive attack ostensibly in order to protect himself. He declares, "War would he have? And he shall have it so!" (II.ii.5). Porrex's readiness to accept Tyndar's counsel and disregard Philander's reasonable advice manifests willfulness in the younger brother. After hearing Tyndar's rumors concerning Ferrex's intentions, Porrex claims:

> His wretched head shall pay the worthy price
> Of this his treason and his hate to me.
> Shall I abide and treat and send and pray
> And hold my yielden throat to traitor's knife,
> While I, with valiant mind and conquering force,
> Might rid myself of foes and win a realm?
>
> (II.ii.57-62)

Porrex, like Ferrex, employs the guise of taking preventive action as a ruse for raising arms against his brother in hope of achieving sole dominance of England. When Porrex exits the stage with the sycophantic Tyndar, leaving the faithful Philander alone, he shows his acceptance of the evil advice to attack and slay his elder brother in order to acquire more power.

Bevington believes that in "the antithetical soul-struggle between their good and evil advisers, Ferrex and Porrex are virtually pawns."[16] Although this assertion is plausible, the converse--that the counselors are the kings' pawns--appears more likely. Both scenes in Act II involve soul-struggles similar to those of the English morality play, yet an important distinction exists: in morality plays, the personifications of good and evil converse directly with the character whose soul they covet and with each other; whereas, according to Wolfgang Clemen, in *Gorboduc*:

> there is no dispute between the speakers; the speeches are an eloquent affirmation of the principles of good and evil, maintained on both sides on general political grounds. The person spoken to, whether it is Ferrex or Porrex, is virtually left out of account; to all intents and purposes the speeches are directed at the audience.

The advisors cannot influence the brothers because the play manifests no character development; the focus lies on the ideas, not the people. Clemen points out that "Most of the spoken scenes are entirely static. We mark time, as it were, or go round in a circle, and it is nearly always obvious from the situation at the beginning of the scene what its ending will be."[17] Ferrex's and Porrex's decisions regarding whether they should select the good or the evil counsel reveal the brothers' natures, for the struggles being recited to the audience actually occur within the minds of the young kings. Ferrex's and Porrex's agreement with the evil counselors, therefore, indicates the brothers' latently ambitious and cruel souls.

On a literal level, Ferrex and Porrex, like Gorboduc, have made up their minds already, yet they ask for their advisors' opinions anyway. The brothers follow the advice that correlates with their opinion, giving the appearance that they heed the words of their counselors when they tyrannically do as they please.[18]   The distinction between this interpretation and that of Bevington signifies that tragedy ensues because the kings act upon their ambitions, not because they permit their parasites to dominate their government. The brothers and not their advisors are blameworthy.

No evident differences exist in the personalities of the brothers; their characters are almost identical. In fact, Thomas Rymer confused Ferrex and Porrex in "A Short View of Tragedy," claiming mistakenly that Ferrex murders Porrex, because the siblings are almost interchangeable.[19] The significant distinction between them lies not in their personalities but rather in their births. The audience may sympathize with Ferrex's situation since the older brother should be the rightful heir--at least from a Renaissance perspective--and should not be forced to share the kingdom with Porrex.

Although Gorboduc, Ferrex, Porrex, and Videna should share responsibility for England's political turmoil, Norton and Sackville, through the voices of Parliament, place more blame on the common people than on the royal family. The nobles express shock that the people murder Gorboduc and Videna: Gwenard says:

> Shall subjects dare with force
> To work revenge upon their prince's fact?
> Admit the worst that may, as sure in this
> The deed was foul, the queen to slay her son,
> Shall yet the subject seek to take the sword,

Arise against his lord, and slay his king?
                                        (V.i.17-22)

The nobles agree then to exact vengeance on the rebels because "There can no punishment be thought too great / For this so grievous crime" (V.i.27-28). In this historical tragedy, vengeance is acceptable only when the revengers belong to the aristocracy. The nobles' (and dramatists') point is that commoners must always be loyal to their king, even when the monarch governs incompetently. But the nobles (as well as Norton and Sackville) fail to realize that since Gorboduc no longer rules the country, his subjects no longer owe him their allegiance.

Although *Gorboduc* emphasizes that commoners should be loyal to their monarch, Norton and Sackville imply that Parliamentary counselors must not allow a ruler to dominate them since their advice is crucial to good government. Norton and Sackville stress the need for rulers to listen to good counsel; if Gorboduc, Ferrex, and Porrex had listened to their trustworthy advisors, the tragic events might have been prevented. In the second quarto of 1570, the only edition approved by the playwrights, printer John Day omits the following eight lines of the play:

That no cause serves whereby the subject may
Call to account the doings of his prince,
Much less in blood by sword to work revenge,
No more than may the hand cut off the head;
In act nor speech, no, not in secret thought
The subject may rebel against his lord
Or judge of him that sits in Caesar's seat,
With grudging mind to damn those he mislikes.
                                        (V.i.42-49)

As Mark Breitenberg notes, the second quarto omits these lines because "this doctrine contradicts earlier extolment of the virtues of 'good counsel,' as well as the ostensible message of the play itself. . . ." This passage advocates monarchical power at the expense of Parliamentary authority, so Norton and Sackville authorized Day to remove it from the play. Such an omission must have held great importance for the playwrights since Day claims in "The Printer to the Reader" that the second quarto was printed to rectify errors in the allegedly corrupt first quarto; yet he used that first quarto as his copy-text and merely omitted the eight lines quoted above.[20] The playwrights, both influential members of Parliament by 1570, did not wish to advocate blind obedience to monarchs; they wanted to dramatize how good counsel could help rulers to govern wisely so that foolish political decisions such as those of Gorboduc, Ferrex, and Porrex might be avoided.

The monarch's self-deposition assumes new meaning when we consider the king an allegorical figure, as in a medieval morality play. Cauthen views Gorboduc as "a morality-like figure who stands for the unity of the commonwealth; when he is killed, the commonwealth passes into anarchy."[21] The first clause of Cauthen's statement is reasonable, for Gorboduc's rule unites the country and the king's self-deposition causes the political turmoil. Norton and Sackville, like many in the Renaissance, advocate the monarchical form of government unequivocally. Anarchy, however, ensues *before* Gorboduc's murder; the deaths that create chaos are those of Ferrex and Porrex, especially the latter's. Videna's murder of Porrex stirs the subjects' wrath, which creates the rebellion in which the commons slay Gorboduc and his wife. The fratricide of Ferrex has less serious ramifications than Videna's murder of her younger son because the former killing deprives England of one of its two kings while the latter leaves the nation with none.

Before Gorboduc divides his realm, his subjects never rebel, for they acknowledge him as the lawful king. By relinquishing the throne, he renders himself a political nonentity; the commons kill him because he has caused the political unrest, not because he possesses political authority. When Gorboduc hears of Porrex's death, he begs Eubulus to "pierce this heart with speed! O hateful light, / O loathsome life, O sweet and welcome death!" (IV.ii.192-93). Gorboduc's despair manifests his unsuitability to govern England. In fact, during the brief period between Gorboduc's discovery of Porrex's murder and his own death, the ex-king never mentions the idea of ruling again. Gorboduc's lack of political clout becomes quite apparent when he learns that Ferrex has taken up arms against Porrex; the former king thinks briefly of raising his own army (III.i.99-105) but reconsiders, he tells us impotently, because the grudge between the brothers will continue and the gods must be appeased. His fatalistic assumption that all authority rests in the gods constitutes a denial of his free will and power. Gorboduc acknowledges his helplessness but attributes it to the will of the gods, when actually his own willfulness and poor judgment deserve blame. The former monarch fails to realize that he has caused the problem by abdicating: he cannot raise an army to restore order because he no longer has subjects; the citizens owe allegiance to either Ferrex or Porrex but not to Gorboduc, as his murder at the hands of the commoners indicates.

Gorboduc's decisions to abdicate and divide the kingdom lead ultimately to the murders of Ferrex, Porrex, Videna, and himself--destroying the entire royal family. Since the elderly monarch's foolhardy plan leaves England without a successor to the throne, anarchy ensues, for ambitious people will risk all when the opportunity arises to seize power. Fergus, the Duke of Albany, declares that he will take advantage of the chaotic situation by attempting to become king:

> If ever time to gain a kingdom here
> Were offered man, now it is offered me.
> . . . .
> No issue now remains, the heir unknown;
> The people are in arms and mutinies;
> . . . .
> Whom shall I find enemies that will withstand
> My fact herein, if I attempt by arms
> To seek the same in these times of broil?
>   (V.i.132-52)

We despise Fergus for capitalizing on the civil unrest for his own profit, but Gorboduc has caused the problem initially. Norton's and Sackville's point is that a kingdom without one rightful successor will suffer through disputes that may result in civil war or foreign invasion. We should consider Fergus's plot to seize authority despicable, for he exploits the turbulent situation in England for his self-aggrandizement, even though he has the ability to help ease the nation's political troubles. Fergus's selfishness and his disregard for the interests of the commonweal indicate his unsuitability to govern England. As the historical tragedy concludes, we cannot determine his success because the playwrights leave the outcome of his usurpation unresolved.[22] Norton and Sackville imply that if Fergus conquers England, Gorboduc's decision to abdicate, his failure to name one lawful successor, and his refusal to listen to Parliament are the causes.

When Gorboduc fails to name one rightful heir to the throne, causing anarchy, he ignores the warnings of history. He is not the first king who foolhardily divides his realm, initiating civil war. When Philander informs the monarch of the ensuing dangers if the king divides the kingdom during his lifetime, the counselor reminds Gorboduc of the civil war with Morgan waged by Cunedag (Gorboduc's ancestor) that occurred after the two nobles usurped Cordelia's power (I.ii.161-65). Although Philander neglects to mention how Cordelia acquired the throne, Gorboduc should know that his ancestor, King Lear, unwisely divided the realm in half during his lifetime, thus precipitating a civil war and a foreign invasion. The Chorus claims that because of his unwise decision to divide the kingdom, Gorboduc "A mirror shall become to princes all / To learn to shun the cause of such a fall" (I.ii.392-93). Lily B. Campbell says that the "idea of holding the mirror up to nature (or to politics) pervaded the whole conception of art during the Elizabethan period. . . ."[23] Monarchs should learn from their predecessors' mistakes in order to rule more effectively. Since many people in Renaissance England believed in the accuracy of the chronicles, writers could employ the past as a means of discussing, analyzing, and possibly influencing the present political situation by holding up "history" as a mirror to contemporary leaders, as in the case of *The Mirror for Magistrates*.[24] Gorboduc's tyranny becomes apparent when the former monarch ignores Eubulus's attempts to dissuade him from dividing the kingdom; Eubulus reminds him of Brutus's similar folly:

> Your grace rememb'reth how in passed years
> The mighty Brute, first prince of all this land,
> Possessed the same and ruled it well in one;
> He, thinking that the compass did suffice
> For his three sons three kingdoms eke to make,
> Cut it in three, as you would now in twain.
> But how much British blood hath since been spilt
> To join again the sundered unity!
>   (I.ii.269-76)

Gorboduc's most heinous sin in the play is his refusal to learn from the mirror of history. If not for the above speech, we might forgive the monarch his division of the kingdom because he might have been unaware of its destructive ramifications; clearly he has faith in his sons' abilities to govern well. He realizes from history that a disaster may ensue if he divides the kingdom, yet he willfully carries through with his plan anyway. The tragedy of the play lies not only in the murders and the civil unrest but also in Gorboduc's refusal to learn from history.

According to the classical humanistic tradition, art forms such as historical drama allow the audience to learn if the work delights and instructs. Drama entertains and teaches its audience more effectively than do other arts because it is visual. Using Hercules as an example, Thomas Heywood discusses how historical drama may cause its audience to emulate dramatic action:

there was in his nonage presented vnto him by his Tutor in the fashion of a
History, acted by the choyse of the nobility of Greece, the worthy and
memorable acts of his father *Iupiter*. Which being personated with liuely and
well-spirited action, wrought such impression in his noble thoughts, that in
meere emulation of his fathers valor (not at the behest of his Stepdame *Iuno*)
he perform'd his twelue labours.[25]

Heywood's example illustrates instruction through emulation. Norton
and Sackville attempt to teach by using the opposite approach--contempt.
Aristotle says that "Through emulation a man prepares himself to win what
is good." Contempt, the converse emotion of equal power, causes one to
shun what is evil. Therefore, Aristotle continues, "men who are in a
condition to emulate or to be emulated must tend to feel contempt for
those who are subject to any evils [defects and disadvantages] that are
opposite to the goods arousing emulation, and to feel it with respect to
these evils."[26] The audience viewing *Gorboduc* should wish to emulate
Eubulus's loyalty and to experience contempt for the monarch's unwise
division of England. Both emulation and contempt function in this
historical tragedy as mirrors to nature; after viewing the play, the audience
should wish to behave as loyally as Eubulus and to avoid acting as
willfully and foolhardily as Gorboduc and his sons.

Historical drama as a mirror acquires political significance when we
consider how people may manipulate history as a means of controlling the
minds and thoughts of others. History can be invented, restored, and
altered in order to propagandize. As we have noticed in chapter one, John
Bale's *King Johan* and William Tyndale's *Obedience of a Christen Man*,
which glorify and martyrize the cruel King John as a function of
Reformation perspective, exemplify this theory. Catholic chroniclers
portrayed John as an evil king, and Protestant historians defended him. Sir
Thomas More's biography of Richard III contains much fiction and greatly
defames the character of the medieval king; we must consider that Henry
VIII, who reigned while More wrote his book, was the son of the ruler
who conquered (and, in a sense, usurped power from) Richard III. A
historical tragedy such as *Gorboduc* could be selected from the chronicles
in order to make a contemporary political statement and influence a
targeted audience, such as members of the Inns of Court, and possibly
Queen Elizabeth herself.

Gorboduc is a propagandistic drama that asserts the need for an English
Protestant successor--perhaps Lady Katharine Grey. After discovering
Fergus's attempt at usurpation, a counselor remarks:

For right will last, and wrong cannot endure.
Right mean I his or hers upon whose name
The people rest by mean of native line,
Or by the virtue of some former law,
. . . .
Such one so born within your native land;
Such one prefer; and in no wise admit
The heavy yoke of foreign governance.

                                    (V.ii.164-72)

Several reasons support the hypothesis that this quotation refers to the
potential succession of Lady Katharine Grey. First, the politically correct
use of the phrase "his or hers," rare in the male-dominated Renaissance,
implies that the dramatists have a female in mind as Elizabeth's successor.
If the playwrights' choice as successor had been either a man or no one in
particular, the dramatists would have used the possessive pronoun "his."
The emphasis on an English-born ruler eliminates Katharine's main
competitor, Mary Stuart.[27] The Queen of Scots became "the subject of
various English attacks at this period. 'Garboduc' [sic] attacked her right
to succeed as an alien."[28]   Contrariwise, Grey, an English great-
granddaughter of Henry VIII, resided frequently at the English court. The
comment regarding a former law refers to the Third Act of Succession
(1544) and Henry's last will, which support Katharine as the rightful
successor to the throne.[29] Henry VIII specified "in his will the succession
(in default of lawful grandchildren) of his niece, Lady Frances Brandon--
who became the mother of Lady Jane and Lady Katharine Grey."
Bevington notes the friendship between the two dramatists and Lady
Katharine's husband, the Earl of Hertford, and Marie Axton suggests that
Robert Dudley helped Norton and Sackville stage *Gorboduc* as a favor to
Grey.[30]   For the aforementioned reasons, we may assume that in
Gorboduc, Norton and Sackville advance the claim of Lady Katharine
Grey as heir presumptive to Elizabeth.

   We must also assume that the playwrights (especially Thomas Norton)
supported Lady Katharine over Mary Stuart because they, like many
Parliamentary counselors, wished for a Protestant successor. We may
allegorize Fergus's villainy as the threat of "Scottish and Catholic invasion
in the name of Mary Stuart."[31] During the Parliament of 1572, Norton
made his position clear on the interrelated issues of the Queen of Scots's
fate and of the need for a Protestant succession; he claimed that the
execution of Mary Stuart was

of necessity. . . If she die not, the Queen is endangered and the succession can never be established with safety: for if an heir apparent is named and kept weak in the interests of Elizabeth's safety, he will never be able to prevail against the Scottish faction.[32]

Norton, a Puritan, later earned the nickname "Rackmaster General" for his torturing of Roman Catholics; the Parliamentarian most probably wrote *A Declaration of Favourable Dealing by her Majesty's Commissioners Appointed for the Examination of Certain Traitors, etc.*, a tract condoning the torture of Catholics.[33] The queen imprisoned him in the Tower in 1581 for vehemently protesting her possible marriage to the Catholic Duke of Alencon.[34] Norton's extreme hatred of Roman Catholics indicates clearly why the propaganda in *Gorboduc* advocates a Protestant successor, such as Lady Katharine.

Norton and Sackville hope that Parliament and Queen Elizabeth, unlike Gorboduc, will learn from history; in fact, the dramatists hope that Parliament and the queen will learn from the history of Gorboduc and realize the necessity of securing an orderly and lawful succession. During the time of the creation and performance of this historical tragedy, there was much debate and anxiety in England regarding the succession to the throne. The crown had passed rapidly from Henry VIII to Edward VI, to Mary, and then to Elizabeth; four monarchs occupied the throne in a mere eleven years (1547-1558). No one could foretell that Elizabeth would reign for forty-five years. Several factions coveted the throne, and some Parliamentarians feared civil war or a foreign invasion from a Catholic country sponsored by Rome. Bevington notes "the determination of the gentry and squirearchy, some of them Puritan in outlook, to control England's political destiny in Parliament. Their clamors for a Protestant successor of their own approving were as much a threat to monarchical supremacy as was Catholic reaction."[35]

Elizabeth's refusal to marry heightened their fears. Because the queen did not produce an heir, Parliamentary advisors expressed the need for her to name a successor in order to prevent the division of the kingdom that occurred in pre-Christian English legendary history, as in the case of Brutus and Gorboduc. Elizabeth, however, did not need a history lesson mirrored for her benefit because she was well aware of the implications of neglecting to name a successor; the queen, unlike her Parliament, viewed the issue from her own best interests. The queen realized "that marriage or announcement of her heir in her precarious first years must fatally yield the balance of power either to an internal faction or to a foreign opponent.

Her availability as a spinster, with its potential reward for the fortunate wooer, became her trump card."[36]

The first performance of *Gorboduc* occurred on January 5, 1562, at the Inns of Court. Cauthen says that Elizabeth learned of the play and commanded the play to be performed again for her consideration; *Gorboduc* "spoke of matters so close to her subjects' hearts--the danger of an unsettled succession to the throne--that it violated her edict (May 16, 1559) forbidding plays which touched on religion or politics, these 'being no meet matters to be written or treated upon but by men of authority, learning, and wisdom, not to be handled before any audience but of grave and discreet persons.'"[37] She obviously realized that the historical tragedy concerning succession related at least indirectly to contemporary political affairs.

Because of Elizabeth's 1559 edict, Norton and Sackville treat the issue of succession carefully and indirectly. Their decision to create a historical tragedy about Gorboduc constitutes, nonetheless, a violation of the queen's prohibition, since the subject matter correlates with Elizabeth's political dilemma. Norton and Sackville employ "history," under the guise of a tragic dramatic entertainment, as a propagandistic tool to influence important people at the Inns of Court and the queen.[38] Norton and Sackville restore and manipulate a legendary tale (from a modern perspective) and dramatize it in order to persuade influential people and the queen herself that Elizabeth should name an English Protestant successor. *Gorboduc* functions also as a mirror to nature since both performances occurred in 1562, before the era of professional actors in England. The gentlemen of the Inner Temple performed the play. The actors playing the parts of Parliamentary counselors who attempt to advise the monarch regarding the issue of succession are actually Parliamentary counselors[39] attempting to convince the queen to choose a successor. The tragedy that occurred in pre-Christian English history could happen again, the play implies, unless Elizabeth heeds the meaning the drama conveys. Thus *Gorboduc* blurs the demarcations between theatre and reality, between past and present, and between history and tragedy.

CHAPTER 8: NOTES

1. Felix E. Schelling, *The English Chronicle Play: A Study in the Popular Historical Literature Environing Shakespeare* (New York: Macmillan, 1902), p. 172.

2. Thomas Nashe, *Pierce Pennilesse, His Svpplication to the Divell*, in *The Works of Thomas Nashe*, ed. Ronald B. McKerrow, 5 vols. (London: A.H. Bullen, 1904; rpt. Barnes & Noble, 1966), I, 213.

3. Irby B. Cauthen, Jr. claims that the dumb show is the first in English drama. Irby B. Cauthen, Jr., ed., *Gorboduc, or Ferrex and Porrex* (Lincoln: University of Nebraska Press, 1970), p. xiii.

4. Thomas Norton, who wrote the first three acts of the play (according to the 1565 quarto), was a devout Protestant. Protestants opposed Catholic images because they were open to diverse interpretations. Norton's dumb shows have explicit meanings, which are accompanied by his statement of their exact meanings and by a spoken version of the dumb show in the play proper. Norton's dumb shows are therefore not open to varying interpretations.

5. Thomas Sackville and Thomas Norton, *Gorboduc, or Ferrex and Porrex*, ed. Irby B. Cauthen, Jr. (Lincoln: University of Nebraska Press, 1970). All quotations from *Gorboduc* are from this edition and are cited parenthetically throughout the text.

6. One may argue that Gorboduc, a pre-Christian monarch, was unaware of primogeniture since the concept, according to John Neville Figgis, originated in the eleventh century; but we must remember that the Renaissance audience was unaware of this fact and interpreted the play from an Elizabethan perspective. See John Neville Figgis, *The Divine Right of Kings* (1914; rpt. New York: Harper & Row, 1965), pp. 22-24.

7. Figgis claims that "The Conqueror introduced, or, at least, crystallized into system all the influences that made for a complete recognition of feudal principles of land-tenure. The king is now not only the national representative, but also supreme landowner; all land is held of him mediately or immediately. This . . . led not only ultimately to the conception of territorial sovereignty, but assimilated the succession of the Crown to the developing law of the inheritance of fiefs" (p. 22). We have seen in the segment on *Richard the Second* (Chapter 7) that Renaissance audiences correlated lawful succession with primogeniture. York pleads with Richard to refrain from confiscating Bolingbroke's possessions,

asking, "for how art thou a king / But by fair sequence and succession?" (II.i.198-99).

8. The lack of communication between Gorboduc and his sons and between the two brothers renders two separate locations necessary, so we should not fault Norton and Sackville, as Sir Philip Sidney does, for failing to preserve the unity of place. See Sir Philip Sidney, *The Prose Works of Sir Philip Sidney*, 4 vols. (1912; rpt. Cambridge: Cambridge University Press, 1962), III, 38.

9. The quoted phrases are Cauthen's; see p. xviii.

10. Franco Moretti, "'A Huge Eclipse': Tragic Form and the Deconsecration of Sovereignty," in *The Power of Forms in the English Renaissance*, ed. Stephen Greenblatt (Norman, Ok.: Pilgrim Books, 1982), p. 11.

11. Moretti, p. 11.

12. The dramatists' explication appears right after the second dumb show and immediately before Act II.

13. David Bevington, *Tudor Drama and Politics: A Critical Approach to Topical Meaning* (Cambridge, Mass.: Harvard University Press, 1968), pp. 144, 145.

14. Baldesar Castiglione, *The Book of the Courtier*, trans. George Bull (1967; rpt. Middlesex, Eng.: Penguin, 1984), p. 323.

15. One may argue that Ferrex is not imperialistic since he never attacks Porrex. We must realize, however, that the younger brother's pre-empted attack and his fratricide prevent Ferrex from launching the latter's impending offensive. We should not consider Porrex the villain and Ferrex the innocent victim.

16. Bevington, p. 145.

17. Wolfgang Clemen, *English Tragedy Before Shakespeare: The Development of Dramatic Speech*, trans. T.S. Dorsch (London: Methuen, 1961), pp. 68, 59.

18. Ferrex's and Porrex's strategy may remind the reader of a later example, in John Milton's *Paradise Lost*. In Book II, Satan organizes a meeting in which he invites suggestions regarding what the devils should do now that the Son has thrown them into Hell. Moloch, Belial, and Mammon speak words that fail to interest Satan. Subsequently, Beelzebub, Satan's second in command, provides the advice that the leader of the devils has already advocated. Satan then agrees with Beelzebub's counsel (the leader has already made the suggestion himself),

giving the appearance that he accepts the advice of Beelzebub and the other fallen angels when they are actually following his plan.

19. Rymer reports in his synopsis of the play that "The Elder Brother Kills the Younger." Actually, Porrex murders Ferrex. Thomas Rymer, "A Short View of Tragedy," in *The Critical Works of Thomas Rymer*, ed. Curt A. Zimansky (New Haven: Yale University Press, 1956), p. 130.

20. Mark Breitenberg, "Reading Elizabethan Iconicity: Gorboduc and the Semiotics of Reform," *English Literary Renaissance*, 18 (1988), 214.

21. Cauthen, p. xviii.

22. Franco Moretti claims that the play concludes with the clear implication that the aristocrats will defeat Fergus; this scholar, however, offers no support for his assertion. See Moretti, p. 8.

23. Lily B. Campbell, *Shakespeare's Histories: Mirrors of Elizabethan Policy* (1947; rpt. San Marino, Cal.: The Huntington Library, 1958), p. 15. The subtitle of her book indicates her belief in the Renaissance use of history as a mirror.

24. Sackville's interest in mirroring history is clear since the writer created the famous Induction for the second edition of *The Mirror for Magistrates* (1563), published one year after the two performances of *Gorboduc*.

25. Thomas Heywood, *An Apology for Actors*, ed. Richard H. Perkinson (New York: Scholars' Facsimiles & Reprints, 1941), sig. B3r. Sir Philip Sidney discusses a similar theme in his "Defence of Poesie": he claims that heroical poetry is significant because "the Image of each Action stirreth and instructeth the minde, so the loftie Image of such woorthies, moste enflameth the minde with desire to bee woorthie: and enformes with counsaile how to bee woorthie" (III, 25).

26. Aristotle, *The Rhetoric of Aristotle: An Expanded Translation with Supplementary Examples for Students of Composition and Public Speaking*, trans. Lane Cooper (Englewood Cliffs, N.J.: Prentice-Hall, 1930), pp. 129, 130. The interpolation is that of the translator.

27. Mary Stuart's son James was born in 1566, four years after the two productions of *Gorboduc*.

28. Antonia Fraser, *Mary Queen of Scots* (1969; rpt. New York: Delacorte, 1970), p. 164.

29. John Guy, *Tudor England* (1988; rpt. Oxford: Oxford University Press, 1990), p. 268.

30. Bevington, pp. 142, 143. Marie Axton, *The Queen's Two Bodies: Drama and the Elizabethan Succession* (London: Royal Historical Society, 1977), p. 46.

31. Bevington, p. 145.

32. Quoted from J.E. Neale, *Elizabeth I and Her Parliaments, 1559-1581*, 2 vols. (London: Jonathan Cape, 1953-57), I, 252-53. Norton uses the male possessive pronoun "his" when referring in 1572 to the successor since Lady Katharine Grey was no longer a potential heir to the throne. Lady Katharine damaged her chance to be named as Elizabeth's successor when she infuriated the monarch by marrying without the queen's consent; Elizabeth and the English court learned of the secret marriage only months after the two productions of *Gorboduc* when Katharine's pregnancy became noticeable. Grey died in 1568. See Guy, pp. 268-69; Neale, p. 130; and Fraser, pp. 163-64, 415.

33. Conyers Read, *Lord Burghley and Queen Elizabeth* (New York: Alfred A. Knopf, 1960), pp. 566, 251.

34. Neale, p. 405.

35. Bevington, p. 143.

36. Bevington, p. 143.

37. Cauthen, p. xii. Elizabeth witnessed the second performance of the historical tragedy at Whitehall on January 18, 1562.

38. The playwrights may even have hoped to influence the queen if they conjectured she would hear about the performance at the Inns of Court (because of their aristocratic status and the political subject matter) and command another staging for her own inspection.

39. Bevington, p. 141.

THE ANONYMOUS *KING LEIR*:

A GALLIMAUFRY OF GENRES

The anonymous *True Chronicle Historie of King Leir and his three daughters* (c. 1593), also known as *the Tragecall historie of kinge Leir and his Three Daughters & c*, shares many similarities with *Gorboduc*.[1] Both plays derive their plots mainly from volume one of Holinshed's *Chronicles*, which records pre-Christian English history; both works involve a division of England into two parts that occurs after an old king foolishly abdicates and relinquishes power to his children; and both dramas focus on the issues of flattery, faithful counsel, and the understanding of the true nature of one's children. The question of genre is more complicated in *King Leir* than in *Gorboduc* since the former possesses elements of several genres. The anonymous drama resembles works that blend history and tragedy (such as *Gorboduc* and *King Lear*), but in other instances the play is similar to Shakespeare's romance, *The Winter's Tale*, and Robert Greene's comedy, *Friar Bacon and Friar Bungay*. The drama contains elements of history, comedy, tragedy, and romance, but we may best classify it as a romantic history.

King Leir is less of a history play than *Gorboduc* since the anonymous work, unlike that of Norton and Sackville, makes no attempt to borrow faithfully from Holinshed's *Chronicles*. The anonymous work takes many liberties with Holinshed's account of the story of Leir. The dramatist concerns himself more with the play's entertainment value and with sentimentalism than with historical accuracy or with a political position. For instance, *King Leir* includes, but does not emphasize (as *Gorboduc* does), the political ramifications of abdication. The anonymous drama neglects also to moralize on the issue of the division of a kingdom--an important topic in *Gorboduc* and *King Lear*, plays with similar plots.

Let us begin with the changes the playwright makes from his main source. The most significant alteration from Holinshed's account is that in the play Leir abdicates in favor of Cornwall and Cambria; in the *Chronicles,* although the king bequeaths the halves of his kingdom to his sons-in-law, Holinshed reports that after Gonorill and Ragan marry, the king "willed and ordeined that his land should be diuided after his death .... After that Leir was fallen into age, the two dukes that had married his two eldest daughters, thinking it long yer the gouernment of the land did come to their hands, arose against him in armour, and reft from him the gouernance of the land. . . ."[2] Holinshed portrays Leir as a victim of the ambitious husbands of Gonorill and Ragan; in the anonymous play, conversely, Leir creates his own misfortunes by abdicating.

By inventing and dramatizing the king's ahistorical abdication, the *Leir* playwright shifts blame from the sons-in-law to the old king. The anonymous dramatist may have altered the chronicle, rendering Leir an unwise king, because one of the dukes in Holinshed's description is Albania (Albany). As noted in the previous segment on *Gorboduc*, the Duke of Albany is associated with Scottish royalty. Although Queen Elizabeth refused to name a successor to the throne, many believed in 1593 that King James of Scotland would replace her; the characterization of a Scottish figure of royalty on the English stage at this time would probably have led the audience to identify Albany with James. Although the anonymous playwright does not portray Ragan's husband as a villain, the writer may have thought it best to dissociate him from the Scottish king. Consequently the dramatist changes the name of the historical figure in Holinshed from Albania to Cambria. Although Cambria is not an evil character, his wife dominates him and he does nothing to help Leir. Furthermore, the dramatist creates the daughters, not the sons-in-law, as the villains who mistreat Leir.

The anonymous dramatist's modification of Holinshed's account may indicate the influence of *Gorboduc*. *King Leir* characterizes the monarch as an old man who, like Gorboduc, relinquishes power for selfish reasons and is therefore blameworthy for the tragic events that consequently befall him. Cambria says that Leir has written to him:

> Being weary of the troubles of his Crowne,
> His princely daughter *Ragan* will bestow
> On me in mariage, with halfe his Seigniories. . . .
>
> (ll. 447-49)[3]

Gorboduc provides a similar reason for his abdication--weariness of the tribulations of governing. The unknown playwright, like Thomas Norton and Thomas Sackville, manifests the dangers of relinquishing power for self-interest. Despite the troubles a king may incur while ruling, he must maintain order by governing until his death out of duty to his subjects and God. When Leir abdicates, he sins against God since the Lord has ordained him as ruler. Since God has selected him as His viceroy, Leir must govern for the remainder of his life. The king's abdication represents a willful dereliction of his obligation to God--a sin for which he must suffer punishment.

Although King Leir is a pre-Christian king, the anonymous playwright transforms the chronicled account of the pagan monarch into a Christian work. Holinshed claims that Leir's reign began in the year 3105 (655 B.C.), yet the playwright creates a contemporary setting for the drama;[4] the characters express Christian ideologies throughout the play. We realize that the characters believe in divine right when Perillus, the king's faithful counselor, warns the messenger-murderer to "beware, how thou dost lay thy hand / Upon the high anoynted of the Lord" (ll. 1695-96). When the murderer attempts to kill Leir, the former king claims that hell "stands gaping wide, / To swallow thee, and if thou do this deed" (ll. 1632-33); divine thunder and lightning reinforces Leir's words, frightening away the murderer and saving the self-deposed monarch's life. God thus defends Leir from evil but punishes him nonetheless for selfishly abdicating the throne.

The divine punishment Leir receives occurs through the destruction of the sociopolitical hierarchy--not only in regard to his life but his entire kingdom as well. We discern the unnatural transformation of power when the king and Perillus board the ship bound for France. The penniless king must exchange his rich clothes, the last remnant of his wealth, with mariners for passage on the ship. The mariner says to Leir: "here's a good strong motly gaberdine, cost me xiiii. good shillings at Billinsgate; give me your gowne for it, & your cap for mine, & ile forgive your passage" (ll. 2008-11). The sight of a former ruler wearing motley and bartering his clothes manifests to the audience the extent of the king's fall. The poverty-stricken monarch now dresses far beneath his royal station (in motley no less) while the mariner's new clothes falsely indicate his wealth. The exchange of clothes implies, especially to an Elizabethan audience familiar with sumptuary laws, that the sociopolitical hierarchy has suffered a drastic reversal.

Since a king towers above his subjects in the social order, Leir's self-deposition causes an upheaval throughout the hierarchy. If the monarch alters his place, the status of others must change as well--almost as if the abdication turns the world upside down. The king becomes his daughters' subject: when the messenger-murderer threatens him, the former monarch attempts pathetically to save his life by saying to the villain:

> if thou have occasion.
> In any thing, to use me to the Queene,
> 'Tis like ynough that I can pleasure thee.
> (ll. 1529-31)[5]

What remains of his power--if it may be called so--rests solely upon his relationship with his two eldest daughters, who despise him. Ironically, the person whom he offers to introduce to Ragan has been hired by her to murder him, indicating Leir's powerlessness. After Leir discovers that Gonorill and Ragan have arranged for his assassination, he attempts to save Perillus's life by kneeling before the murderer, begging for mercy. The sight of a king on his knees in a posture of supplication to a messenger indicates to the audience the extreme reversal of power that Leir has created.

Leir relinquishes both political and familial power to Gonorill and Ragan. Since the former monarch mistakenly equates love with obedience and expects reciprocity for kindnesses rendered, he believes Gonorill and Ragan will treat him well after he vacates the throne. He fails to realize that when he dispossesses himself of the crown, he loses his political authority. His daughters become queens and his sons-in-law, kings, but he has rendered himself a deposed monarch, merely a subject. As we have discerned in *Gorboduc*, when a king transfers his political sovereignty to his children, he relinquishes his familial authority over them as well.

The changes in familial relationships parallel the alterations in the social order. After he abdicates, Leir acts no longer as father to his children but rather like a son. Gonorill and Ragan possess complete power over him, an assertion supported by the above quotation in which he offers to introduce the messenger to Ragan. They may also strip him of his retainers at will, as Gonorill does. Upon realizing his misjudgment of his daughters, Leir asks himself why he has lived "to see / The course of nature quite reverst in me" (ll. 860-61). Although Cordella behaves benevolently towards Leir, their relationship endures a role reversal also. Cordella acts as a mother figure to Leir. When Leir hungers for food upon his arrival in France, Cordella feeds him at the banquet as a mother does a child, and she and her husband must restore him to power since he lacks the authority to do so himself.

After Leir relinquishes power to his sons-in-law, we find that they do not rule, for their wives govern them. Gonorill and Ragan rule their dominions and their husbands. Ragan declares in a soliloquy:

> I rule the King of Cambria as I please:
> The States are all obedient to my will;
> And looke what ere I say, it shall be so;
> Not any one, that dareth answere no.
>   (ll. 930-33)

We witness the wife's power over her husband when the ambassador from France arrives. Cambria welcomes him courteously, but when Ragan (knowing that she herself has arranged Leir's murder) insists--without justification--that the ambassador has murdered her father, Cambria immediately agrees with her: he does as she bids. Cordelia Sherman points out that by controlling their husbands, Gonorill and Ragan "further outrage the laws of nature by ruling, however subtly, the men to whom they are bound by that law to be subservient."[6] An Elizabethan audience, familiar with men as leaders of families in their patriarchal society, would have viewed a wife governing her husband as unnatural and atypical.[7]

Although Leir's abdication results in the reversal of the sociopolitical order, Providence restores it. *King Leir* is a Christian play in which God re-creates order out of chaos and protects the virtuous. Despite his abdication and his harsh treatment of Cordella, the former monarch is a benevolent person who does not deserve the cruel treatment he receives from Gonorill and Ragan; impoverished, hungry, powerless, and ill-treated, he discovers Providence in the guise of the Gallian (French) King and Cordella.

In an unusual scene indicative of the complexity of the play's genre, France invades England, and the Elizabethan audience, we may assume, would have cheered for the French. The audience may have sympathized somewhat with Cornwall, out of nationalistic duty, when the duke asks the French King, "how darest thou / Presume to enter on our Brittish shore?" (ll. 2550-51); in the anonymous play, however, justice and Providence supersede nationalistic sentiments. The Gallian King, along with the self-deposed English monarch and Cordella, attacks England in order to restore Leir to his divinely ordained and rightful English throne; he would receive, therefore, the support of the Elizabethan audience.[8] The playgoers would have sympathized with the Gauls since they do not slay any Englishmen and since they have the approval of the English nobles, who address Leir as follows:

> Long have you here bin lookt for, good my Lord,
> And wish'd for by a generall consent:
> And had we known your Highnesse had arrived,
> We had not made resistance to your Grace:
> And now, my gracious Lord, you need not doubt,
> But all the Country will yeeld presently,
> Which since your absence have bin greatly tax'd,
> For to maintayne their overswelling pride.
>   (ll. 2519-26)

We may assume that if the English nobility cheerfully accepts the Gallian army, the Elizabethan audience would also--especially since the French are restoring a divinely ordained English king to the throne.

The Gallian King says that with God on their side they will

> easily arrive on Brittish shore,
> Where unexpected we may them surprise,
> And gayne a glorious victory with ease.
> Wherefore, my loving Countreymen, resolve,
> Since truth and justice fighteth on our sides,
> That we shall march with conquest where we go.
>   (ll. 2393-98)

An Elizabethan audience, like any group of playgoers, would have probably supported the army with God, truth, and justice on its side--especially a force including virtuous English royalty such as Leir and Cordella--even if that army consists of French soldiers. In the context of *King Leir*, France's attack on England is justifiable and the success of the French army, providential.

The French invasion is historical since the playwright derives the information regarding the event from Holinshed's *Chronicles*, an account the audience would have accepted as truth. Because the play dramatizes Leir's restoration to the throne through divine help, we may classify the invasion as providential history. The action is tragic from the perspective of an Elizabethan audience, for France conquers England. Yet the scene is also comedic because of its humor; none die or suffer injuries; the hero is the nobleman-clown Mumford who divides his time between pursuing English soldiers and chasing naked Englishwomen; and Leir repossesses the throne, to the satisfaction of the English nobility.

The nobles respect Leir because he has ruled benevolently for many years before his abdication and his banishment of Cordella. We must bear in mind that he makes these errors immediately after the death of his wife, and he is not, as he admits, capable of understanding his daughters without her advice:

> Although our selves doe dearly tender them,
> Yet are we ignorant of their affayres:
> For fathers best do know to governe sonnes;
> But daughters steps the mothers counsell turnes.
>   (ll. 17-20)

He then attempts to replace himself as king by marrying off his daughters to neighboring dukes, thus combining his paternal and political responsibilities. The anonymous playwright blends effectively the historical and romantic genres in Leir's unwise conflation of his political and familial duties. The king's decision to segment the realm is political, so he possesses no right to coerce Cordella into marrying a man she does not love. The monarch's device to entrap his favorite daughter by "proving" her love through marriage with a man of his choice is manipulative. Leir foolishly decides to bestow political realms upon his children in accordance with their love to him, wrongly confusing politics and family. We may classify Leir's banishment of Cordella and reconciliation with her most accurately as romance, one that foreshadows Leontes's relationship with Perdita in *The Winter's Tale*.

The monarch's decision is also faulty since, as Leir discovers, one cannot measure the emotion of love--especially by rhetoric. Skalliger informs Gonorill and Ragan of the secret that their father will marry them to dukes with whom they wish to unite and that Leir will request that Cordella marry a duke she does not love. The two sisters then flatter their father and place Cordella in a precarious situation by promising him:

> should you appoynt me for to marry
> The meanest vassayle in the spacious world,
> Without reply I would accomplish it:
> In briefe, commaund what ever you desire,
> And if I fayle, no favour I require.
>   (ll. 2248-52)

Gonorill and Ragan realize that they may pledge unequivocal duty to their father since he will unwittingly do their bidding and since he will expect similar obedience from Cordella. The duty of the two elder daughters consists merely of words; they never perform any deed that demonstrates their loyalty to Leir.

The king never asks Cordella if she will marry the King of Hibernia (Ireland) since she refuses to flatter him with the hyperbolic rhetoric of filial duty. Cordella says that she "cannot paynt my duty forth in words, / I hope my deeds shall make report for me" (ll. 277-78). We cannot discern the father's initial reaction since Gonorill and Ragan immediately criticize Cordella, falsely complaining that she has insulted their father and acted disobediently. Their reactions influence Leir, incurring his wrath towards his youngest daughter. Leir, unlike Gorboduc, Ferrex, and Porrex, is a three-dimensional character whom others may persuade. The monarch, accepting Gonorill's and Ragan's assertions that Cordella does "not wish my fathers good" (l. 310), banishes and disinherits his youngest and favorite daughter. Cordella and Perillus disapprove of Leir's game, but she speaks her criticisms in asides, and he says nothing at that time. Gonorill and Ragan may control their father successfully with their counsel because no one counters with opposing advice. We may liken the king in this scene to a character in a morality play whose bad angel corrupts him but whose good angel has yet to appear. Leir's misjudgment of his children, his anagnorisis, and his subsequent reconciliation with Cordella in France stray from the chronicle accounts and from standard political ideology but work rather effectively as a romance.

King Leir, unlike *Gorboduc* and *King Lear*, contains little political moralizing, and Leir's role as king is not essential to the plot. The play, therefore, is not a chronicle history play but rather a mixture of genres. Since *King Leir* contains tragic elements, we should not be surprised that in 1605 Simon Stafford entered the play in the Stationers' Register as *the Tragecall historie of kinge Leir and his Three Daughters & c.*[9] We should remember that John Heminges and Henry Condell, the editors of the first folio of Shakespeare's plays, classify *Cymbeline* as a tragedy; this drama, like *King Leir*, involves legendary English history and, despite its potential for tragedy, concludes happily. Horace Howard Furness and E.K. Chambers believe the play is tragic, for "If the spectacle of a respectable elderly king, reduced to such an extremity of hunger as to induce his faithful attendant to offer him his bare and living arm as an article of diet, be not tragic, it is difficult to say what tragedy is."[10]

Hardin Craig and Frederick Gard Fleay disagree, and the former describes the drama as "a rather bright and cheerful play."[11] No one suffers injuries or dies in the play, and the comic relief scenes are light-hearted, quite unlike the dark comedy of the Fool in Shakespeare's later version of the story. Sherman, who assumes that the playwright had "an orthodox Anglican faith in the justice of Heaven," notes that "Leir sins through folly and anger, but is inevitably restored to grace and his kingdom, because he accepts his punishment with humility and true penitence."[12] After Leir trusts in God's Providence and repents his mistreatment of Cordella, he acquires the ability to resume power, with her help and that of the Gallian King. The rectification of Leir's political situation parallels his spiritual redemption. The religious aspects of this "successful theological play"[13] influence the genre of the drama, for Providence and Leir's faith in God insure that the potentially tragic plot will end comically. We may thus justify Craig's and Fleay's interpretation as well as that of Furness and Chambers.

These conflicting conceptions of the drama's genre, which occur because scholars concentrate on certain aspects and sections of the work while deciding on its generic form, indicate why the play also appeared in the Stationers' Register in 1594 as *The most famous Chronicle historie of Leire kinge of England and his Three Daughters*, and in 1624 as *Leire and his Daughters*.[14] The 1594 entry interprets the play as a chronicle history because of its employment of historical sources while the 1624 title implies a domestic drama concerning a man and his children. The play is a history because many in the audience would have accepted the story as historical fact. Irving Ribner concurs with the latter classification: *King Leir* "uses legendary history merely for the sake of sentimental romance."[15] Although *King Leir* examines a political situation involving a king and the issue of succession, the playwright employs the historical account (based on Holinshed's *Chronicles*) in his dramatization of Leir's relationships with his daughters; since the historical aspects of the play work effectively as the premise of a familial story involving the restoration of a man's bond with his favorite daughter through his spiritual redemption, we may classify the anonymous drama as a romantic history.[16]

The genre of the play helps us determine its political perspective. Since *King Leir* concludes happily, with the divinely ordained king's providential restoration to the throne, we realize the conservative nature of the dramatist's political stance. Although one may argue that the tragic elements of the play--consequences for which Leir bears responsibility--indicate subversion, the comic ending supersedes them. One may argue that Leir's abdication and his misjudgment of his daughters indicate his inability to rule since his selfish and foolish decisions result in a foreign invasion, the unhappiness of the nobles, and Cordella's banishment. We must remember, however, that no one dies during the battle; England regains its sovereignty; and Leir, with God's help, recovers the throne from his two evil daughters, to the delight of his nobles, and reunites with Cordella. In fact, the conclusion of the play is rather comic since it follows the potential tragedy: the contrast intensifies the comedy. *King Leir* is romantic since the play moves from tragedy to comedy through the king's anagnorisis, spiritual redemption, and consequent political and familial restoration. This movement towards the reinstatement of the divinely sanctioned leader is clearly politically conservative.[17] In contrast, Shakespeare's tragic ending, which purposely alters the historical legend by denying Leir's restoration to the throne and darkening his character, is more subversive politically than the anonymous play.

CHAPTER 9: NOTES

1. Cordelia Caroline Sherman, ed., *A Critical Edition of King Leir*. Diss. Brown University, 1981, p. 26. The earliest possible date is 1590 (the publication of the first three books of Edmund Spenser's *Faerie Queene*); Henslowe records a performance of *King Leir* on April 8, 1594; see R.A. Foakes and R.T. Rickert, eds. *Henslowe's Diary* (Cambridge: Cambridge University Press, 1936), p. 21. The play must have been written, therefore, between 1590 and 1594. Sherman points out that since the playhouse manuscript was kept by a stationer during the period 1594-1605 and the Queen's Men could not afford to purchase new scripts in 1594, "we may hypothesize that *Leir* was written at least as early as 1593" (p. 26).

2. Raphael Holinshed, *Holinshed's Chronicles of England, Scotland, and Ireland*, 6 vols. (London: J. Johnson, et al., 1807-08), I, 447.

3. Geoffrey Bullough, ed., *The True Chronicle Historie of King Leir and his three daughters.*, in *Narrative and Dramatic Sources of Shakespeare*, 8 vols. (London: Routledge and Kegan Paul; New York: Columbia University Press, 1957-75), VII, 337-402. All quotations from the anonymous *King Leir* are from this edition and are cited parenthetically throughout the text by line number.

4. Holinshed, I, 446.

5. The period after the word "occasion" at line 1529 is problematic. The three lines should be read as one sentence. E.B. Everitt, Joseph Satin, and Cordelia Caroline Sherman place no punctuation after the word in their editions of the play. See E.B. Everitt, ed., *The True Chronicle History of King Leir and His Three Daughters, Goneril, Ragan, and Cordella*, in *Six Early Plays Related to the Shakespeare Canon* (Copenhagen: Rosenkilde and Bagger, 1965), p. 40 (ll. 1529-31); Joseph Satin, ed., *King Leir*, in *Shakespeare and His Sources* (Boston: Houghton Mifflin, 1966), p. 497 (ll. 1484-86); Sherman, p. 117 (ll. 87-89).

6. Sherman, p. 43.

7. Although one may argue that a queen ruled England at this time, women did not hold positions of authority on other levels of society. Parliament, for instance, consisted exclusively of men, and social laws supported the dominance of men.

8. Although an Elizabethan audience might have supported the Gallian invasion, they would not have sympathized with Leir's gratitude to the Gallian

King: after they conquer England, Leir shows his appreciation to Cordella's husband by offering him England as a reward (ll. 2555-64).

9. Sherman, p. 1. We should not overlook the possibility that Stafford used the word "tragecall" in his 1605 entry of the title in order to profit from the popularity of Shakespeare's *King Lear.* This theory depends on the assumption that Shakespeare's play appeared on stage in 1605 (before the entry of *King Leir* in the Stationers' Register) and not 1606 (as other critics believe, because of Gloucester's reference to recent eclipses). For more information on this complex issue see Edmond Malone, ed., *The Plays and Poems of William Shakespeare, with the Corrections and Illustrations of Various Commentators: Comprehending A Life of the Poet, and An Enlarged History of the Stage,* 2 vols. (London: Rivington, et al., 1821), II, 404-05; Robert Adger Law, "On The Date of King Lear," *PMLA*, 21 (1906), 462-77; Frederick Gard Fleay, *A Chronicle History of the Life and Work of William Shakespeare: Player, Poet, and Playmaker* (New York: Scribner and Welford, 1886), p. 237; and Sherman, pp. 3-13, 30.

10. Horace Howard Furness, ed., *King Lear, A New Variorum Edition of Shakespeare* (1880; rpt. New York: Dover, 1963), p. 378. See also E.K. Chambers, *William Shakespeare: A Study of Facts and Problems* 2 vols. (Oxford: Clarendon, 1930), I, 469.

11. Hardin Craig, "Motivation in Shakespeare's Choice of Materials," *Shakespeare Survey,* 4 (1951), 32; see Fleay, p. 237.

12. Sherman, pp. 28, 34.

13. Sherman, p. 46.

14. Sherman, p. 1.

15. Irving Ribner, *The English History Play in the Age of Shakespeare.* rev. ed. (New York: Barnes & Noble, 1965), p. 247.

16. Shakespeare later experimented with the romantic history genre in approximately 1610 with *Cymbeline.* This play, like *King Leir,* employs chronicle history as a means of dramatizing a romantic situation.

17. We must realize that *King Leir* is a much less political play than *Gorboduc* and *King Lear.* The anonymous dramatist concerns himself more with the story's entertainment value and its ability to be financially successful than with a political agenda. Marie Axton says that "The very absence of political elements in the earlier play [*King Leir*] points up their force and coherence in Shakespeare's."

Marie Axton, *The Queen's Two Bodies: Drama and the Elizabethan Succession* (London: Royal Historical Society, 1977), p. 138.

CHAPTER 10

"As flies to wanton boys are we to th' gods. . . .":

KING LEAR AND SHAKESPEARE'S DENIAL OF PROVIDENTIAL HISTORY

Shakespeare's 1608 quarto, *The True Chronicle History of the life and death of King Lear and his three Daughters,* later published in the first folio of 1623 as *The Tragedie of King Lear*, employs the anonymous *King Leir* (c. 1593) as a primary source.[1] The romantic history by the unknown dramatist is, as we have seen, somewhat apolitical, and the parts of the work that deal with politics imply the author's conservatism. Shakespeare's *King Lear*, first performed in approximately 1605, concerns itself with politics more than does its predecessor and questions religious and political ideologies in a manner that suggests a certain subversiveness. In this bitter, perhaps even nihilistic, drama, the playwright challenges the notions of divine Providence and of a king's ability to rule his subjects adequately; it may even undermine the Renaissance concept of monarchy as an efficacious form of government. The earlier play is an English romantic history play, but Shakespeare, by interrogating the established beliefs in God's justice and in the effectiveness of monarchical government, merges the "historical" story of King Lear with tragedy.

According to Holinshed's *Chronicles,* another of Shakespeare's sources for the main plot, when Lear found it difficult to rule well because of his advancing age, "he thought to vnderstand the affections of his daughters towards him, and preferre hir whome he best loued, to the succession ouer the kingdome."[2] The chronicler implies that Lear intended to employ this test as a means of dividing the country fairly. Yet, his method of asking his daughters how much they love him was foolish, as noted in the section on *King Leir*. Furthermore, the division of a kingdom leads almost inevitably to disaster, a commonplace Renaissance belief that Norton and Sackville had dramatized in *Gorboduc*. The king's motive in the *Chronicles* for testing his children's affection (to reward his daughters for their love) was more plausible than in *King Lear*, especially since Holinshed does not imply that this test occurred publicly.

In the first scene of Shakespeare's drama, the king attempts to reaffirm his authority by pressuring his daughters into announcing their love for him in front of the court. The dramatist's portrayal of Lear is negative because the king causes his daughters to embarrass themselves by declaring private emotions in a public and political forum in order to gratify his pride. Since we understand from Kent and Gloucester that the monarch has divided the kingdom equally *before* his test begins (I.i.1-7), that Lear has already drawn the divisions on his map before his daughters speak (I.i.37-38), and that Lear bestows one-third of his kingdom upon Goneril and Regan after each speaks (without waiting to hear Cordelia's words), we comprehend the pointlessness of the king's charade.[3]

King Lear's plan backfires when Cordelia refuses to play her father's game. The humiliated monarch views her behavior as an attack on his political power, for the confrontation occurs in front of the court; he cannot expect allegiance from his subjects when his own children refuse to obey him. The king attempts then to re-establish his authority by disinheriting and disowning his favorite daughter. Jonathan Dollimore says that kings punish perverse or unnatural behavior, for "control of the threat becomes the rationale of authoritarian reaction in a time of apparent crisis."[4] One of Lear's major errors is his misjudgment of the perverse element he must destroy. By equating sincere love with hyperbolic rhetoric, he misunderstands the true nature of his daughters' love for him and attempts to destroy his favorite child although he "thought to set [his] rest / On her kind nursery" (I.i.213-24). Consequently, he banishes Cordelia and Kent, who love him the most, and empowers his evil daughters and their husbands, the perverse threats.

The furious monarch in Shakespeare's play attempts to demonstrate his power by humiliating the daughter he considers unnatural: he punishes Cordelia by depriving her of land, power, and dowry while in her presence bestowing his kingdom solely upon his two eldest daughters and their husbands. Ironically, Lear's display of power involves his concomitant relinquishment of that authority. The king evinces his power by showing how much he loses by surrendering the kingdom. By manifesting his authority, he renders himself powerless.

This scene, which borrows from the anonymous *King Leir*, deviates from Holinshed's *Chronicles*. Shakespeare, like the anonymous creator of *King Leir*, ignores Holinshed's assertion that the monarch ordered the kingdom divided *after* his death and that the dukes seized the throne during his lifetime. According to Holinshed's account, we cannot blame Lear for his loss of power since his sons-in-law usurp his authority forcefully. Shakespeare's monarch, however, willingly abdicates so that he may "shake all cares and business from our age" (I.i.39).[5] His self-deposition implies his selfishness and his misunderstanding of the role of kingship: he considers the monarchy a possession he may dispose of at will; he fails to recognize the lifelong obligations that the position entails. Marie Axton claims that "Lear makes an utter travesty of kingship by not only dividing the realm, giving away the power of his office and sundering the crown, but by retaining the name of king and thus the responsibility for all the ensuing disasters."[6] Lear, however, is culpable not because he maintains his title (as Axton suggests) but rather because he relinquishes the power that God has ordained him to possess. Lear's failure to comprehend his monarchical responsibilities and their importance indicates his unsuitability as king.[7]

In Shakespeare's play, as in *Gorboduc* and *King Leir*, the monarch's wrongful abdication results in an unnatural reversal of power. King Lear becomes a subject of, and hence inferior to, his two eldest daughters, as the Fool points out on several occasions. The Fool remarks that Lear has made his "daughters [his] mothers, for when [he gives] them the rod, and put[s]. . . down [his] own breeches," the king reverses his relationship with Goneril and Regan (I.iv.169-71). The Fool adds that Lear becomes subservient to his daughters; when the former monarch tells Goneril that she frowns much lately, the jester says to him, "Thou wast a pretty fellow when thou hadst no need to care for her frowning; now thou art an O without a figure. I am better than thou art now" (I.iv.188-90). Lear's abdication creates a topsy-turvy situation, as when the cart draws the horse (I.iv.220-21):

> The man that makes his toe
>   What he his heart should make
> Shall of a corn cry woe,
>   And turn his sleep to wake.
>   (III.ii.31-34)

The heart is a more essential part of the anatomy than the toe, for people use the latter merely for physical movement while the former is an integral organ necessary for survival, often associated with human feelings and with the soul. The toe, unlike the heart, is an external, sensory body part; Lear and Gloucester initiate their own tragedies by relying upon their sensory organs (ears and eyes, respectively) instead of basing their decisions on what their hearts say.[8] The Fool's song implies that Lear, who has placed baseness above worthiness, has created his own dilemma by inverting the social order.

By portraying reversals of power, Shakespeare demonstrates that subjects do not necessarily owe their allegiance to their legitimate monarch. Richard Strier points out that *King Lear* "can be seen, in part, as an extended meditation on the kinds of situation in which resistance to legally constituted monarchy becomes a moral necessity, and in which neutrality is not a viable possibility."[9] After the king abdicates, Goneril/Albany and Regan/Cornwall become the rightful leaders; Lear becomes a mere subject. Thus, when Gloucester aids Lear and possesses the letter regarding the French invasion, his comportment is morally correct yet treasonous. Strier notes that when Gloucester arrives on the heath to comfort Lear, "he speak[s] the language of morally mandated disobedience to 'superior powers,' of higher than immediate duty."[10] The punishment that Cornwall exacts from the earl is cruel yet technically justified, for Gloucester, by supporting his former king and disobeying Cornwall's order, commits treason. The reprehensible Oswald, contrariwise, always obeys his monarch, and thus Cornwall saves him from the wrath of Kent, who carries a missive from Lear (Cornwall's subject). Oswald follows the orders of his queen (Goneril) while Kent attempts to subvert those commands. Oswald is not a superior subject to Gloucester and Kent; rather, Shakespeare demonstrates that during certain times, such as when the hierarchy has been inverted, rebellion against legitimate forms of authority are morally acceptable. The presentation of a situation onstage that invites support for the insurrection against a lawful monarchy is subversive.

The reversal of power reaches a climax when Lear visits Regan's castle. Regan and Cornwall permit Oswald, Goneril's servant, to treat the former king rudely; Oswald's insult of Lear (I.iv.45-54) symbolizes the reversal of power since the messenger no longer owes obedience to the former king but rather to the self-deposed monarch's daughters and their husbands--not because he is Goneril's servant but because they possess authority over her father. Consequently, Regan and Cornwall may flaunt their power over Lear by siding with Oswald against Caius (Kent); they may also put Kent in the stocks, punishing Lear as well as his servant. When Goneril and

Regan exert their authority over their father once again, insulting him by reducing his train (the last vestige of his authority), Lear leaves Regan's house during the fierce storm. Earlier we have witnessed the king forcing Cordelia to leave; this time, in contrast, Lear must depart since he has transferred his authority to his children and their husbands. Shakespearean scholars have frequently compared the storm into which Lear flees to that which rages within the man. Instead, we may conjecture that the unnaturally fierce storm is the macrocosm for which the reversal of the sociopolitical hierarchy is the microcosm; in other words, the imbalance in nature reflects the imbalance of power that Lear himself has brought about. During the storm, the self-deposed king goes mad, which is another indication of the imbalance of power--one that correlates with another anatomical metaphor. In *The Trew Law of Free Monarchies* (1598), King James employs the commonplace analogy of a human head when he discusses kingship; the ruler governs his realm as a head controls the body:

> For from the head, being the seate of judgement, proceedeth the care and foresight of guiding, and preuenting all euill that may come to the bodie, or any parte thereof. The head cares for the bodie: so doth the King for his people. As the discourse and direction flowes from the head, and the execution according thervnto belongs to the rest of the members. . . .[11]

Lear, the head in James's metaphor, precipitates the tragic events with his lack of intelligence and foresight. After the monarch goes mad, his former subjects, such as Kent, Cordelia, and the doctor, must care for him since he cannot think for himself; the body and the head reverse roles. The body assumes more importance than the head, as the toe acquires dominance over the heart in the Fool's metaphor. Part of the reason for Lear's madness is his realization that Goneril and Regan, two members of the political body, now rule as the head, and he has rendered himself an obsolete segment of the body--a huge demotion from his position as monarch.

In the first two acts of Shakespeare's play, Lear possesses a monarch's title and power but fails to act like a good king. He conflates political and familial matters, and he manifests his egocentricity by assuming that his subjects exist for his benefit instead of he for them. But we should not be surprised that a man of royal blood, who presumably has been groomed for the throne since his birth and who has spent his life atop Fortune's wheel, should be selfish and intolerant of contradiction. The monarch's error, unlike that of the ruler in the anonymous play, is typical of the king's personality.[12] Lear's misguided attitude towards power is quite similar to that of most of the kings in Shakespeare's other English history plays-- monarchs such as King John, Richard II, and Richard III.

The ruler's foolish decision to depose himself causes him to fall to the bottom of Fortune's wheel, thus permitting him to realize what makes a good king. Upon arriving on the heath during the storm, the powerless Lear wonders how the impoverished survive such horrendous weather. The former ruler, unfamiliar with the sight of poverty since he has dwelled exclusively among the rich, appears shocked. He admits, "Oh! I have ta'en / too little care of this" (III.iv.32-33). Lear most probably would not have made such a realization nor such a comment had he retained his power. Shakespeare implies in *King Lear* that those in authority distance themselves from the poor and starving classes. Dollimore asserts:

> in a world where pity is the prerequisite for compassionate action, where a king has to share the suffering of his actions in order to 'care', the majority will remain poor, naked, and wretched. The point of course is that princes only see the hovels of wretches during progresses (walkabouts?), in flight, or in fairy tale.[13]

Now powerless, the once egocentric ruler gains a new altruism while on the heath, and his charitable behavior manifests his humanity (as opposed to his spiritual body and authority). Although Lear wishes to remain outside during the storm in order to maintain his sanity, he agrees to venture inside the hovel because he pities the Fool, and the former monarch allows the boy to enter first, which may be the first time anyone has preceded him anywhere.[14] In a selfless gesture, Lear removes his clothes in order to clothe Poor Tom (III.iv.111-12). Leonard Tennenhouse says that "When Lear strips off his clothes to reveal himself as 'unaccommodated man,' Shakespeare boldly reveals the natural body of the king as one that appears to bear little value in its own right. . . . In and of itself, it is powerless."[15] The scene is bold, for Shakespeare dramatizes a king who is no different from other human beings. As Lear strips off his clothes, the playwright strips away the metaphysical nature of kingship to reveal its cultural manifestations. Lear remarks later that "Through tatter'd clothes small vices do appear; / Robes and furr'd gowns hide all" (IV.vi.164-65).[16] The king's physical body is identical to that of others, and his spiritual body lies in his clothes, not in divine selection. Lear philosophizes more on the similarities between those who have and those who lack authority: "See how yond justice rails upon yond simple thief. Hark in thine ear: change places, and, handy-dandy, which is the justice, which is the thief" (IV.vi.151-54). The judge's robe and title, not his abilities or his deserts, separate him from common people; furthermore, in Lear's era (and to some extent in Shakespeare's) the monarch is also the highest ranking judge in society, so his statement implies that kings and subjects are essentially identical, the only difference lying in the exterior manifestations of monarchy.

Although the theme of authority preoccupies the former king, he no longer covets it. On the heath, Lear forgets about his train (courtiers who exist simply to enhance his prestige) and his power; instead he helps his people. Ironically, his concern for his subjects emerges when they are no longer his subjects. In order for a monarch to comprehend how to treat his poverty-stricken subjects properly, he cannot be in power; authority blinds a ruler since class demarcations prevent him from seeing beyond his own privileged situation. By losing his crown, Lear acquires the ability to think and govern well; he has, however, lost the authority to rule. Lear loses his power, yet, unlike the situation in Shakespeare's sources, he never regains power after he learns how to rule. Shakespeare implies in this dark play that the ability and the authority to govern are not coextensive; inevitably, those in power rule ineffectively. Since monarchs possess royal blood and thus dissociate themselves from their subjects, the monarchical form of government functions poorly.

We have discerned also that the division of a kingdom works improperly also since it leads to civil strife, as in the dissension between Cornwall and Albany, which Kent mentions to the Gentleman (III.i.19-31). In Shakespeare's bleak tragical history, perhaps no effective form of government exists; any type of rule will lead to disaster.

Let us now anatomize the court that Lear has left behind--or rather that has left him behind. After Lear divides the kingdom, a civil strife occurs between Cornwall and Albany, and Goneril and Regan fight over the bastard Edmund. Gloucester, by misinterpreting the perverse and unnatural force he must overcome, falls victim to the ambitious ruler Cornwall, who cruelly plucks out his eyes. Cornwall's abuse of his newly acquired power causes his servant to murder him. When we contrast the impoverished and "mad" court on the heath during the storm with this bloody aristocratic court, the former appears more suitable and even more pleasurable; we may even wish to question which court is the insane one.

The court that has banished Lear, placed Kent in the stocks, and blinded Gloucester is clearly evil, yet surprisingly strong. In Holinshed's *Chronicles* and in the anonymous *King Leir*, the French army, with Cordella and Leir in its retinue, defeats this evil kingdom, and Leir regains the throne; we may interpret the outcome as divine justice. In *King Lear*, the evil force emerges victorious initially but then destroys itself because of the ambition and lust of the leaders. Shakespeare includes no battle scene, and the war occurs between V.ii and V.iii; in other words, the playwright allows no time to elapse for the battle, as if to indicate a brief and easy victory for the evil force. Evil is stronger than virtue, the play implies, but when it becomes too powerful, it self-destructs. Good cannot defeat evil: only evil can destroy evil. Ultimately, sinister and chaotic forces succumb, and order is restored, but the price that must be paid is the death of virtue and innocence (Cordelia and, to some extent, Lear and Gloucester).

Shakespeare deviates purposefully from his sources to portray a world void of Providence that mocks its inhabitants. Gloucester notes, "As flies to wanton boys are we to th' gods, / They kill us for their sport" (IV.i.36-37). Although Edgar's attempt to prove the existence of divine authority succeeds with his gullible father, it is rather unconvincing. Edgar convinces Gloucester that he has led him to the edge of a precipice and watches as the blind man falls. Now disguised as a citizen of the town below, Edgar declares that the duke's survival represents a manifestation of divine aid: "Think that the clearest Gods, who make them honours / Of men's impossibilities, have preserved thee" (IV.vi.73-74). The trick dupes the old man into thinking that the gods have saved his life, but we, who have eyes, realize that no cliff exists. Gloucester's life is in no danger and cannot therefore be preserved. Even though Edgar shares his intent with us, this scene implies, according to William R. Elton, that miracles demonstrating divine authority are frauds that deceive the gullible.[17]

We may discern a glimmer of divine intervention when Edgar defeats Edmund and declares that "The Gods are just, and of our pleasant vices / Make instruments to plague us" (V.iii.170-71). There are secular reasons for Edgar's victory, however, such as his superior upbringing; he is Gloucester's eldest and only legitimate son: a noble's heir received an education that included lessons in swordsmanship.[18] Furthermore, Shakespeare's audience would have accepted a legitimate son defeating a bastard rather than the reverse situation. More significantly, as Edgar remarks on the equity of the Gods, Edmund's officer executes the innocent Cordelia, thus undermining and destroying any prospect for divine justice.

There was a growing distrust of Providence in Renaissance England, according to Elton. This scholar cites a plethora of books written during Shakespeare's playwriting career whose purpose was to defend the concept of Providence from the increasing number of "atheists" and advocates of

Epicurus and Lucretius.[19]   Paul W. Miller claims in his discussion of Marlowe's "Hero and Leander" that John Carpenter writes *A Preparative to Contention* (1597) to prove "That the concept of an unjust God was dangerously prevalent in England" at the time the author wrote the poem.[20] Carpenter laments in his treatise the "deepe distrust of *the divine Providence*, by faith in the which, men have a chief comfort in this life, and without the which, they run into a labyrinth of errors. *Diagoras* the Atheist hath within his Schoole manie shrewd Schollers."[21]

Luther advocates the idea of *Deus absconditus*, the belief that God not only fails to better life on earth but also acts antagonistically towards man. Montaigne and Calvin advance the concept of *debilitas rationis* (the limitation of human reason); Montaigne and Calvin argue that Providence exists but that God's actions are beyond the understanding of postlapsarian human beings. Such a theory cannot be proven and may be considered paradoxical: human beings must accept the belief that what they know about Providence is beyond their comprehension. Calvin believes that because of *debilitas rationis*, man must obey God blindly and ignore the apparent lack of Providence. Those in power could employ this ideology to convince their subjects to accept their lot in life passively and to conform to both religious and secular laws.

In the Renaissance, some questioned the idea of Providence instead of accepting the belief that divine justice was beyond human reason. This interrogation of the ideology appears in dramatic works with tragic endings, such as *King Lear*. Arthur Sewell claims:

> Tragedy finds its origin not in a Christian idea of imperfection but in 'Renaissance anarchism'. . . . Shakespearian tragedy is the product of the change in men's minds--the Renaissance change--by which men came to feel themselves separate from God; by which, indeed, the idea of God receded from men's habitual certitudes and became no more and often less than an intellectual construction, a merely credible hypothesis, a Being remote and not certainly just or beneficent, perhaps the Enemy.[22]

Shakespeare's altering of his sources contradicts the providential history exhibited in Holinshed's account and in *King Leir*; in Shakespeare's play, God is not just. By dramatizing the deaths of Cordelia and of Lear, Shakespeare denies the importance of English history and of Providence. Playwrights often conflate or change time, minor characters and events, but Shakespeare's alteration of the fate of Cordelia and Lear is shocking and disturbing. Samuel Johnson claims:

I was many years ago so shocked by *Cordelia's* death, that I know not whether I ever endured to read again the last scenes of the play till I undertook to revise them as an editor. . . . *Shakespeare* has suffered the virtue of *Cordelia* to perish in a just cause, contrary to the natural ideas of justice, the hope of the reader, and, what is yet more strange, to the faith of the chronicles.[23]

Shakespeare's questioning of history and of Providence renders *King Lear* a subversive play since Renaissance monarchs employed providential history as a means of legitimizing their right to wear the crown. For instance, many considered Henry VII's victory over Richard III at Bosworth Field to be providential since Henry's triumph destroyed the evil Richard Crookback, united the houses of Lancaster and York, and ended the alleged curse on England that resulted from Bolingbroke's usurpation of Richard II's power. Rulers during the Tudor dynasty interpreted Henry of Richmond's historical victory as providential. According to the propagandistic Tudor myth, God (believing England had suffered enough during the War of the Roses to atone for Bolingbroke's usurpation) ensured that good (Richmond) would defeat evil (Richard III). In Shakespeare's *King Lear*, however, "the wicked prosper, and the virtuous miscarry. . . ."[24] The gods disregard the occurrences on Earth, forcing people to control their own destinies. *King Lear*, unlike its predecessor by the anonymous playwright, contains no happy ending or restoration--just deaths and sorrow. As Lear dies, Kent says:

> He hates him
> That would upon the rack of this tough world
> Stretch him out longer.
>   (V.iii.318-20)

The same feeling holds true for all the characters in the play since no character has anything or anyone to live for because of the lack of divine intervention.

The doubting of Providence in *King Lear* allows the audience to question the theory of the divine right of kings, an ideology perpetuated by Tudor monarchs and by King James, England's ruler when Shakespeare wrote *King Lear*. According to *An Homily against Disobedience and Wylful Rebellion* (1570), which clergymen read from the pulpit to congregations who were required to attend Church, the Holy Scriptures and the Old Testament state frequently that kings "reign by God's ordinance, and that subjects are bound to obey them; that God does give princes wisdom, great power and authority; that God defends them against their enemies and destroys their enemies horribly; that the anger and displeasure of the prince is as the roaring of a lion. . . ."[25]

The action in Shakespeare's play contradicts the above description of the divine right ideology, subverting the homiletic theme of allegiance to a monarch. King Lear cannot "reign by God's ordinance" if his world lacks the presence of a Supreme being (as the tragical history appears to do). The homily asserts that God provides kings with wisdom; yet we have seen that Lear's foolish political decisions (such as his abdication, division of his kingdom, and his disinheritance of Cordelia) bring England to the brink of ruin. We may concur with the Fool when he calls the former king a fool, adding that "All thy other titles thou hast given away; that thou wast born with" (I.iv.147-48). God has not bestowed much wisdom upon this king. The homily claims that "God defends them against their enemies . . . ." Lear receives no divine defense in Shakespeare's play; in fact, God appears to aid the king's foes. We have observed an example of Providence in the anonymous play when divine thunder rescues Leir and Perillus from the messenger-murderer. Conversely, while Shakespeare's Lear stands on the heath, the thundering storm compounds his troubles and precipitates his madness. The storm, whether natural or supernatural, assists the malevolent designs of Goneril, Regan, and Cornwall. In his apostrophe to the stormy elements, Lear calls them:

> servile ministers,
> That will with two pernicious daughters join
> Your high-engender'd battles 'gainst a head
> So old and white as this.
>
> (III.ii.21-24)

Thus, the action in *King Lear* calls into question the ideologies perpetuated in the homily regarding divine right and the necessity of subjects' allegiance to monarchs.

We should not conclude from the above interpretation of *King Lear* that Shakespeare was an atheist--in either the Renaissance or the twentieth-century meaning of the word. Shakespeare's denial of Providence in the play is an exploration, an experiment but not an affirmation. Yet Lear must bear the responsibility for his actions since the fault is not in the gods but in himself. In Lear's world, which we would now classify as existential, people must pay the consequences for their actions. By altering information from Holinshed's *Chronicles* and *King Leir*, Shakespeare suggests dramatically that people must fend for themselves since royalty and the virtuous cannot count on divine aid. Shakespeare's undermining of providential history transforms the story of Lear from a history to a tragic history.

English chronicle history was important politically since kings employed it to legitimize their right to govern. For instance, Richard, Duke of York, used history as a means of claiming the throne, causing the War of the Roses.[26] Upon acquiring the throne, Henry VII attempted to justify his right to govern by tracing his lineage from John of Gaunt. Monarchs used the historical past to legitimize the present so that their authority would appear to possess a metaphysical (as opposed to a cultural) origin. History is, therefore, an essential propagandistic political tool.

In the transitions from *Gorboduc* to *King Leir* to *King Lear*, a growing distrust of English chronicle history exists. Norton and Sackville rely on Holinshed's account of Gorboduc and follow it rather faithfully. The anonymous author of *King Leir* takes a few liberties with Holinshed's story since he concerns himself more with sentimental interests and entertainment than with politics and historical accuracy; yet the dramatist maintains the same plot, conclusion, and tone of the chronicled account. In *King Lear*, Shakespeare employs a skeleton of his sources but creates a new story in which he alters the plot and completely changes the conclusion and the tone of Holinshed's historical report. Shakespeare dramatizes a story with which his audience would have been familiar but manipulates the plot as if history and fable are interchangeable. Shakespeare's version is almost a totally different story; it demystifies history by dramatizing how easily the past may be altered and created for any purpose, thus questioning the use of history to legitimize kingship.

CHAPTER 10: NOTES

1. In the past decade, much scholarship has been written on the subject of the two versions--the 1608 quarto and the 1623 folio. Gary Taylor, Stanley Wells, Michael Warren, and Steven Urkowitz have contributed much to the study of the disparities between the two texts. In fact, Stanley Wells's and Gary Taylor's edition of Shakespeare's *Complete Works* (Oxford: Clarendon, 1986) includes both versions of *King Lear*. The folio *King Lear* has been widely accepted as Shakespeare's revision of the 1608 quarto after the playwright saw the drama staged. The disparities between the two texts are, however, not as significant as these scholars suggest. For the purposes of this chapter (which does not focus on any of the revisions), the Bevington edition, which conflates the two versions, is quite satisfactory and is the text employed for all quotations throughout the chapter: *The Complete Works of Shakespeare*, ed. David Bevington (Glenview, Ill.: Scott, Foresman, 1980).

2. Raphael Holinshed, *Holinshed's Chronicles of England, Scotland, and Ireland*, 6 vols. (London: J. Johnson, et al., 1807-08), I, 447.

3. We also know that King Lear has divided the kingdom already since Burgundy and France know Cordelia's dowry before the scene begins (I.i.195-96).

4. Jonathan Dollimore, "Transgression and Surveillance in *Measure for Measure*," in *Political Shakespeare: New Essays in Cultural Materialism*, eds. Jonathan Dollimore and Alan Sinfield (Ithaca: Cornell University Press, 1985), p. 5.

5. Annabel Patterson suggests that Lear's desire to relinquish his political duties may be a subtle attack by Shakespeare on his new monarch, King James. James was notorious for "his abandonment of the cares of government for the pleasures of hunting." Patterson mentions other similarities between Lear and James, such as the possession of a notable fool and the "use of the [royal] prerogative" (p. 59). James or his censors could have interpreted the portrayal of Lear as an attack on the monarch. Patterson indicates, however, that King Lear would not have insulted the king and would have been approved by the censors because the play manifests the dangers of dividing a kingdom. The play was performed before the king on St. Stephen's Day (December 26), 1606--during James's struggle to win support for the Union, the joining of England with Scotland. Patterson notes that a play, to escape the censors, may attack and praise in different sections of the same drama (pp. 59-60). Annabel Patterson, *Censorship and Interpretation: The Conditions of Writing and Reading in Early Modern England* (Madison: The

University of Wisconsin Press, 1984). For more information on King Lear and the Union, see Marie Axton, *The Queen's Two Bodies: Drama and the Elizabethan Succession* (London: Royal Historical Society, 1977), pp. 131-37, 143-45.

6. Axton, p. 139.

7. In the anonymous play, King Leir commits the same error, but we should consider him a good king, nonetheless. We may forgive Leir's mistake since it appears to be a rare one--an error that occurs immediately after the burial of his wife. No extenuating circumstances exist in Shakespeare's drama, and Regan and Goneril claim that he has always comported himself rashly and immoderately (I.i.294-300). The comic ending of *King Leir* and the tragic conclusion of Shakespeare's play manifest clearly the contrasted worthiness of the two elderly kings.

8. Lear loves Cordelia more than his other two daughters yet banishes her and rewards Goneril and Regan because of what he hears from them during his test of their affections; Gloucester loves Edgar much more than Edmund, but he disowns his legitimate son and places his faith in his bastard because of the forged letter he reads. It is no coincidence that Gloucester's punishment consists of his blinding, for, as the duke admits later, "I stumbled when I saw" (IV.i.19). Both Lear and Gloucester err by trusting their sensory organs instead of their hearts.

9. Richard Strier, "Faithful Servants: Shakespeare's Praise of Disobedience," in *The Historical Renaissance: New Essays on Tudor and Stuart Literature and Culture*, eds. Heather Dubrow and Richard Strier. (Chicago: The University of Chicago Press, 1988), p. 104.

10 . Strier, p. 118.

11. *King James VI (and I), Minor Prose Works of King James VI and I,* ed. James Craigie (Edinburgh: Scottish Text Society, 1982), p. 74.

12. Since *King Leir* is a politically conservative play and a romantic comedy that emphasizes sentimental appeal and entertainment value more than historical accuracy, the playwright characterizes Leir as a magnanimous ruler.

13. Jonathan Dollimore, *Radical Tragedy: Religion, Ideology and Power in the Drama of Shakespeare and his Contemporaries* (Chicago: University of Chicago Press, 1984), p. 191.

14. Lear believes that by remaining outside during the storm he may suppress his anger towards his daughters, for he will not think of their ingratitude.

15. Leonard Tennenhouse, *Power on Display: The Politics of Shakespeare's Genres* (New York: Methuen, 1986), p. 139.

16.   In the passage, Bevington relies on the 1608 quarto; in the 1623 folio, Shakespeare changes "small vices" to "great Vices." See William Shakespeare, *The Tragedie of King Lear* (IV.v.2367) in *The Complete Works*, eds. Stanley Wells and Gary Taylor (Oxford: Clarendon, 1986), p. 1093. It is line 2367 of the play, not of IV.v.

17. William R. Elton, *"King Lear" and the Gods* (1966; rpt. Lexington: The University Press of Kentucky, 1988), p. 93.

18. The concept of education, such as Edmund's education in a boarding school (I.i.32-33), is anachronistic, and reflects Renaissance education rather than pre-Christian schooling.

19. See Elton, pp. 9-33.

20. Paul W. Miller, "The Problem of Justice in Marlowe's 'Hero and Leander,'" *Notes and Queries* N.S. 4 (1957), 163-64.

21. The quotation from Carpenter's book appears in Elton's *"King Lear" and the Gods*, p. 22.

22. Arthur Sewell, *Character and Society in Shakespeare* (Oxford: Clarendon, 1951), pp. 120-21.

23. Samuel Johnson, *Johnson on Shakespeare*, in *The Yale Edition of the Works of Samuel Johnson*, ed. Arthur Sherbo, 15 vols. (New Haven: Yale University Press, 1958-85), VIII, 704.

24. Johnson, VIII, 704.

25. *An Homily Against Disobedience and Wylful Rebellion*, in *Divine Right and Democracy: An Anthology of Political Writing in Stuart England*, ed. David Wootton (Middlesex: Penguin, 1986), pp. 95-96.

26. See Shakespeare's *2 Henry VI* (II.ii.10-58).

CONCLUSION

During the course of this study, we have noticed a growing distrust of established ideologies such as the divine right of kings and the king's two bodies, as well as the truthful and providential nature of history. Early English history plays generally support the concepts that monarchs employed to justify their authority. In *Magnificence*, Skelton does not staunchly defend monarchy because of the playwright's anger towards Henry VIII, but the dramatist blames evil flatterers more than he does the ruler, and the king maintains his authority. John Bale's *King Johan* clearly advocates the theory of divine right and unwavering allegiance to one's monarch. *Gorboduc* supports the reign of Elizabeth while advocating the importance of Parliament and while warning the queen of the necessity of naming an English Protestant as heir to the throne.

As the years progress, playwrights increasingly question religious and political ideologies that relate to kingship. The anonymous *Woodstock*, Christopher Marlowe's *Edward II*, and Shakespeare's *Richard II* dramatize the reigns of weak and incompetent kings who misgovern their realms and mistreat their nobles. We view *Woodstock* mostly from the perspective of the dukes and are always on their side against Richard and his flatterers (who possess power throughout the drama). In the plays by Shakespeare and Marlowe our sympathies lie initially with the nobles but shift to the monarchs as they lose power; we are content at first that the depositions should occur, but our empathy for the usurpers disappears once they practice their new authority. As the audience of these three works, we almost always support those who do not possess the crown, not those who do. The three plays contain a note of political subversion, for they cause us to sympathize with those who lack power and they posit the question of whether nobles have the right to depose a king who leads his nation to ruin. Furthermore, *Edward II* and *Richard II* manifest clearly a trend towards tragedy as we pity the monarchs once they lose power--even though we may acknowledge the necessity of deposition.

A similar movement towards subversion and tragedy exists in the canon of Shakespeare's history plays.[1] In Shakespeare's first tetralogy (*1, 2,* and *3 Henry VI* and *Richard III*), which encompasses the War of the Roses, the playwright dramatizes the unfortunate repercussions of disobeying the king and of civil strife. David Riggs claims that "If providential history may be identified with the element of moral teleology that Shakespeare, like most Elizabethans, professed to see in the succession of reigns that led to the union of Lancaster and York, then there is, beyond question, a providential theme in *Henry VI* which is duly consummated in *Richard III*."[2] In *Richard III*, Shakespeare employs the negative portrayal of the title character that the Tudor monarchs and their loyal followers such as Sir Thomas More had fostered. By perpetuating the historical distortions of Richard III, the playwright supports Queen Elizabeth implicitly since her grandfather replaced the humpbacked king after defeating him at Bosworth Field in 1485.

Shakespeare dutifully characterizes Henry of Richmond as a benevolent noble who will restore order to England--order that has been lacking since the deposition of Henry VIII. Richmond will reunite the houses of York and Lancaster through his marriage:

> We will unite the white rose and the red.
> Smile heaven upon this fair conjunction,
> That long have frown'd upon their enmity!
> . . . .
> O, now, let Richmond and Elizabeth [daughter of
> Edward IV and grandmother of Queen Elizabeth],
> The true succeeders of each royal house,
> By God's fair ordinance conjoin together!
> And let their heirs, God, if thy will be so,
> Enrich the time to come with smooth-fac'd peace,
> With smiling plenty, and fair prosperous days!
> (V.v.19-34)[3]

Shakespeare characterizes Richmond's triumph as providential; Henry is God's instrument to restore harmony to England after civil unrest caused by Bolingbroke's usurpation of England's divinely ordained king.

Riggs, however, focuses on the first tetralogy; his comment about teleological order in the first tetralogy would not hold true for the second. In *Richard II*, from Shakespeare's second tetralogy, we must question whether the playwright still views history as providential. We may challenge whether war and chaos occur because of Richard's deposition and subsequent regicide, or whether civil strife would have occurred anyway. Furthermore, the glorious reign of Henry V and his divinely aided triumph at Agincourt undercut the possibility of a curse. Shakespeare also undermines the Bishop of Carlisle's prophetic words regarding divine retribution by challenging the ideologies of divine right and the king's two bodies.

The increasing political subversiveness of these dramas exemplifies the growing distrust of the institutions that held power in Renaissance England --the monarchy, the court, and the Anglican church.   In fact, the questioning of the competence and virtues of these institutions exists in all the plays in this book--most noticeably in the dramas written during the latter part of the Tudor dynasty. This distrust continued throughout the first forty years of the seventeenth century and culminated in the dissolution of the government, the English Revolution, and the subsequent beheading of Charles I.   We understand the ramifications of the challenging of these political institutions when we consider "the putting of a king on trial in the name of 'the people of England', on a charge of high treason for violation of 'the fundamental constitutions of this Kingdom'. This was something which had never been done before. The Revolution involved not merely the substitution of one king for another but the abolition of the institution of monarchy."[4]

Most of the plays in this study concern the issue of deposing a king in favor of another.   In Part One, King John encounters the threat of deposition by the corrupt Catholic church, his nephew, and his nobles. Deposition is a significant issue in Part Two because kings misgovern after they subjugate themselves to flatterers. Part Three concerns voluntary abdication and the concomitant division of the realm. The playwrights question the rulers and the ideologies that legitimize kingship, but they do not challenge monarchical rule. In *King Lear*, however, which is the latest of the ten plays I treat (c. 1605), Shakespeare challenges the effectiveness of the monarchical system of government.   This challenge becomes stronger in the decades that follow Shakespeare's great tragical history play--a challenge culminating in the trial for treason and the execution of Charles I.   We should ponder whether Charles or the monarchy was actually on trial and found guilty.

Andrew Marvell's description of the execution of Charles manifests the poet's astute conflation of history with tragedy:

That thence the *Royal Actor* born
The *Tragick Scaffold* might adorn:
   While round the armed Bands
   Did clap their bloody hands.
He nothing common did or mean
Upon that memorable Scene:
   But with his keener Eye

> The Axes edge did try:
> Nor call'd the *Gods* with vulgar spight
> To vindicate his helpless Right,
>   But bow'd his comely Head,
>   Down as upon a Bed,
> This was that memorable Hour,
> Which first assur'd the forced Pow'r.[5]

Marvell compares this historical event to a play and Charles to an actor. As Shakespeare does in *King Lear*, Marvell blends history with tragedy, for he describes the historical event as if it were a tragedy. The historical scene is tragic partly because the actor is of royal blood and also because of the king's political impotence. The scene also possesses tragic possibilities because the institution of monarchy, as well as Charles, suffers execution. Franco Moretti claims that "new ages are not brought into being merely through the development of new ideas: the dissolution or overthrowing of old ideas plays an equal part in their emergence."[6] The politically subversive dramas we have discussed challenge the ideologies of kingship and thus influence their audiences. The Commonwealth would agree with the latter assertion since the new government deemed it necessary to close the theatres in 1642 because of what they considered its negative moral effects upon its patrons. The political dramas of the Renaissance, therefore, possess a role in the political turbulence that culminates in the dissolution of the English government and in the subsequent English Revolution.

CONCLUSION: NOTES

1. I do not count *Henry VIII*, first, because Shakespeare may have only written part of the play (collaborating with John Fletcher) and, second, the drama appears well after the prime of his career.

2. David Riggs, *Shakespeare's Heroical Histories: "Henry VI" and Its Literary Tradition* (Cambridge, Mass.: Harvard University Press, 1971), p. 5.

3. David Bevington, ed., *The Tragedy of King Richard the Third*, in *The Complete Works of Shakespeare*, 3rd ed. (Glenview, Ill: Scott, Foresman, 1980), p. 719.

4. Lawrence Stone, *The Causes of the English Revolution 1529-1642.* (New York: Harper & Row, 1972), p. 49.

5. H.M. Margoliouth, ed., "An Horatian Ode upon Cromwel's Return from Ireland," in *The Poems and Letters of Andrew Marvell*, 3rd ed. 3 vols. (Oxford: Clarendon, 1971), I, 92-93; ll. 53-66.

6. Franco Moretti, "'A Huge Eclipse': Tragic Form and the Deconsecration of Sovereignty," in *The Power of Forms in the English Renaissance*, ed. Stephen Greenblatt. (Norman, OK: Pilgrim, 1982), p. 7.

BIBLIOGRAPHY

PRIMARY SOURCES

"The Alleged Articles of 1308." Eds. H.G. Richardson and G.O. Sayles. *The Governance of Mediaeval England from the Conquest to Magna Carta.* Trans. H.G. Richardson and G.O. Sayles. Edinburgh: Edinburgh UP, 1963. 466-69.

An Homily against Disobedience and Wylful Rebellion. In *Divine Right and Democracy: An Anthology of Political Writing in Stuart England.* Ed. David Wootton. Middlesex: Penguin, 1986. 94-98.

Bale, John. *King Johan.* Ed. Barry B. Adams. San Marino: The Huntington Library, 1969.

---. *Kyng Johan.* Ed. Edmund Creeth. *Tudor Plays: An Anthology of Early English Drama.* New York: W.W. Norton, 1972. 97-213.

---. *King Johan.* In *The Complete Plays of John Bale.* Ed. Peter Happe. Vol. 1. Cambridge: D.S. Brewer, 1985-86. 2 vols.

---. *King Johan.* Ed. John Henry Pyle Pafford. Oxford: Oxford UP, 1931.

Brown, Rawdon, Ed. *Calendar of State Papers.* Venetian II. No. 1287, 1867-69.

Bullough, Geoffrey. See listings under *The Troublesome Raigne of King John* and *The True Chronicle Historie of King Leir and his three daughters.*

Castiglione, Baldesar. *The Book of the Courtier.* Trans. George Bull. 1967. Middlesex: Penguin, 1984.

Devereux, Walter Bourchier. *Lives and Letters of the Devereux, Earls of Essex: In the Reigns of Elizabeth, James I, and Charles I., 1540-1646.* Vol. 1. London: John Murray, 1853. 2 vols.

Gairdner, James, Ed. *Letters and Papers, Foreign and Domestic, of the Reign of Henry VIII. Preserved in the Public Record Office, the British Museum, and Elsewhere in England.* London: Eyre and Spottiswoode, 1892.

Hardyng, John. *The Chronicle of Iohn Hardyng. Containing an Account of Public Transactions from the Earliest Period of English History to the Beginning of the Reign of King Edward the Fourth. Together with The Continuation by Richard Grafton, To the Thirty Fourth Year of King Henry the Eighth.* Ed. Henry Ellis. 1812. New York: AMS, 1974.

Heywood, Thomas. *An Apology for Actors; A Refutation of the "Apology for Actors."* New York: Garland, 1973.

---. *An Apology for Actors.* Ed. Richard H. Perkinson. New York: Scholars' Facsimiles & Reprints, 1941.

Hobbes, Thomas. *Leviathan.* Ed. C.B. Macpherson. 1968. Harmondsworth: Penguin, 1983.

Holinshed, Raphael. Holinshed's *Chronicles of England, Scotland, and Ireland.* Vols. 1, 2. London: J. Johnson, 1807-08. 6 vols.

King James VI (and I). *The Trew Law of Free Monarchies.* In *Minor Prose Works of King James VI and I.* Ed. James Craigie. Edinburgh: Scottish Text Society, 1982.

Machiavelli, Nicholas. *Machiavelli's The Prince: An Elizabethan Translation.* Ed. Hardin Craig. Chapel Hill: U of North Carolina P, 1944.

Mankind. In *Medieval Drama.* Ed. David Bevington. Boston: Houghton Mifflin, 1975. 901-38.

Marlowe, Christopher. *Edward the Second.* Ed. W. Moelwyn Merchant. 1967. London: A. & C. Black; New York: W.W. Norton, 1989.

---. *Tamburlaine: Part One.* In *The Complete Plays of Christopher Marlowe.* Ed. Irving Ribner. Indianapolis: Bobbs-Merrill, 1963. 49-111.

Marvell, Andrew. "An Horatian Ode upon Cromwel's Return from Ireland." *The Poems and Letters of Andrew Marvell.* Ed. H.M. Margoliouth. 3rd ed. Vol. 1. Oxford: Clarendon, 1971. 3 vols.

Milton, John. "Eikonoklastes." *Complete Prose Works of John Milton.* Ed. Don M. Wolfe. Vol. 3. New Haven: Yale UP, 1953-82. 8 vols.

Nashe, Thomas. *Pierce Pennilesse His Svpplication to the Divell.* In *The Works of Thomas Nashe.* Ed. Ronald B. McKerrow. Vol. 1: 137-245. 1904. London: Barnes & Noble, 1966. 5 vols.

Richardson, H.G., and G.O. Sayles, Eds. "The Alleged Articles of 1308." See listing under "Alleged Articles."

Roger of Wendover. *Roger of Wendover's Flowers of History.* Trans. J.A. Giles. Vol. 2. London: Henry G. Bohn, 1849. 2 vols.

Rossiter, A.P., Ed. *Woodstock: A Moral History.* See listing under *Woodstock.*

Sackville, Thomas, and Thomas Norton. *Gorboduc, or Ferrex and Porrex.* Ed. Irby B. Cauthen, Jr. Lincoln: U of Nebraska P, 1970.

Shakespeare, William. *The Complete Works of Shakespeare.* Ed. David Bevington. 3rd ed. Glenview: Scott, Foresman, 1980. All quotations from *King John, Richard the Second, King Lear,* and other Shakespeare plays are from this edition.

---. *The Tragedie of King Lear.* In *The Complete Works.* Eds. Stanley Wells and Gary Taylor. Oxford: Clarendon, 1986.

Sidney, Sir Philip. "The Defence of Poesie." *The Prose Works of Sir Philip Sidney.* Vol. 3: 1-46. 1912. Cambridge: Cambridge UP, 1962. 4 vols.

Skelton, John. *Magnificence.* Ed. Paula Neuss. Manchester: Manchester UP; Baltimore: The Johns Hopkins UP, 1980.

---. *The Poetical Works of John Skelton: With Notes, and Some Account of the Author and His Writings.* Ed. Alexander Dyce. Vols. 1, 2. 1843. New York: AMS, 1965. 2 vols.

The Troublesome Raigne of King John. In *Narrative and Dramatic Sources of Shakespeare.* Ed. Geoffrey Bullough. Vol. 4: 72-151.London: Routledge and Kegan Paul; New York: Columbia UP, 1957-75. 8 vols.

The True Chronicle Historie of King Leir and his three daughters. Narrative and Dramatic Sources of Shakespeare. Ed. Geoffrey Bullough. Vol. 7: 337-402. London: Routledge and Kegan Paul; New York: Columbia UP, 1957-75. 8 vols.

The True Chronicle History of King Leir. In *Shakespeare and His Sources.* Ed. Joseph Satin. Boston: Houghton Mifflin, 1966. 458-526.

The True Chronicle History of King Leir and His Three Daughters, Goneril, Ragan, and Cordella. In *Six Early Plays Related to the Shakespeare Canon.* Ed. E.B. Everitt. Copenhagen: Rosenkilde and Bagger, 1965.

Tyndale, William. *The Obedience of a Christian Man.* In *Doctrinal Treatises and Introductions to Different Portions of The Holy Scriptures.* Ed. Rev. Henry Walter. Cambridge: Cambridge UP,1848. 127-344.

Vernon-Harcourt, L.W, Ed. "Hic annotatur quis sit senescallus Angliae et quid ejus officium." *His Grace The Steward and Trial of Peers: A Novel Inquiry into a Special Branch of Constitutional Government: Founded Entirely upon Original Sources of Information, And Extensively upon Hitherto Unprinted Materials.* Trans. L.W. Vernon-Harcourt. London: Longmans, Green, 1907.

Walter of Guisborough. *Chronicle of Walter of Guisborough.* Ed. H. Rothwell. 3rd ser. 89. London, 1957.

Woodstock: A Moral History. Ed. A.P. Rossiter. London: Chatto and Windus, 1946.

SECONDARY SOURCES

Adams, Barry B., Ed. Introduction. *King Johan*. By John Bale. San Marino: The Huntington Library, 1969. 1-69.

Aristotle. *The Rhetoric of Aristotle: An Expanded Translation with Supplementary Examples for Students of Composition and Public Speaking*. Trans. Lane Cooper. Englewood Cliffs: Prentice-Hall, 1930.

Axton, Marie. *The Queen's Two Bodies: Drama and the Elizabethan Succession*. London: Royal Historical Society, 1977.

Baker, Herschel. Introduction. *King John*. In *The Riverside Shakespeare*. By William Shakespeare. Gen. Ed. G. Blakemore Evans. Boston: Houghton Mifflin, 1974.

Battenhouse, Roy. "King John: Shakespeare's Perspective and Others." *Notre Dame English Journal* 14 (1982): 191-215.

Beaurline, L.A. Appendix. *King John*. By William Shakespeare. Cambridge: Cambridge UP, 1990.

Bevington, David, Ed. Footnote. *Complete Works of Shakespeare*. By William Shakespeare. 3rd ed. Glenview: Scott, Foresman, 1980.

---. *Tudor Drama and Politics: A Critical Approach to Topical Meaning*. Cambridge, MA.: Harvard UP, 1968.

Black, J.B. *The Reign of Elizabeth 1558-1603*. 2nd ed. Oxford: Clarendon, 1959.

Blackstone, Sir William. *Commentaries on The Laws of England: In Four Books; With an Analysis of the Work*. Vol. 1. New York: W.E. Dean, 1836. 2 vols.

Braunmuller, A.R. Introduction. *The Life and Death of King John*. By William Shakespeare. Oxford: Clarendon, 1989. 1-93.

Breitenberg, Mark. "Reading Elizabethan Iconicity: *Gorboduc* and the Semiotics of Reform." *English Literary Renaissance* 18 (1988): 194-217.

Bushnell, Rebecca W. *Tragedies of Tyrants: Political Thought and Theater in the English Renaissance*. Ithaca: Cornell UP, 1990.

Campbell, Lily B. *Shakespeare's Histories: Mirrors of Elizabethan Policy*. 1947. San Marino: The Huntington Library, 1958.

Candido, Joseph. "Blots, Stains, and Adulteries: The Impurities in *King John*." In "*King John*": *New Perspectives*. Ed. Deborah T. Curren-Aquino. Newark: U of Delaware P; London: Associated UPs, 1989. 114-125.

Cauthen, Irby B., Jr., Ed. Introduction. *Gorboduc, or Ferrex and Porrex.* By Thomas Sackville and Thomas Norton. Lincoln: U of Nebraska P, 1970. xi-xxx.

Chambers, E.K. *The Elizabethan Stage.* Vol. 4. Oxford: Clarendon, 1951. 4 vols.

---. *William Shakespeare: A Study of Facts and Problems.* Vol. 1. Oxford: Clarendon, 1930. 2 vols.

Clemen, Wolfgang. *English Tragedy Before Shakespeare: The Development of Dramatic Speech.* Trans. T.S. Dorsch. London: Methuen, 1961.

---. "Past and Future in Shakespeare's Drama." *Proceedings of the British Academy* 52 (1966)

Craig, Hardin. *The Enchanted Glass: The Elizabethan Mind in Literature.* New York: Oxford UP, 1936.

---. "Motivation in Shakespeare's Choice of Materials." *Shakespeare Survey* 4 (1951): 26-34.

Dollimore, Jonathan. "Introduction: Shakespeare, Cultural Materialism and the New Historicism." *Political Shakespeare: New Essays in Cultural Materialism.* Eds. Jonathan Dollimore and Alan Sinfield. Ithaca: Cornell UP, 1985. 2-17.

---. *Radical Tragedy: Religion, Ideology and Power in the Drama of Shakespeare and his Contemporaries.* Chicago: U of Chicago P, 1984.

---. "Transgression and Surveillance in *Measure for Measure.*" *Political Shakespeare: New Essays in Cultural Materialism.* Eds. Jonathan Dollimore and Alan Sinfield. Ithaca: Cornell UP, 1985. 72-87.

Edwards, H.L.R. *Skelton: The Life and Times of an Early Tudor Poet.* 1949. Freeport: Books for Libraries Press, 1971.

Elliot, John R. "Shakespeare and the Double Image of King John." *Shakespeare Studies* 1 (1965): 64-84.

Elton, William R. *"King Lear" and the Gods.* 1966. Lexington: The UP of Kentucky, 1988.

Everitt, E.B., Ed. Introduction. *The Troublesome Reign of John, King of England . . . In Six Early Plays Related to the Shakespearean Canon.* Copenhagen: Rosenkilde and Bagger, 1965.

Figgis, John Neville. *The Divine Right of Kings.* 1914. New York: Harper & Row, 1965.

Fleay, Frederick Gard. *A Chronicle History of the Life and Work of William Shakespeare: Player, Poet, and Playmaker.* New York: Scribner and Welford, 1886.

Foakes, R.A., and R.T. Rickert, Eds. *Henslowe's Diary*. By Philip Henslowe. Cambridge: Cambridge UP, 1936.

Forker, Charles R. *Fancy's Images: Contexts, Settings, and Perspectives in Shakespeare and His Contemporaries.* Carbondale: Southern Illinois UP, 1990.

Foucault, Michel. *The Order of Things: An Archaeology of the Human Sciences.* New York: Vintage, 1973.

Fraser, Antonia. *Mary Queen of Scots.* 1969. New York: Delacorte, 1970.

Fryde, E.B., et al. *Handbook of British Chronology.* 3rd ed. London: Office of the Royal Historical Society, 1986.

Furness, Horace Howard, Ed. Appendix. *King Lear, A New Variorum Edition of Shakespeare.* By William Shakespeare. 1880. New York: Dover, 1963. 353-491.

Goldberg, Jonathan. "Sodomy and Society: The Case of Christopher Marlowe." *Staging the Renaissance: Reinterpretations of Elizabethan and Jacobean Drama.* Eds. David Scott Kastan and Peter Stallybrass. New York: Routledge, 1991: 75-82.

Greenblatt, Stephen. "Invisible Bullets: Renaissance Authority and its Subversion, *Henry IV* and *Henry V.*" *Political Shakespeare: New Essays in Cultural Materialism.* Eds. Jonathan Dollimore and Alan Sinfield. Ithaca: Cornell UP, 1985. 18-47.

---. Introduction. *The Power of Forms in the English Renaissance.* Norman: Pilgrim, 1982. 3-6.

Guy, John. *Tudor England.* 1988. Oxford: Oxford UP, 1990.

Hamilton, J.S. *Piers Gaveston, Earl of Cornwall, 1307-1312: Politics and Patronage in the Reign of Edward II.* Detroit: Wayne State UP; London: Harvester-Wheatsheaf, 1988.

Happe, Peter, and John N. King. Introduction. *The Vocacyon of Johan Bale.* By John Bale. Binghamton: Medieval & Renaissance Texts & Studies, 1990.

Heinemann, Margot. "Political Drama." *The Cambridge Companion to English Renaissance Drama.* Eds. A.R. Braunmuller and Michael Hattaway. Cambridge: Cambridge UP, 1990: 161-205.

Heiserman, A.R. *Skelton and Satire.* Chicago: U of Chicago P, 1961.

Helgerson, Richard. *Forms of Nationhood: The Elizabethan Writing of England.* Chicago: U of Chicago P, 1992.

Hertzbach, Janet Stavropoulus. "From Congregation to Polity: The English Moral Drama to Shakespeare." Diss. Indiana University, 1978.

Hodgdon, Barbara. *The End Crowns All: Closure and Contradiction in Shakespeare's History.* Princeton: Princeton UP, 1991.

Holderness, Graham. *Shakespeare's History.* Dublin: Gill and Macmillan; New York: St. Martin's, 1985.

Holt, J.C. *Magna Carta and Medieval Government.* London: Hambledon, 1985.

Honigmann, E.A.J. Introduction. *King John.* By William Shakespeare. London: Methuen, 1973. xi-lxxv.

Hosley, Richard. "Shakespeare's Use of a Gallery over the Stage." *Shakespeare Survey* 10 (1957): 77-89.

House, Seymour Baker. "Cromwell's Message to the Regulars: The Biblical Trilogy of John Bale, 1537." *Renaissance and Reformation* 15 (1991): 123-38.

Hurstfield, Joel. "The Politics of Corruption in Shakespeare's England." *Shakespeare Survey* 28 (1975): 15-28.

Hutchison, Harold F. *The Hollow Crown: A Life of Richard II.* London: Eyre and Spottiswoode, 1961.

James, Mervyn. *Society, Politics and Culture: Studies in Early Modern England.* Cambridge: Cambridge UP, 1986.

Jenks, Edward. *The Book of English Law.* London: John Murray, 1928.

Johnson, Samuel. *Johnson on Shakespeare.* In *The Yale Edition of the Works of Samuel Johnson.* Ed. Arthur Sherbo. Vol. 8. New Haven: Yale UP, 1958-85. 15 vols.

Jones, Richard H. *The Royal Policy of Richard II: Absolutism in the Later Middle Ages.* Oxford: Basil Blackwell, 1968.

Kantorowicz, Ernst H. *The King's Two Bodies: A Study of Medieval Political Theology.* 1957. Princeton: Princeton UP, 1981.

Kelly, Henry Ansgar. *Divine Providence in the England of Shakespeare's Histories.* Cambridge, Mass.: Harvard UP, 1970.

Kinney, Arthur F. Introduction to "Homily on Obedience (1559)." *Elizabethan Backgrounds: Historical Documents of the Age of Elizabeth I, Newly Edited, With Introductions.* Hamden: Archon, 1975. 44-59.

---. Introduction to "The Honorable voyage unto Cadiz, 1596 (1598)." *Elizabethan Backgrounds: Historical Documents of the Age of Elizabeth I, Newly Edited, With Introductions.* Hamden: Archon, 1975. 276-83.

Lacey, Robert. *Robert, Earl of Essex.* New York: Atheneum, 1971.

Law, Robert Adger. "On the Date of *King Lear.*" PMLA 21 (1906): 462-77.

Leacroft, Richard, and Helen Leacroft. *Theatre and Playhouse: An Illustrated Survey of Theatre Building from Ancient Greece to the Present Day.* London: Methuen, 1988.

Lever, J.W. *The Tragedy of State.* London: Methuen, 1971.

Levin, Carole. *Propaganda in the English Reformation: Heroic and Villainous Images of King John. Studies in British History.* Lewiston: Edward Mellen, 1988.

Levin, Harry. *The Overreacher: A Study of Christopher Marlowe.* 1952. Gloucester: Peter Smith, 1974.

MacDonald, Ronald R. "Uneasy Lies: Language and History in Shakespeare's Lancastrian Tetralogy." *Shakespeare Quarterly* 3 (1984): 22-39.

Malone, Edmond, Ed. *The Plays and Poems of William Shakespeare, with the Corrections and Illustrations of Various Commentators: Comprehending A Life of the Poet, and An Enlarged History of the Stage.* By William Shakespeare. Vol. 2. London: Rivington, 1821. 2 vols.

Manheim, Michael. *The Weak King Dilemma in the Shakespearean History Play.* Syracuse: Syracuse UP, 1973.

Marcus, Leah S. *Puzzling Shakespeare: Local Reading and Its Discontents.* Berkeley: U of California P, 1988.

Matchett, William. Introduction. *King John.* By William Shakespeare. New York: Signet, 1966.

---. "Richard's Divided Heritage in *King John.*" In *Essays in Shakespearean Criticism.* Eds. James L. Calderwood and Harold E. Toliver. Englewood Cliffs: Prentice-Hall, 1970. 152-70.

McCoy, Richard C. *The Rites of Knighthood: The Literature and Politics of Elizabethan Chivalry.* Berkeley: U of California P, 1989.

McCusker, Honor. *John Bale: Dramatist and Antiquary.* Diss. Bryn Mawr University, 1942.

Merchant, W. Moelwyn, Ed. Footnote. *Edward the Second.* By Christopher Marlowe. 1967. London: A.& C. Black; New York: W.W. Norton, 1989.

Miller, Paul W. "The Problem of Justice in Marlowe's 'Hero and Leander.'" *Notes and Queries* N.S. 4 (1957): 163-64.

Moretti, Franco. "'A Huge Eclipse': Tragic Form and the Deconsecration of Sovereignty." *The Power of Forms in the English Renaissance.* Ed. Stephen Greenblatt. Norman: Pilgrim, 1982. 7-40.

Neale, J.E. *Elizabeth I and Her Parliaments, 1559-1581.* Vol. 1. London: Jonathan Cape, 1953-57. 2 vols.

Neuss, Paula.   Introduction. *Magnificence.* By John Skelton. Manchester: Manchester UP; Baltimore: The Johns Hopkins UP, 1980. 1-64.

Packe, Michael. *King Edward III.* London: Ark Paperbacks, 1985.

Pafford, John Henry Pyle, Ed. Introduction. *King Johan.* By John Bale. Oxford: Oxford UP, 1931.

Patterson, Annabel. *Censorship and Interpretation: The Conditions of Writing and Reading in Early Modern England.* Madison: U of Wisconsin P, 1984.

Phillips, J.R.S. *Aymer de Valence, Earl of Pembroke 1307-1324: Baronial Politics in the Reign of Edward II.* Oxford: Clarendon, 1972.

Plowden, Alison. *Danger to Elizabeth: The Catholics Under Queen Elizabeth I.* New York: Stein and Day, 1973.

Potter, Robert. *The English Morality Play: Origins, History and Influence of a Dramatic Tradition.* London: Routledge & Kegan Paul, 1975.

Rackin, Phyllis. "Patriarchal History and Female Subversion in *King John.*" In *"King John": New Perspectives.* Ed. Deborah T. Curren-Aquino. Newark: U of Delaware P; London: Associated UPs, 1989. 76-90.

---. *Stages of History: Shakespeare's English Chronicles.* Ithaca: Cornell UP, 1990.

Ramsay, R.L. Introduction. *Magnyfycence.* By John Skelton. *Early English Text Society* ("Extra Series." Vol. XCVIII), 1908.

Read, Conyers. *Lord Burghley and Queen Elizabeth.* New York: Alfred A. Knopf, 1960.

Ribner, Irving. *The English History Play in the Age of Shakespeare.* Rev. ed. New York: Barnes & Noble, 1965.

Ridley, Jasper. *Henry VIII.* London: Constable, 1984.

Riggs, David. *Shakespeare's Heroical Histories: "Henry VI" and Its Literary Tradition.* Cambridge, MA: Harvard UP, 1971.

Robinson, Ian. *"Richard II" & "Woodstock."* Doncaster: Brynmill, 1988.

Rossiter, A.P. *English Drama from Early Times to the Elizabethans: Its Background, Origins and Developments.* New York: Barnes & Noble, 1959.

---, Ed. Preface. *Woodstock: A Moral History.* London: Chatto and Windus, 1946. 1-76.

Rymer, Thomas. "A Short View of Tragedy." *The Critical Works of Thomas Rymer.* Ed. Curt A. Zimansky. New Haven: Yale UP, 1956.

Saccio, Peter. *Shakespeare's English Kings: History, Chronicle, and Drama.* New York: Oxford UP, 1977.

Scarisbrick, J.J. *Henry VIII.* Berkeley: U of California P, 1968.

Schelling, Felix E. *The English Chronicle Play: A Study in the Popular Historical Literature Environing Shakespeare.* New York: Macmillan, 1902.

Sen Gupta, S.C. *Shakespeare's Historical Plays.* London: Oxford UP, 1964.

Sewell, Arthur. *Character and Society in Shakespeare.* Oxford: Clarendon, 1951.

Shepherd, Simon. "Shakespeare's Private Drawer: Shakespeare and Homosexuality." *The Shakespeare Myth.* Ed. Graham Holderness. Manchester: Manchester UP, 1988: 96-110.

Sherman, Cordelia Caroline, Ed. Introduction. *A Critical Edition of King Leir.* Diss. Brown University, 1981.

Smallwood, R.L. Appendix. *King John.* By William Shakespeare. Middlesex: Penguin, 1974. 365-74.

Smith, Bruce R. *Homosexual Desire in Shakespeare's England: A Cultural Poetics.* Chicago: U of Chicago P, 1991.

Smith, Lacey Baldwin. *This Realm of England, 1399-1688.* 3rd ed. Lexington, MA: D.C. Heath, 1976.

Stone, Lawrence. *The Causes of the English Revolution 1529-1642.* New York: Harper & Row, 1972.

Strier, Richard. "Faithful Servants: Shakespeare's Praise of Disobedience." *The Historical Renaissance: New Essays on Tudor and Stuart Literature and Culture.* Eds. Heather Dubrow and Richard Strier. Chicago: The U of Chicago P, 1988. 104-33.

Summers, Claude J. *Christopher Marlowe and the Politics of Power.* In *Salzburg Studies in English Literature: Elizabethan and Renaissance Studies.* Ed. James Hogg. Salzburg: Institut Fur Englische Sprache und Literatur, 1974.

Tennenhouse, Leonard. *Power on Display: The Politics of Shakespeare's Genres.* New York: Methuen, 1986.

Ure, Peter, Ed. Introduction. *King Richard II.* By William Shakespeare. 1961. London: Methuen, 1969. xiii-lxxxiii.

Vaughan, Virginia M. "*King John*: A Study in Subversion and Containment." In *"King John": New Perspectives.* Ed. Deborah T. Curren-Aquino. Newark: U of Delaware P; London: Associated UPs, 1989. 62-75.

Walker, Greg. *John Skelton and the Politics of the 1520s*. Cambridge: Cambridge UP, 1988.

Warren, W.L. *King John*. London: Eyre & Spottiswoode, 1961.

Wilson, John Dover, Ed. Introduction. *King John*. By William Shakespeare. Cambridge; Cambridge UP, 1969.

INDEX

NOTE ON THE AUTHOR

Eric Sterling earned his B.A. degree in English at Queens College in New York. He received his M.A. and Ph.D. in English, with a minor in Drama and Theatre, from Indiana University in Bloomington. He has published articles on Edmund Spenser, William Shakespeare, Martha Moulsworth, Rolf Hochhuth, Nelly Sachs, Arthur Miller, and Edward Albee. He is an Assistant Professor at Auburn University at Montgomery in Alabama, where he lives with his wife, Jill.